PRINCIPLES OF SOCIAL AND POLITICAL THEORY

BY

ERNEST BARKER

*Honorary Fellow of Merton College, Oxford
and of Peterhouse, Cambridge*

OXFORD UNIVERSITY PRESS

Oxford University Press, Amen House, London E.C.4

GLASGOW   NEW YORK   TORONTO   MELBOURNE   WELLINGTON

BOMBAY   CALCUTTA   MADRAS   KARACHI   KUALA LUMPUR

CAPE TOWN   IBADAN   NAIROBI   ACCRA

FIRST PUBLISHED BY THE CLARENDON PRESS 1951
REPRINTED 1952
REPRINTED LITHOGRAPHICALLY IN GREAT BRITAIN
AT THE UNIVERSITY PRESS, OXFORD
FROM SHEETS OF THE SECOND IMPRESSION
1953, 1956
FIRST ISSUED IN OXFORD PAPERBACKS 1961

PREFACE

THIS book is based on a course of lectures regularly delivered in the University of Cambridge during the latter years of my tenure of the Chair of Political Science. (The course was last delivered in the academic year 1938-9.) Encouraged by some of those who originally attended the lectures, and especially by one or two who have since become teachers and lecturers in the subject, I have turned some eighty pages of crabbed manuscript notes, packed with additions and alterations, into something which may seem new and strange to those who knew the argument in its original form. It has been a little like putting the pieces of pith called 'Japanese flowers' into water; but it has taken much more time and very much more mental effort. I despaired again and again in the course of writing the book (the arteries of the mind are hardened by the time one reaches the middle seventies); but somehow I got to the end, and I now present to the reader the testament of my old age.

I had written the major part of this book when I came across a passage in one of Professor Whitehead's books which comforted me greatly. It is a sentence in one of the essays in his *Aims of Education*, and it runs as follows: 'It should be the chief aim of a University professor to exhibit himself in his own true character—that is as an ignorant man thinking, actively utilising his small store of knowledge.' I was the more comforted by these words, and especially by the word 'ignorant', because I was very conscious of my want of that sort of knowledge of politics which comes from actual experience. But my mood changed when I noted that Mr. Amery, in the introduction to his *Thoughts on the Constitution*, had quoted a sentence from Spinoza which could not but be depressing to the theorist of the study. 'It cannot be doubted that politicians themselves have written much more happily than philosophers about political matters.' Professor Whitehead had comforted me. Could I think of any comfort in the face of Spinoza's dictum?

A reflection occurred to my mind, which I drew from my master Aristotle. In a passage in the third book of his *Politics* he draws a distinction between those who are 'executants', or 'men of directing skill', in any given field of activity, and those who are simply 'cultivated', or possessed of some general knowledge; and he then goes on to suggest that persons belonging to the latter class may be credited with a power of judgement which entitles them to be heard. It is on this ground that he bases an argument for the right of the ordinary citizen to have some say in politics. On the same ground, perhaps, the ordinary student, who has sought to acquire some share of general knowledge, and to utilize it, as best he can, in thinking about the problems of social and political theory, may venture to submit his thoughts to the consideration of others. At any rate I have done so; and here is the result.

These excuses are perhaps superfluous; but they are some relief to the mind and some satisfaction of the conscience. There is another acknowledgement which I desire to make, with more confidence in its propriety. It is an acknowledgement of the debt which I owe to the students who attended my lectures. They not only encouraged me to think by their presence: they also stimulated me, by their questions, to revise and correct my thoughts. In the latter years of my lecturing I formed the habit of inviting questions at the end of each lecture; and I tried, at the beginning of the next lecture, to give some answer to the questions I received. I gained a good deal in this way; and though I cannot, after all these years, identify the passages in the book which are all the better for the questions I was asked and sought to answer, I know that they are numerous. I do not forget my debt.

I ought to explain, as I end, why the preamble to the Constitution of India is printed after the table of contents. It seemed to me, when I read it, to state in a brief and pithy form the argument of much of the book; and it may accordingly serve as a key-note. I am the more moved to quote it because I am proud that the people of India should begin their independent life by subscribing to the principles of a political tradition which we in the West call Western, but which is now something more than Western.

E. B.

August 1950

CONTENTS

PREAMBLE

TO THE CONSTITUTION OF INDIA

WE, THE PEOPLE OF INDIA, having solemnly resolved to constitute India into a SOVEREIGN DEMOCRATIC REPUBLIC, and to secure to all its citizens:

JUSTICE, social, economic and political;

LIBERTY of thought, expression, belief, faith and worship;

EQUALITY of status and of opportunity;

and to promote among them all

FRATERNITY assuring the dignity of the individual and the unity of the Nation;

IN OUR CONSTITUENT ASSEMBLY this twenty-sixth day of November 1949 do HEREBY ADOPT, ENACT AND GIVE TO OURSELVES THIS CONSTITUTION.

BOOK I

STATE AND SOCIETY

*An Historical View of the Relation of State and Society and
of Theories about their Relation*

§ 1. THE IDEAS OF 1789

BURKE, in his *Reflections on the Revolution in France*, laid down
the proposition, 'Society is indeed a contract ... but the
State ought not to be considered nothing better than a partnership agreement in a trade ... it is a partnership in all science; a
partnership in all art; a partnership in every virtue, and in all perfection'.[1] The proposition suggests two reflections. The first is that
Burke, sliding unconsciously from a mention of 'society' into a
mention of 'the State', implies that the two are one. The second is
that he views this single and unitary system (which we may call a
'society-state') as a total and all-inclusive partnership which is
competent for every purpose: not only the legal purpose of
enunciating and enforcing a scheme of law and order (a purpose which he does not mention, because it may be assumed as
self-evident), but also the economic purpose of 'trade', the cultural purpose of 'science' and 'art', and the moral and religious
purpose of 'every virtue' and 'all perfection'. What then, we
may ask, of the Church? Is it not also a partnership, a separate
partnership, directed to a religious purpose which involves and
includes connected purposes such as the promotion of education?
Burke would reply that by virtue of 'a state religious establishment' the Church is welded into the State to form one consecrated commonwealth which embraces both church and
state.[2] But what, we may also ask, of bodies such as trade unions?
Are they not also partnerships, separate partnerships, which beginning from economic 'agreement in a trade' may rise to wider
charitable and even cultural purposes? In 1790, when Burke
was writing his *Reflections*, trade unions were sparse and strug-

---

[1] *Reflections*, pp. 105–6 (edition of the *Works of Burke* in the World's Classics,
vol. ii).
[2] Ibid., pp. 100–3.

gling bodies, already illegal (or at any rate of dubious legality) under the common law, as being 'conspiracies in restraint of trade' and therefore contrary to 'public policy', but made more illegal still, only a few years later, by the Combination Acts of 1799–1800, which added the force of statute and legislative prohibition to the disabilities already imposed by the rules of the common law. The state thus seemed (but only *seemed*, as we shall see later) to stand alone in conservative Britain at the end of the eighteenth century: alone, and all-comprehensive.

But it seemed to be equally solitary, and no less comprehensive, in revolutionary France. Article 3 of the *Déclaration des droits de l'homme et du citoyen*, promulgated in 1789 and prefixed to the Constitution of 1791, laid it down that 'le principe de toute souveraineté réside essentiellement dans la nation [that is to say, in the national state]; nul corps, nul individu ne peut exercer d'autorité qui n'en émane expressément'. This principle of national sovereignty was carried into effect for the Church by the 'Civil Constitution of the Clergy', which turned the Catholic Church in France at once into a branch and a copy of the new revolutionary State, deriving authority from that State and modelled upon it, point by point, in its organization. The principle was equally, or even more stringently, applied in the same year (1790) to trade unions, by a law which declared combinations of workers to be 'inconstitutionnelles, attentatoires à la liberté et à la Déclaration des droits de l'homme et du citoyen, et de nul effet'.

§ 2. IDEAS TODAY

TODAY we generally distinguish between Society and the State. Our starting-point, when we use either term, is the given and historical fact of the nation. We assume, as the basis of our thought, a distinctive space, or territory, inhabited by a distinctive human stock (racially mixed, as a rule, but none the less distinctive), which is engaged in a nexus of co-operative activity. We then go on to the further assumption that this unit or nation —this amalgam of space and stock, with its nexus of co-operative activity—behaves in two ways, or as two orders, and does so concurrently and simultaneously. It acts in a social or voluntary way, as a social order or Society. It acts in a legal or compulsory way, as a legal order or State.

(*a*) By 'Society' we mean the whole sum of voluntary bodies, or associations, contained in the nation (and even ramifying beyond it by the connexions which they establish with similar bodies in other nations), with all their various purposes and with all their institutions. Taken together, and regarded as a whole, these associations form the social substance which goes by the general and comprehensive name of 'Society'. Taken separately, and regarded in themselves, they generally show and share two features: first, they are essentially *voluntary* in origin: secondly, they are essentially *specific* in purpose, each existing for some one purpose—religious, economic, educational, charitable, or 'social' in that narrower sense in which we speak of any of the purposes of our ordinary human intercourse (such as the common enjoyment of sport or the common cultivation of leisure) as being a 'social purpose'. But if each, taken separately, thus exists for a specific purpose, all taken together exist for a number and a variety of purposes. In view of the many and various purposes of its parts, we may accordingly say that Society does, in Burke's words, constitute 'a partnership in *all* science, . . . in *all* art, . . . in *every* virtue and in *all* perfection'; and we may even say that, so conceived, Society is in a sense total or 'totalitarian'. But to say that is not to say—indeed it is a very different thing from saying—that the State, which has its own separate basis and its own peculiar character, is also 'totalitarian'.

(*b*) What, then, is the separate basis and the peculiar character of the State? By 'the State' we mean a particular and special association, existing for the special purpose of maintaining a compulsory scheme of legal order, and acting therefore through laws enforced by prescribed and definite sanctions. The State, as a rule, is national in its scope (though a given State may be multi-national), just as Society also is national: in other words, most States are what we call 'national States'. But if, on this point, the State agrees with Society—or, more exactly, is coextensive with Society—it also differs (and differs profoundly) from the associations other than itself which we call, in their sum, by the name of 'Society'. It differs in two respects. First, it includes *all* the members of the stock which inhabits its space or territory, and it includes them all as a matter of necessity: other associations include only *some* (though a national church, in Sweden for instance, may include nearly all), and they include these on a voluntary basis. Secondly, the State has the power of using legal coercion, the power of enforcing obedience, under the sanction of punishment, to ordained rules of behaviour; other associations, in virtue of their voluntary basis, can apply only social discipline, and can expect only voluntary obedience to agreed ways of behaviour, obedience enforced in the last resort by the sanction of exclusion from membership. We may therefore say of the State that while it is an association like other associations, in the sense of being a union of men for the purpose of acting as *socii* or partners in the realization of a common purpose, it is also an association which is unlike other associations, in the sense of having a unique *purpose* (the purpose of maintaining a compulsory scheme of legal order) which gives it the unique *scope* of including compulsorily all the persons resident in a given territory and the unique *power* of making law and using legal coercion.

The distinction here stated is a problem, or rather a cause of problems, as well as a distinction. On the argument which has been followed a nation is simultaneously, and coextensively, two things in one. It is a social substance, or Society, constituted of and by a sum of voluntary associations, which have mainly grown of themselves—in the sense that they have been formed by voluntary and spontaneous combination—and which desire to act and to realize their purposes as far as possible by themselves. That is one side of the nation. The other side (which we may call either the reverse or the obverse, according to our preference) is that it is a political, or, as it is perhaps better called, a legal substance; a single compulsory association including all, and competent, in all cases where it sees fit, to make and enforce rules for all. This double nature of the nation—this simultaneity and coextension of its social and its legal aspect—raises a threefold problem. (1) What are the things which belong to the nation in its legal aspect, as an organized State? (2) What are the things which belong to the nation in its social aspect, as a sum of voluntary associations? (3) What control should the nation, as organized in a State (and therefore competent to deal with all persons and judge in all cases *in the legal sphere*), exercise over itself as organized in a society of voluntary associations acting *in the social sphere*?

The totalitarian states which have appeared—and disappeared—in recent years (if indeed they have disappeared, and if communism be not a new incarnation of their spirit) gave a simple answer to all these problems. They denied the distinction between State and Society and shelved the questions which it raises. They integrated the nation in the State, and made the State the solitary and total expression of the nation. This was not a revolution: it was rather a reversion. The history of the past can furnish us with many examples of totalitarianism. But it can also furnish us with examples of divergencies from, or reactions against, the theory of the solitary and total State. We may, therefore, attempt an historical retrospect, and seek to attain an historical view both of the relation between State and Society in the past and of the theories of the past about their relation.

§ 3. THE GREEK CITY-STATE

THE Greek city-state is still of importance, and a living part of the living past, because it has left us a theory, expressed in the writings of Plato and Aristotle, which still lives in our minds and colours our thoughts. Though it bore the name of 'Polis', which we naturally associate with politics, the city-state was something more than a political system; and it went far beyond the legal purpose of declaring and enforcing a body of rules for the control of legal relations. It was State and Society in one, without distinction or differentiation; it was a single system of order, or fused 'society-state', of the type unconsciously assumed by Burke in the theory of his *Reflections*. Because the Polis was more than a state—because it was also, over and above that, a religious confession and an ethical society; because it was also, into the bargain, an economic concern for the purpose of production and trade; because it was also, in addition to that, a cultural association for the common pursuit of beauty and truth— because it was all these things, Plato expects it, in his *Republic*, to formulate the true idea of God and the rules of moral behaviour, to regulate economic life, and to control all art and science by its system of education. Aristotle is less far-reaching: he is even willing to recognize the Polis as an 'association of associations'. But even to Aristotle the political association is sovereign and all-inclusive, embracing and regulating all the others; and the science of this association—the science of politics—is a master-science which 'determines what other sciences should be studied in states, which of them should be learned by each group of citizens, and to what extent they should be learned'.[1] When he speaks of man as being by his nature a *politikon zōon*, he does not mean that 'man is by nature a political animal', in the sense of having a natural interest in what we call politics and a natural instinct for indulging that interest. He means that man is a being who is intended by the capacities of his nature for life in a Polis, as bees are intended by their capacities for life in a hive: a being who *must* live in a Polis if he is to develop his capacities, for the simple reason that those capacities can only grow from 'potency' to 'act' in a general and generous environment which includes not only what we call politics, but also art and science and 'every virtue and all perfection'.

But the very fact that the Polis was something more than a State is a reason why we should approach with caution the lessons of Greek political theory. They are noble lessons; but they are the lessons of a theory which was something more than political. It was a theory, we may say, of an omnicompetent 'Society-State'. Our modern theory, based on our own experience of life, which is different from that of the Greeks, is more in a single dimension. It is simply a theory of the competent State—that is to say, of a State which is competent simply and solely for its specific purposes, which are essentially legal purposes. The State, in our experience, is a guarantor of rights and duties. It has in its hands the instrument of law; and it does whatever can be done by the use of that instrument. Its strength is as the strength of law; and it can avail no more, and no farther, than law. The State of our theory is accordingly a State which legally declares and legally guarantees the rights and duties of its members, whether those members are individuals or societies of individuals. It can declare and guarantee the rights and duties of religious societies; but it is not itself a religious society. It can declare and guarantee the rights and duties of authors, teachers, and all other persons who are engaged in the creation and transmission of culture; but it is not itself the creator and inculcator of culture. It can declare and guarantee

[1] *Nicomachean Ethics*, Book I, c. ii., § 6.

the rights and duties of all the agents engaged in the area of economic production and distribution: indeed it can even become itself an agent in that area, if a due guarantee of the rights of the labouring classes and the duties of their employers cannot be otherwise provided; but it offends against its own nature, and it injures its own primary legal function, if it loads itself with any large burden of direct economic activity. It is the supervisor of activity, and not the generator. It is the author of a framework of rights and duties, but not itself the whole framework of life.

§ 4. THE IMPACT OF CHRISTIANITY

THE rise and spread of the Christian religion made a great break in the antique system of ideas: the system enshrined in the Greek Polis (and still visible in the Parthenon), and similarly enshrined in the parallel *civitas Romana*, which beginning on the Tiber (and still visible in the Roman Forum and on the Capitol) gradually made the whole of the Mediterranean world one 'city' and styled it the *imperium Romanum*. Beneath the ancient city-state there grew the catacombs; and from the catacombs there emerged an authority—the authority of the Church—which stood distinct from, and over against, the authority of a city-state now magnified into a city-empire. There is dynamite in the text, 'Render . . . unto Caesar the things which are Caesar's; and unto God the things that are God's' (Matthew xxii. 21).[1] Ultimately, it meant the sundering of the sphere of Society from the sphere of the State; and we may even say that in the field of social and political theory (though that is only one field, and the explosive emergence of the Christian religion was felt in other and wider fields) this was the great result of the teaching of Christ. Immediately, and indeed for long centuries, which begin with the recognition of Christianity as a *religio licita* by Constantine, and extend into and through the Middle Ages, the effect of Christianity was the emergence of the doctrine of the two ends—the temporal end, which alone belongs to the State, and the eternal end which belongs to, and is the prerogative of, the Church.

What was the Christian doctrine of the nature of the temporal

[1] See below, Book VI, § 7, *ad finem*. The Latin of the Vulgate runs, 'Reddite . . . quae sunt Caesaris, Caesari: et quae sunt Dei, Deo'.

end? It was eventually formulated, like so much else, by St. Thomas Aquinas in the thirteenth century. His theory is that it involves four things, which thus belong to the State—all else, as a matter of the eternal end, belonging to the Church. The first of these four things is security and sufficiency of life: in other words, freedom from the threat of death and freedom from the threat of starvation. The second thing, rising in the scale, is a legal scheme of order and justice: a scheme of law, proceeding from the people or from a competent authority acting on their behalf, with a correlative scheme of administrative order. The third thing, rising still further in the scale, is what may be called the promotion of a minimum standard of morality, in aid of, and subsidiary to, the major moral activity of the Church, which has the general custody of moral life *sub specie aeternitatis*: the State, which acts in the order of time and in temporal society, being thus concerned, and only concerned, with immoral acts which excite repulsion in the majority of the members of such a society or undermine the very foundations of its existence. The further and last thing, at the top of the scale, is the protection of religion, as a function ancillary to the life of the Church: the State being bound, by a due respect for the eternal end, to secure for its members the conditions in which they can exercise the faculty of contemplating eternal truth under the wing and guidance of the Church.

Corresponding to the doctrine of the two ends, there is the parallel doctrine of the two powers (*duo fines, ergo duae potestates*). The doctrine of the two powers is first clearly expressed by Pope Gelasius I (492–6), when he writes of 'Duo . . . quibus principaliter mundus hic regitur: auctoritas sacrata pontificum, et regalis potestas'. In the development of this doctrine the authority of the State (*regalis potestas*) becomes a specifically *legal* authority, with a subsidiary moral and an ancillary religious function; and on the other hand the authority of the Church, while primarily religious, becomes in addition a moral and an educational (or cultural) authority. The scope of the authority of the Church is indicated by the triple power regarded as inherent in the clergy—the religious *potestas ordinis*, in all matters concerning the sacraments; the moral *potestas jurisdictionis* (though, as we shall have occasion to notice, clerical jurisdiction came also to cover cases outside the category of morals); and the educational *potestas docendi*. Armed with this triple power, the Church divides the regimen of the world with the State on a system of dyarchy. In the original theory of Gelasius, that system is still regarded as a system of parity: the Popes in Rome have still some deference for the imperial authority, though that authority has come to reside beyond the seas in Constantinople; and their idea is still an idea of equality, parity, or parallelism. Each authority is equal to the other in its own sphere. Not only so, but each authority is dependent on the other when once it enters the sphere of the other; the clergy depending as much on the governors of the State in temporal matters as the governors of the State depend on the clergy in matters spiritual. It is a nice balance—each equal to the other when acting in its own sphere: each equally dependent on the other when acting in the sphere of the other. But there is already a shadow of coming disturbance, and a certain oscillation of the nicely adjusted balance. Gelasius notes that the burden of the clergy is the heavier of the two, inasmuch as they have to render account even for the rulers of the State at the final day of judgement. The 'heavier burden' may easily become a 'greater power'.

There are two further things to be noted. The first is that though, in the new conception, there are two *authorities*, there is still a single *community*. The two authorities rule simultaneously the same community. That community—Rome having achieved an oecumenical unity of the Mediterranean world—is a universal community of all Christian men, *respublica Christiana*, which is at one and the same time a Church and a State, with coextensive and identical membership: a Church, when regarded as pursuing the eternal end; a State, when regarded as pursuing the end which is an end in time. One community, but two governments—two governments corresponding to the two ends of the community—this is the first thing to be noted. The second, in logic at any rate, is consequential on the first. If there was one community, it was natural that one of the two governments should attempt, in spite of theories of dyarchy, to make itself supreme, by reducing 'government' as well as 'community' to the sovereign principle of unity:[1] and it was

[1] Dante stated the sovereign principle of unity in the *De Monarchia* (I, c. viii): 'Humanum genus bene se habet et optime, quando secundum quod potest Deo

further natural that the clerical government, as being charged with the greater end and bearing the heavier burden, should be the government which made this attempt. Accordingly, from Pope Gregory VII to Pope Boniface VIII (or, roughly, from 1150 to 1300), the clergy begin to enter the sphere of the end which is an end in time, and to take over temporal causes from the authority of the State. Legalizing itself in the process, the Church moves into the area of legal order and justice. In matters civil, for instance, it attempts to stop usury, and to enforce just prices on traders, by its courts and their canon law: in matters criminal it attempts to control the perennial feuds of fighting nobles by the institution of the 'truce' or 'peace' of God; in matters international, it attempts to bring even kings, and their wars and policies and treaties, under the jurisdiction of the papal *curia*. The Church is the judge of sin (*peccatum*); and what are the bounds of sin? When a king, for instance, has broken a treaty, has he not committed the *peccatum* of perjury (this was the argument of Innocent III), and must he not therefore be judged for his sins by the Church? Sin thus becomes an engulfing conception. It absorbs breaches of contract, breaches of the peace, and other contraventions of the general scheme of law. The boundary between morality and legality begins to fade; and the guardian of morality thus becomes the general guardian even of law.

This is a return, on a far larger scale and under far different auspices, of the old totality of the city-state. The Church, which had begun with a division of spheres, and had taught the doctrine of the two ends and the correlative doctrine of the two powers, had ended by the time of Boniface VIII in a new junction of spheres and an implicit rejection of any division. Indeed Boniface VIII had *explicitly* rejected division. The terrene power, he had said in the Bull *Unam Sanctam Ecclesiam* of 1302, shall be judged by the spiritual; but the supreme spiritual power shall be judged by God alone. It is a *divina potestas*, given by the word of God to St. Peter and his successors; and whoever therefore resists this power, thus ordained of God, resists the ordinance of God, 'nisi duo, sicut Manichaeus, fingit esse principia, quod

---

adsimilatur. Sed genus humanum maxime Deo adsimilatur quando maxime est unum; vera enim ratio unius in solo illo est.' But Dante himself did *not* deduce one government, and one only, from this sovereign principle of unity.

falsum et haereticum esse judicamus'. Here dyarchy has gone; and here, we may even say, Gelasianism has been turned into and condemned as Manichaeism, or a recognition that the principle of evil is equal to the principle of good. Thus the policy of the medieval church, at its apogee or rather its extremity of logic, would bring all human life under a single *lex divina* enforced in the last resort by the supreme authority of the Papacy, acting through an array of ecclesiastical courts and institutions. (The registrar of the Roman chancery headed the Bull of Boniface VIII with the rubric 'Declaratio quod subesse Romano pontifici est omni humanae creaturae de necessitate salutis', which is a summary of its concluding words.) This may fairly be called the return of the omnicompetent 'Society-State', with its undifferentiated unity and its single controlling authority. But the Greek and Roman city-state had really controlled all life with an integrated authority. The medieval polity of which the Popes dreamed—a polity with supreme authority integrated in a theocracy—might claim a similar authority. But it could only claim; and the claim was confronted by facts of life and factors of power before which it collapsed in the moment of its statement. A medieval king, Philip IV of France, showed by the success of the measures which he took against Boniface VIII that the power of territorial kingship, however limited its area, was greater than the claims of the Universal Church, however wide its scope.

§ 5. MEDIEVAL KINGDOMS AND ESTATES

THE Middle Ages proper—the 'middle' Middle Ages, from the eleventh to the thirteenth century—were a period of turbulence and germination. They contained, and developed, other facts and factors besides the theoretical polity of a single *respublica Christiana*, whether that polity was conceived as conducted on the principle of dyarchy or viewed as reduced to unity under the supreme power of a theocracy. Two of these facts demand special notice for their bearing on the future development of Europe.

The first is the *regnum*. Though theory (which was mainly or even exclusively a theory expounded by the clergy), basing itself on the ancient fact of a universal Roman Empire, proclaimed the existence of a single universal community, which in its temporal aspect was a single *Regnum* or empire, as in its spiritual aspect it was a single *Ecclesia* or church—though theory ran in this channel of unity, life itself ran in the channels of diversity. Actually there were many *regna*, territorial or regional *regna*, at any rate in the West. Soon after the end of the thirteenth century the lawyers were even beginning to claim that each territorial king was the emperor of his kingdom (*rex in regno suo est imperator regni sui*): in other words, they held that the territorial or regional *Rex* excluded the 'emperor' of the would-be universal *Regnum* from the bounds of his own particular *regnum*, and was himself (as his lawyers styled our Richard II) 'the entire emperor of his realm'. Externally the claim might have some force, as a rebuttal of imperial claims of sovereignty: internally, in view of domestic turbulence, it was as yet an idle claim. It is true that the territorial or regional *regnum* was the area in which, with the development of nationalism and the rise of powerful national monarchies during the course of the sixteenth century, new national States would arise, and modern history (which is the history of such States) would take its beginning. But there was little of a national State—indeed there was little of any sort of State—in the territorial *regnum* of the Middle Ages. It was a paradise of Estates rather than the pattern of a State.[1]

The second fact which demands our notice is this fact of Estates. Whatever the lawyers might say about his being 'the entire emperor of his realm', the king of each *regnum* had to face three serious competitors within his realm. In the first place there was the territorial branch of the Church Universal (the *ecclesia Anglicana*, or the *ecclesia Gallicana*), claiming for itself the privilege of immunity from the royal courts in a range of cases both civil and criminal, and able to appeal to the authority of the Papacy if its claim were challenged. (Not that the position was simple, or that a king might not sometimes be allied with the church of his territory to defend its liberties against the Papacy, or sometimes, again, with the Papacy to defend—and share—the lucrative prerogatives of patronage and taxation which the Popes sought to exercise over each territorial church.)

[1] The same Latin word *status* (in the sense of a 'station' or 'standing') is the origin both of 'Estate' and 'State'. It may be said to be one of the great turning-points of history that in the sixteenth century the word ceased to mean *États* or Estates, and came to mean what Machiavelli calls *lo Stato*. On the general history of the word in medieval and modern times see below, Book III, § 1.

In the second place, there were the feudal nobles, who individually acted as sovereigns, so far as they could, in their local fiefs, and collectively formed a baronage ready to dispute authority at the centre as a body of rival kings. Finally, there were the *communitates*, the local communities or 'commons', particularly in the towns, which locally sought autonomy for their municipal governments and their various merchant and craft guilds, and centrally, if they were joined together in an assembly of 'the Commons', might join the baronage in challenging the king—or the king in challenging the baronage.

These three competitors of the king (some of whom, however, might on occasion act as his interested allies)—the clergy, the baronage, and the commons—were loosely organized, and came to be known, as Estates. As they took shape, the medieval kingdom became an 'Estates-State': a State of the three Estates. Such a State, because by its nature its authority was disputed, or we may even say divided, was hardly competent, as it stood, for the specific purpose which any form of State must fulfil if it is to be worthy of the name: the purpose of making and enforcing a single scheme of law and order. In brief, there was an abundance of 'Society' in the territorial kingdoms, or 'Estates-States', of the Middle Ages; but there was very little 'State'. Associations in various forms—clerical, baronial, municipal: whether based on religion or class or calling—became so many factotums, each making its own law and order in a time of general self-help; and the authority of the State, as represented by the king and his courts, was penned into a corner.

§ 6. THE SIXTEENTH CENTURY AND THE NATIONAL STATE

THE later centuries of the Middle Ages presented a sharp antithesis, or even self-contradiction: on the one hand, the ideal, or the theory, of a universal society under the regimen of a single theocracy: on the other, the fact of a number of quasi-national, or potentially national, kingdoms, all seeming to be disintegrated into so many polyarchies. In the age of the Renaissance, Reformation, and Reception—one of the great turning-points in the course of human history—a movement emerges, and gathers weight, towards the formation of unified national States. These States not only vindicate for themselves the province of law and order: they also annex, so far as they can, the province of religion; they assert a protectorate over the sphere of education and culture; and they gradually invade, under the banner of mercantilism, the territory of economics. The State reacts against the medieval invasion of its province by Society: it proceeds, in turn, to invade Society. Such is the swing of the pendulum, and such the recurrence of thesis in the face of antithesis.

Various causes contributed to foster the movement towards the formation of unified national States. There was a political cause: the rise of national feeling (particularly in the Western Kingdoms), partly in reaction against the divisions and miseries of civil war, partly in response to the challenge of foreign adventures and expansion; a feeling which demanded some centre of stability and loyalty, and was content to find that centre in the absolutism of a new monarchy ready to play on the strings of a feeling which suited its aims. There was an economic cause: the new development of trade and commerce fostered by the great discoveries (in Africa, America, and Asia), and the demand of traders and merchants for an effective central system of law and administration as the necessary condition of their economic success. There was an intellectual cause: the recovery of classical ideas, and especially the vogue and spread (the Reception as it is called) of the civil law of Rome, with its traditions of the sovereign city-state and the sovereign 'majesty' of the *princeps*. Finally there was a religious cause: the Reformation, which allying itself, or drawn into alliance, with the other tendencies of the time produced in England, and in some of the principalities of Germany, the system of the State-Church, independent of Rome and the Papacy, but dependent on the State and its prince, who thus added to his headship of the State a headship of the Church under the style of 'supreme governor' or *summus episcopus*.

By the action of these causes the medieval Estates-State was turned into a national monarchical State; and a return was made to the classical unity of the Greek city-state and the Roman Empire, with their integration of human life in a single embracing and compelling community. The State now becomes, at any rate in the area of the Anglican and the Lutheran Reformation (but not, or not to the same extent, in the area of

Calvinism), a Church as well as a State: it may even be said to become Society as well as the State, the one and total organization of human life. A new emphasis on the notion of sovereignty—the old *majestas* of the Romans—accompanies this development. In contradistinction from the medieval Estates-State, the national monarchical State of the sixteenth century gravitates towards autocracy and a system of absolutism: it is a 'Prince-State'. It is true that the notion of sovereignty had already been apprehended and emphasized by medieval Popes. Bodin said of Innocent III that 'he knew best of all men the rights of sovereignty', and we have already seen that Boniface VIII could proclaim those rights in resounding terms. But this was a proclamation of the rights of a spiritual autocracy; and it was a new thing when Machiavelli and Bodin proclaimed the rights of secular sovereignty. Machiavelli was a 'statist', in the sixteenth- and seventeenth-century sense of the word; and for 'reason of State' he preached in his *Prince* (composed in 1515) the doctrine that 'the prince'—though he was thinking especially and mainly of a *nuovo principe*, seeking to create a new unity and order in a disordered Italy—may go to work against religion and morals in order to establish the absolute executive sovereignty which is the supreme end of the State, or rather the supreme means to its end of unity and order. Bodin was rather the legist; and in his *République* (first published in 1577) he lays it down that in every State there must exist a legislative sovereignty, or *majesté*, which may be defined as 'a supreme power over citizens and subjects, free from the laws' (though itself the author of laws)—except, he adds, 'fundamental laws' such as the Salic Law of France. Machiavelli may be said to arm the executive sovereign, and Bodin the legislative; but armed by both the sovereignty of the State is clad in full panoply, so far as concerns the temporal sphere of which they were both mainly thinking.

But what of the spiritual sphere? In his *Ecclesiastical Polity* (of which the first four books were published in 1594) Hooker enunciates two propositions. The first is that 'in a . . . Christian State or Kingdom . . . one and the self-same people are the Church and the Commonwealth'. In other words a *populus*, or nation, is at once an *ecclesia* and a *respublica*: all the members of the *respublica* are *ipso facto* members of the *ecclesia*, and citizenship and churchmanship are therefore coextensive: there is only one community, which is both a Church and a State, and which is both simultaneously and in one. This, as has already been noted, had also been the view of the Middle Ages; but Hooker's one community, instead of being universal, as the Middle Ages had thought, was a national body or *populus* living in a national State or kingdom. If this first proposition marks one great change, Hooker's second also marks another. 'It is expedient', he states, 'that their sovereign . . . in causes civil have also in ecclesiastical affairs a supreme power'. The supreme power of the civil sovereign is thus extended to the ecclesiastical sphere; and though we may think of 'a personal union' (as when one king rules two different kingdoms under two separate titles), the result remains that the same authority controls the Church and the State.

The sixteenth century thus issues in a sovereignty which, besides possessing an absolute executive and an equally absolute legislative authority in the temporal sphere, is also possessed of 'a supreme power', if not in 'the religious sphere' at any rate in 'ecclesiastical affairs' (it would be a nice distinction to determine the difference between the two, as it would equally be to determine the difference between the nature of supreme power in 'civil' and its nature in 'ecclesiastical' affairs). The idea grows of the State as the one form of human grouping, and of that State as controlled and determined by an absolute sovereignty which is its essence.[1] But the idea did not go unchallenged; and indeed a number of challenges appeared. In England, although the Tudor commonwealth was largely shaped by its royal masters in the new pattern, there was always Parliament, to which Sir Thomas Smith, in his *De Republica Anglorum* (published in 1583), ascribes 'the most high and absolute power of the realm'; and during the course of the seventeenth century the power of this Parliament grew and grew, as there also grew along with it a system of local government, almost of a voluntary type, in the hands of unpaid Justices of the Peace. Again, in the area of the Roman Church the idea began to be developed, to meet the case of a Protestant sovereign (though it was not confined to that case), that the Church was a separate society

[1] It may even be said that, according to this idea, sovereignty *is* the State, and the State is sovereignty: see below, Book III, § 1.

with rights of its own inherent in its own distinctive nature. This idea attained its most notable expression in the theory of the Spanish Jesuit Suarez; and even in the days when the Spanish Inquisition was still serving as the instrument of Spanish monarchical policy, he was already teaching (in his *Tractatus* of 1611) a doctrine of 'Community' which not only made the church a *communitas politica vel mystica*, based on divine foundation and on that basis transcending communities of human invention, but also ranked some secular groups, such as knightly orders and local communities, in the category of 'perfect communities capable of political government', and thus placed them on an equal footing with the State. Last, but not least, in the area of Calvinism there was an abundance of dissidence from the idea of the all-inclusive State. Triumphant Calvinism might indeed proclaim the no less rigorous idea of the all-inclusive Church, answering the claims of autocracy by the similar claims of theocracy, and seeking to make kings 'God's silly vassals'. But Calvinism was seldom, or long, triumphant: it was generally the faith of minorities: and it gradually came into line with the 'sects' (Congregationalists, Baptists, and others) who stood for the cause of minorities and the rights of the 'gathered' Free Church based upon voluntary compact. This is a development which mainly belongs to the seventeenth century; but even earlier, in the latter half of the sixteenth, the struggling Calvinists of France had already challenged any idea of the all-inclusive State. The *Vindiciae Contra Tyrannos* of 1579 is a Huguenot argument against the *Machiavellani* of absolutism, and a plea for the contracted rights of the people; and the Huguenots were even ready to ally themselves with old ideas of the 'Estates-State', alleging against the King of France the ancient rights both of the nobility of the provinces and of the commons of the cities, in the knowledge that Huguenot nobles and townsfolk were the necessary stay and support of their cause.

§7. THE FRENCH REVOLUTION

THE idea of the all-inclusive monarchical State, which had emerged in the sixteenth century, was still active in the eighteenth; and indeed it may seem to have attained its crown and consummation in the enlightened despots of the latter half of

that century. The French Revolution, at the first blush, appears
as a great reaction and a swing of the pendulum to the opposite
extreme. It *was* a reaction and a swing of the pendulum, but by
no means a reaction to the opposite extreme. It rejected the
adjective 'monarchical'; but it retained the more crucial adjective 'all-inclusive'. National sovereignty (*la souveraineté nationale*)
was a cardinal tenet of the Revolution; and national sovereignty
meant the absolute might of the nation, acting through its representatives, or even through a single plebiscitary first consul or
emperor, to do whatever it thought fit to do—regulating the
Church; suppressing guilds and annulling combinations of
workers; annihilating ancient provinces; controlling all education; in a word, omnicompetent.

From this point of view the Revolution was at one with enlightened despotism; and indeed it issued in the most enlightened
(and the most despotic) of all the despots. But it had also its
other side. It was based on the democratic idea that the nation
should make, or at any rate approve, a government representative of itself; and not only that, but that it should also make, or
at any rate approve, its own constitution or permanent scheme
of political life. (Not that the schemes proved permanent; but
their very impermanence meant a renewal, again and again, of
national making or national approval.) This was a genuine
revolution. Moreover, the Revolution produced, as the very first
of its fruits, a Declaration of the Rights of Man; and that
declaration too was destined to repeated renewal. On the other
hand, the Declaration of the Rights of Man may also be said
to be little more than a catalogue of exceptions to the action of
an otherwise absolute State. Nor is that all. The exceptions are
only in favour of individuals, and not of groups or associations.
It is possible to exaggerate the significance of article 10 of the
Declaration, that 'nul ne doit être inquiété pour ses opinions,
même religieuses, pourvu que leur manifestation ne trouble pas
l'ordre public établi par la loi'. But this article, at the best, can
hardly be said to be a recognition of religious liberty. It is not
so much the proviso or *pourvu* that matters: religious liberty
must always make its account with the demands of public
order. It is rather that the word *nul* is an individualistic word,
and that religious liberty is not only, or even mainly, a liberty
of individuals. It *is* indeed that; but it is also the liberty of

religious *societies*—and not merely their liberty to worship, but also their liberty to educate, to persuade, and to conduct their mission. The French Revolution, not only in its immediate but also in its long-time effects, which have lasted into the twentieth century, has not been tender to religious societies; and if it has not disquieted the individual for his opinions, *mêmes religieuses*, it has not always left the group in peace. The revolutionary theory of France has generally remained a theory which, if it professes to be democratic, and to respect the rights of man, is still a theory of the State as the one organization—and the only organizer.

§8. GERMAN ROMANTICISM AND IDEALISM

DIFFERENT as is the German theory of the early nineteenth century from that of the French Revolution, it has some fundamental similarities; and indeed it was partly drawn from Rousseau (the prophet not of the rights of man, but of the sovereignty of the general will) and from the spirit of the Revolution. But German theory has its own genius; and that genius may perhaps be expressed in the word 'romanticism'. It was the tendency of German thinkers to make a romance or *Märchen* out of the State and the *Volk* or Folk (which is something different from *la nation*) that stood behind the State. They were in the mood depicted by Heine: 'Ich weiß nicht was soll es bedeuten' (there generally *was* a haze about their thought), but

> Ein Märchen aus altern Zeiten
> Das kommt mir nicht aus dem Sinn.

The romantic thought of Germany began by idealizing the Folk, primarily the early Teutonic folk 'of old times', and then, by a natural extension (the more natural in view of national reaction against the French Empire) the German Folk of the present. It regarded the Folk as a maker of folk-lore, of folk-songs and folk-music, of folk-law, and of a general folk-intuition-into-the-world-and-life (*Weltanschauung*): it made the Folk an entity, a being, even a person, which sang, made ballads, created law, and directed the march of history. Well and good, we may say—so long as the Folk is not also the State, or still retains some being apart and distinct from the State; so long as Folk is another word (which we may not like, but may allow to serve) for what we prefer to call 'Society'—the community acting for itself in its own general social way, and as such distinct from the State with its particular and legal way of action. But this was not the line which was followed by German thought. The romanticized Folk, just because it is made an entity, a being, and even a person, can readily be identified (at any rate by the synthetic mind) with the entity, being, or person of the State—that is to say with the Government—that is to say, when we come to the last resort, with the person of the Governor (*der Herrscher*). This is what actually happened: this is Hegelianism, on its political side; and here the political romanticism of Germany touches one of the trends of the political realism of France—the trend towards *souveraineté nationale* and the vesting of that sovereignty in a single plebiscitary ruler called first consul or emperor. (But there were other trends also in France.)

The political philosophy of Hegelianism, an outcome of German romanticism, may be summarily regarded from two different but complementary points of view. It lifts the Folk up into being a Mind, and not only a Mind, but also an incarnation of the Eternal Mind. It pulls the Folk down into being a State, and not only a State, but also a monarchical State of the Prussian type. From the first point of view we may see the eternal consciousness expressing itself, in the course of its eternal process of movement or 'becoming', through Folk-minds which are the operative organs of God in time and space, and indeed are God Himself as He operates in time and space. These Minds are therefore divine: as such, they cover the whole range of life; as such, again, they are final and right, within their space and time, for everything which they cover. From the second point of view we see the Folk-mind, while still remaining an organ and expression of the Eternal Mind, identified first with the general being and action of *the* State, and then, by a further extension, with the particular being and action of *a* State, a particular form of State, a monarchical State of the Prussian type.

To understand the first of the two identifications just made—the identification of the Folk-mind (or *Volksgeist*) with the general being and action of the State—we must turn to the Hegelian method, which is a method that goes, as it were, in threes: first the thesis, then the antithesis, and then the synthesis of both in a higher unity. In the sphere of moral and political philosophy the thesis is Law, or the external realization of Right; in other words, it is a system of rules for controlling outward relations—partly in the field of family-life, with its rules of marriage and the descent of property, but mainly in the greater field of 'bourgeois' relationships (*die bürgerliche Gesellschaft*), the field of industry and commerce, with its nexus of economic interests and all the rules implied in the nexus. This Law, or external realization of Right, is the mark and constituent force of the State in the lower and cruder form in which it first appears: indeed we may even say that, apart from the field of family-life, the State in its lower and cruder form is simply the system of 'bourgeois' relationships *regarded as producing law* (from and through the necessities of its nexus of interests) *and as controlling itself by the law which it produces*. So far of the thesis of Law. The antithesis is Morality, or the internal realization of Right: in other words, it is the system of rules made by the individual conscience for the control of its inward self. The divergence between the thesis of outward Law and the antithesis of inward Morality demands a synthesis and reconciliation. This is to be found in a third conception: that of Social Ethics (*Sittlichkeit*), which consists of the whole system of rules, disciplines, and influences—the union of the legal and the moral—controlling in harmony the whole of life both inward and outward. The vehicle of this system of rules, disciplines, and influences is the fully developed State; and thus the State, in its lower form the vehicle of Law, becomes in its higher form the vehicle of a system of Social Ethics. But if the developed State is the vehicle of such a system, so transcending Law and Morality, and so uniting them both in a single spiritual texture, this State may be regarded as merged in, and may be identified with, the Folk which is the operative organ of the eternal consciousness; or vice versa (and this is perhaps the better mode of expression) the Folk may be regarded as merged in, and may thus be identified with, the general being of the developed State.

This is the first identification. The second follows; and by this second identification the Mind of the Folk, already merged in the general being of the State (in its higher and developed form), is further merged in the particular being of a particular form of State, the Prussian monarchical form; which means, in effect, the identification of the Mind of the Folk with the mind of a Prussian King. How was this second merger achieved? The answer is that the essence of the higher form of State consists in its being a higher and reconciling unity, and that such unity is best secured in 'an active individual, in the will of a decreeing individual, in monarchy'. The king stands above the play of 'bourgeois' relationships and outside the nexus of economic interests: he is the organ of impartiality—but above all he is the focus of unity.

If this summary account is just, it follows that Hegelianism is a version, and possibly the extremest version, of the unified 'Society-State'. Hegelianism makes the State the vehicle of a system of social ethics, which is law and morality in one; and by making it the vehicle of such a system it makes it all-inclusive. It identifies the State, so regarded and so conceived, with the Folk which is an operative organ of God; and it then proceeds to identify this Folk-State with the monarch, who thus becomes an organ of God in his turn. Finally, by deifying this Folk-State-Monarch—by making the Folk-State God's organ, and the Monarch, through it, God's commissary—it makes the amalgam absolute: absolute both within and without. The amalgam is absolute within, because it admits no democratic rights of the collective people and no civil rights of the individual man and citizen: the collective people is absorbed in and contained by the Monarch, and the individual man and citizen is absorbed in and contained by the State's system of Social Ethics. Absolute within, the amalgam is equally absolute without, and it is so because—being deified, and therefore infinite and un-limited—it knows no international society of States and none of the rules and duties imposed by such a society upon its consti-tuent members. There is just the solitude of the State; and the State is all in all.

None the less, there are elements in Hegelianism which look in other directions, and may be pleaded in aid of other causes, than that of the absolute State. There is, for instance, the idea of the system of 'bourgeois' relationships (*die bürgerliche Gesellschaft*); the idea of the play and counterplay of its economic interests; the idea of its connexion with the development of law. This, as we shall have occasion to notice, was a starting-point of Marxian theory; and indeed it is a commonplace that Marx built on Hegelian foundations—even though, as he said himself, he had first turned them 'upside down' by substituting the process of Matter, and the conception of dialectical materialism, for Hegel's process of Mind, and his conception of dialectical idealism. But however it might be modified or turned 'upside down' for the purpose, Hegelianism could certainly be used to support not only the cause of absolutism, but also that of socialism. Perhaps this could be done the more easily because there is, after all, some measure of kinship between the two, and because, in some of its forms, socialism tends to the absolute. On the other hand, there are also elements in Hegelianism which may be pleaded in aid of the cause of liberalism; and here there can be no question of any kinship with absolutism. The *political* theory of Hegel is indeed inimical to liberalism; but his general *philosophical* theory is none the less not wholly unfavourable to liberal ideas. His conception of the eternal debate of thesis and antithesis, and of the opposition of thought to thought in the operation of Mind, involves the necessary conclusion that debate and discussion must always be at work in any society of minds, now emphasizing *this* idea, and now emphasizing *that*, but always seeking to achieve a synthesis, or, as we also say, in one of our common English terms, 'to find a compromise'. If we think of political parties as representing thesis and antithesis, and of Parliament as seeking to find a reconciling synthesis, we can defend parliamentary democracy in terms of Hegelian ideas. We can even argue that Hegel himself was untrue to his own ideas when he became a political absolutist. He failed to see that the sovereign thing in political thought, as in all the thought of the world, is the *process* of thought itself, as it works its way between the clashing rocks of thesis and antithesis. Distrusting, or rather forgetting, the *process* (and the essence of liberalism is reliance upon it), he turned instead to an *organ* or instrument; and for the natural synthesis of debate he substituted the artificial synthesis of 'a decreeing individual'.

§ 9. ENGLISH INDIVIDUALISM

IN the course of the argument there have appeared a variety of expressions of the unified and all-inclusive 'Society-State': first the classical City-State; then the theocratic Church-State of the dreams of Boniface VIII; then the Prince-State of the sixteenth century; then the Nation-State of the French Revolution, with its assertion of national sovereignty; and then the monarchical Folk-State of German romanticism. All along—from the first explosive emergence of Christianity to the Jesuit and Calvinist thinkers of the seventeenth century, and from them to our own days—all along there has been at work a leaven of Christian thought; and that leaven has been a cause of constant fermentation. 'Render . . . unto Caesar the things which are Caesar's; and unto God the things that are God's.' Sometimes, it is true, the leaven has ceased to be true to its nature: it has been a rennet that curdles rather than a leaven of fermentation: it has sought to bind Church and State together in one inclusive whole, either, at one extreme, by making the Church also a State, and thus instituting some form of theocracy, or, at the other extreme, by making the State also a Church, and thus arming the ruler of the State with a final and supreme power in affairs ecclesiastical. On the whole, however, and in the main, the influence of Christian thought, in its long-time operation, has been the influence of a solvent, which has made for the opening of any 'closed' system of social organization; and this is true not only of the reformed branches of Christianity, but also (and this in spite of the Inquisition and the Index) of the general spirit and tendency of the Roman Catholic Church since the age of the Reformation and the Counter-Reformation.

But there is also a secular factor which must be taken into the reckoning when we seek to trace the development of the relation between State and Society and the growth of men's ideas about the nature of their relation. That factor is the individualism (but it is something more than individualism, and the name is really a misnomer, for there is something more in question than individuals and their rights) which for the last three centuries and more has inspired so much of English life, not only 'within the realm', but also in the many settlements planted 'overseas' on the continent of America and under the southern stars. The matter is not only a matter of Britain: it is also a matter of the whole British Commonwealth: it is even a matter of the United States of America, which was cradled in the Commonwealth. Here, however, we must restrict our scope to Britain, and even to England, for it was in the conditions of English life in the seventeenth century that the temper of life and the method of action of Anglo-Saxon 'individualism' began to develop.

The England of the sixteenth century had cherished the conception of the one undivided commonwealth ('the very and true commonweal', as one writer calls it)—with religious life under a State-Church; with economic life regulated by a system of State-protection at the ports, and by a State labour code (the Statute of Artificers of 1563) in the towns and shires; and even with moral life supervised by the courts of the State-Church, which punished sexual immorality and other moral offences. 'This realm of England', so runs the beginning of the Statute for the Restraint of Appeals (1533), 'is . . . governed by one supreme head and king, . . . unto whom a body politic, compact of all sorts and degrees of people divided in terms and by names of spiritualty and temporalty, be bounden and ought to bear, next to God, a natural and humble obedience.' Some of the lawyers went even farther: instead of speaking of a body politic annexed to (but yet distinct from) the King, they spoke of the King himself as having, or being, a body politic, of which the 'members' were his subjects, and in which he and they were so united that they formed one corporation. We already begin to see the Leviathan of Hobbes when we read in Plowden's reports (about the year 1550) that 'he and his subjects together compose the corporation, . . . and he is incorporated with them, and they with him, and he is the head and they are the members, and he has the sole government of them'.[1]

English history in the seventeenth century is the history of the disintegration of this inclusive corporation, or rather of the progressive differentiation, and the progressive liberation, of bodies of opinion and bodies of men which move outside the orbit of the 'body politic'. But the inclusive 'commonwealth', the single 'body politic', the one 'corporation', had never been so united as it is assumed to be in the statutes and law reports of the sixteenth century. There were two inheritances from the Middle Ages which could not be absorbed in the body of Leviathan. The first was the system of the common law, and the legal profession behind that system. The system of the common law was a firm deposit of rules and processes largely intended, and generally effective, for the protection of the rights of the subject:

[1] Plowden, 234, quoted in Maitland's *Collected Papers*, iii, p. 250.

a deposit too hard, and too unmalleable, to be dissolved by any new absolutism. The legal profession, pivoted on the Bar, and on barristers who had long been organized in their own voluntary Inns of Court, was largely an autonomous profession, engaged (along with judges who had themselves been barristers in their day) in developing rules of law and methods of legal procedure on its own professional lines, and confronting the King and his ministers with the collective weight of its professional opinion. But there was also a second inheritance. This was a 300-year-old Parliament, with its own deposited procedure and its own system of ideas (largely, it is true, derived from the lawyers, who had always played a large part in Parliament from the earliest days of that 'High Court'); and this too confronted the King and his ministers with its collective weight.

This legal and political basis of the common law and the high court of Parliament provided the ground and the opportunity for the new developments which began to appear in the seventeenth century. They are developments which are partly religious and partly economic; but the two are interconnected. Between them they achieved, gradually and almost unconsciously, a progressive differentiation of the unified commonwealth and a progressive liberation of social groups.

The great religious fact is the existence and growth of the 'free churches'. It is true that the free churches, as groups or societies, only achieved recognition of their right to exist, and to assemble for worship, by the Toleration Act of 1689: it is true that their members, as individuals, only won the right to full citizenship by the repeal of the Test and Corporation Acts in 1828, and only gained admission to the two old Universities by the Universities Tests Act of 1871: it is true that it was a long slow process, covering almost the whole of three centuries, which at last established the equality of the members of the free churches with the members of the State-Church. But the thing that matters is the struggle itself, even more than the achievement. From the reign of Elizabeth onwards the free churches were always there, and always seeking to vindicate the principle of the freedom of the religious group against the idea and practice of the inclusive 'body politic'. Nonconformity was to the English national state what early Christianity was to the Roman imperial state: indeed we may even say that, never having been adopted by the English State, as early Christianity was by the Roman empire, it was even more. It steadily stood for the principle that the State had nothing to do with religion, so far as churches other than the State-Church were concerned: it vindicated the conception of religion as something apart from, and independent of, the State: and it thus prepared the way for the general principle and practice of the distinction between State and Society. Nonconformity is wrongly judged as a religion of individualism, and as a simple plea for the individual right of the solitary conscience. It had indeed a solitary quality and a tough fibre of individualism; but it had also something more, and something at least as great. It was a religion of 'the society' (Baptist, Quaker, or Methodist), and a plea for the collective right of the freely 'gathered' group. Here, as elsewhere, what is called individualism is something more than individualism; and if the obverse side is the unit, the reverse side is the group.[1]

If religious developments thus followed the banner of Free Religion, economic development similarly followed the banners of Free Trade and Free Labour—free trade, as against the old State-protectionism: free labour, as against the old State labour-code. Nonconformity prepared the way for this trend of economic development, partly in virtue of the simple fact that it was vindicating a parallel cause in its own field of religion, and partly because it was Nonconformists who largely constituted the trading class which demanded free trade and were the backbone of the working class which later demanded free labour. Free Trade—which is here to be understood not in its narrow sense of freedom from the imposition of tariffs, but in the broad sense in which it means the freedom of trade and industry to develop themselves, without state-regulation by means of exclusively chartered companies and restrictive monopolies—Free Trade in this broader sense is anterior to the repeal of the Corn Laws in 1846. It is a cause as old as the parliaments of the

[1] It is only fair to add that today, by one of the paradoxes of history, it is the State-Church, or a large section of that church, which is vindicating the principle of the freedom of religious society. Many of the leaders of the Church of England are champions of the cause of 'life and liberty', and advocates of the conception that the Church should be free to change its ritual, to alter its articles of religion, and to manage generally its organization and discipline, independently of the State and the Parliament of the State.

reign of Charles I: it won some triumphs after the Restoration of 1660: it may be said to have consolidated itself with the Revolution of 1688. It may seem to be pure individualism, and indeed it is more individualistic than the parallel cause of Free Labour; but at any rate it encouraged the action of social (and not merely private) enterprise, and it promoted the formation of voluntary social groups, or companies, for the conduct of such enterprise. (Lloyd's and the London Stock Exchange, both originally associations based on the social life of city coffee-houses in the eighteenth century, may serve as examples of these groups.) The cause of Free Labour, struggling for existence in the eighteenth century, emerged to light in 1824–5, with the repeal or drastic modification of the Combination Laws of 1799–1800; and here, especially in the subsequent growth of trade unions and their organization, the collective side of a demand which begins with a claim of the rights of men is obvious to every eye. Free Labour means the claim of a right for organized labour groups to bargain collectively and in the last resort to strike collectively; and Free Labour doubles its group production when it creates, by way of reaction and answer, organized employer-groups on the other side. Taken together, Free Trade and Free Labour mark another large development of Society, parallel to the religious development, and another stage in the process of differentiation between Society and the State.

Such was the general process which began its course in the conditions of English life in the seventeenth century, and such were the results towards which it moved. We may therefore agree with a modern historian that 'the main feature of British history since the seventeenth century has been the remoulding of a State by a powerful Society', which has at once differentiated itself from the State and then acted upon it and even in it. (Parties, after all, are social formations: the Whig party began its life in a city inn, just as Lloyd's and the Stock Exchange began in coffee-houses; and the social formations called parties, though they belong to the area of society, act in and upon the State.) We may also agree, when we reflect on the Virginia and Massachusetts 'Companies' which laid the foundations of what is now the United States of America, that 'the expansion of England in the seventeenth century was an expansion of Society, and not of the State'.[1] The general process, at home and abroad, was a process by which Society grew round the State—surrounded it indeed, with growths—and yet left it as the hard core and legal substance of organization, affecting all the growths, and affected by all the growths, in a constant interaction.

§ 10. MARXIAN SOCIALISM: HEGEL TO LENIN

THE very term 'socialism' would seem to suggest another and perhaps alternative way of the disengagement of Society. But does the theory of Marxian socialism, as it was developed in Germany during the nineteenth century, and afterwards amplified and exemplified in Russia during the first half of the twentieth, correspond to the suggestion of the term? Names and terms can be veils as well as mirrors; and we shall do well to study the actual evolution of socialism before we attach any credence to the suggestion of its name.

The evolution begins in the theory of Hegel's *Philosophy of Right*,[2] and especially, as has already been noticed, in Hegel's conception of 'burgess' or bourgeois society. It was on this theory and this conception that Marx and Engels built, as Lenin, in his turn, built again on the structure which they had raised. According to Hegel's theory the system of 'bourgeois society'—or, as we may also call it, the 'nexus of economic relationships', or the 'community of economic interests'—was something which supervened, in the course of the dialectic of history, on the original and natural kin-group for the purpose of providing more abundant means of subsistence than the kin-group was able to provide, and of doing so by means of the institutions of private property and accumulation of capital. The ways of providing the means of subsistence being various, bourgeois society accordingly became a various system of different classes, or orders, or estates. Hegel distinguishes three of these classes: the class of those engaged in dealing with the immediate products of nature; the class of those engaged in the further manufacture of such products, and in the general opera-

---

[1] The two passages quoted are both taken from the late Professor Unwin's *Studies in Economic History*, p. 28 and p. 341.

[2] See the essay on the relation of Fichte and Hegel to Socialism in Professor W. Wallace's *Lectures and Essays*.

tions of distribution; and the class of those concerned in securing the general interests of the whole society. Tracing the development of this system of classes, Hegel proceeds to argue that it turns itself, in the process of its development, into what may be called the first or lower form of the State, and does so by the process of evolving a body of laws. These laws, however, represent only the *de facto* rules of the actual proceedings of the society: they follow the lines of the natural course of social development, which, if it is natural, is not necessarily just: they solidify and sanction, rather than elevate and control, the existing system of order. Along with this body of laws, and in order to give it support, the system of classes or orders—turning itself still further into a form of State—also develops an organized police, and with it adds a further sanction and a firmer solidity to the existing order. Laws and police—these are the State, and these are the foundations and pillars of 'bourgeois society'.

So far, and if he had stopped at this point, Hegel was handing the keys of the State to the impending siege of the Marxians. He had spoken of bourgeois society turning itself into a form of State, and buttressing itself by a body of laws and an organized police in order to consecrate an existing system of economic order which was a system of private property and the accumulation of capital. But Hegel's argument went farther; and it reached a higher stage. He argued that in the later and developed form of State (which would seem to be identical with the Prussia of his day) two further things were added; one of them from above, and the other from below. From above there came the reconciling and the humanizing force of a system of State protection and a system of State education, the one regulating the clashes and the other supplementing the defects of the bourgeois system of classes. From below there came the development of corporations or guilds, each inspired by a sense of honour and a pride in good workmanship; each, accordingly, moved by a disposition to do its best for the benefit of the whole; and all thus concurring to provide a new moral root of the State and the foundation of a system of 'Social Ethics'. (Incidentally, it should be noted that in his view of the nature and functions of corporations Hegel may be regarded as a parent of the corporative State of Italian Fascism as well as of the socialist State of the Russian Soviet system; and it should be noted that, just as in Italy a century later, his corporations are all to be authorized or chartered—for 'no association has existence and place in society, except such as are legally constituted and acknowledged'.) It follows that from above and below the original bourgeois society is endowed with a new moral character; and on this basis the true State, the State in its developed and rational form, can build that system of social ethics which, as has already been noted, is the synthesis of the external rules of bourgeois society with the inner morality of conscience. Elsewhere, Hegel argues (he means elsewhere than in Prussia, and he refers in particular to England), the mere play of Society is left to its unchecked action, with no true State for its guidance, but merely with a parliament which, if it is called representative, is representative only of social factors and economic interests; and here there ensues, on the one hand, an unregulated accumulation of wealth, and on the other, the depression of a rabble (*Pöbel*, or proletariate) below any decent standard of subsistence. It follows that a society of this order does not possess, for all its accumulation of capital, the means of preventing the miseries of poverty: it is accordingly driven to colonization and commerce with backward territories, and it slides into what, in the language of a later day, is styled by the name of 'imperialism'. The moral is that a bourgeois society which fails to rise to the level of a true State, by attaining a system of social ethics, is a poor thing likely to perish, weakened by its own abundance.

Omit Hegel's theory of the 'true State' (but that is a large omission), and you have here the essential elements of Marxianism. The nature of the building which can be constructed from these elements is clear from the argument of Lenin's pamphlet on 'the State and Revolution'. That argument may be resumed in some five propositions. (1) Society, in the sense of economic society, is driven by the collision of its opposing interests to institute a State, *seemingly* above itself, which will moderate the force of collision by keeping it within the bounds of a form of law and order; and professional armed forces, serving in lieu of a 'self-acting armed organization of the population', are attached by it to that State. (2) But since this State is the result of collision, it is *actually*, and as a matter of fact, no more—and no less—than the strongest of the colliding interests, the interest of the class engaged in manipulating accumulated capital; and thus, instead of standing above society, a State of this order is really immersed in the play of society and dominated by its dominant interest—being, in effect, the organized domination of the strongest class, which is that of the capitalists, for the purpose of exploiting the weakest class, which is that of the manual workers. (3) Even the democratic Republic, with its system of universal suffrage, is still a means of capitalist domination: indeed, it is 'the best possible political form for capitalism', since it enables the omnipotence of wealth to assert itself indirectly—but all the more effectively—through the bribery of officials and representatives, the control of the Press, and the influence of the Stock Exchange on the policy of government. (4) On the other hand, the process of economic development, as it expands the range of its operations and multiplies the number of its operatives, is steadily tending to lift the proletariate—that is to say, the manual workers in urban industries—into the position of the strongest class, closely knit together by propinquity and solidly organized in their own unions; and thus, though the democratic Republic is 'the best possible political form for capitalism', it is also 'the best form of the State for the proletariate under capitalism', since it gives its members the best opportunity of organizing themselves for political objects. (5) So organized, the urban proletariate, in the day when it is the strongest and conscious of its own strength, will capture the State from capitalism by revolution and the use of force, as capitalism in its day had captured the State from the other interests and classes of society by the same method and the same means. It is all a matter of collision. The grinding of collision is the process of history; and the results of the grinding are at once inevitable and right.

So far the argument of Lenin is an analysis of the historical process and an interpretation of the past. But history does not stop; and the past flows into the future. What does Lenin see when he puts his hand to his brow and under it scans the horizon of the future? He sees no perpetuity of the proletarian State of the workers. The proletariate will maintain the State for a time, but only for a time. It will maintain it temporarily for the two necessary—but also transitory—purposes of suppressing the capitalist class and guiding the semi-proletariate (the peasant and the lower middle classes) along the path of reconstruction. These two purposes once achieved, the State—even the proletarian State, which will now have done its work and exhausted its mission—will 'wither away'. In the new era there will be no classes; and since the State, by its nature, is an organ of class (this class or that, but always *some* class) there will be no State. There will be nothing but society, community, communism— a society, community, communism destitute of classes and free from even the shadow of force; a society, community, communism where there are neither lions nor lambs, and all are 'accustomed to observing the elementary conditions of social existence without force and without subjection'. Thus the proletarian State—the State of 'socialism'—is only a phase. The consummation of history, on the horizon of the future, is the negation of the State, even in its socialist form, and the emergence of a pure society no longer vexed by collision, but knit together in the spontaneous harmony of a natural and unforced communism. The end of socialism is, we may say, the ending of socialism (for even socialism presupposes the State), and the inauguration in its place—if also by its means—of a perpetual reign of pure society under the style of communism.

It may thus be said that Marxian Socialism, in Lenin's interpretation, means the use of the categories of 'State' and 'Society' for the purpose of argument; but the argument which they serve is an argument (1) that there has never been any real distinction of State and Society during the centuries of struggle (on the contrary the State has always been, and must always be, the organ of a social interest), and (2) that in the final millennium there will be no distinction at all, because there will be no State. In neither phase, the pre-millennial or the millennial, is there any room for distinction between Society and the State. *Omnia reducuntur ad unum*: it would be Manichaeism, as Pope Boniface VIII said in 1302, to allege two principles. In the pre-millennial phase the State is immersed in Society, and is indeed a function of Society—capitalistic when Society is capitalistic and under the dominance of the capitalist class; proletarian when Society is proletarian and under the dominance of the proletariate; but always a function of Society and indistinguishable from Society. In the millennial phase the State has gone: unity drops the disguise (which was never more than a disguise) of its Janus mask: there is one organization of human life, and only one.

But it is not always easy to distinguish the millennial from the pre-millennial in the theory of Marxian Socialism. The pre-millennial, in its last stage of the socialist State or proletarian dictatorship, has a way of becoming itself millennial. (The future will come, and will be better than the present; but meanwhile the present is good.) If we stop our inquiry, as perhaps we may, at the stage of the socialist State, it would appear that Marxianism, like the doctrine of Hegel, combines and confuses State and Society in a single and total organization of all human life. It only differs from the doctrine of Hegel in abandoning the idea of a controlling system of social ethics in favour of the idea of a controlling system of social economics—which means, in effect, that Marxianism stops short at Hegel's first or lower form of State, and refuses to proceed to the true or higher State in its developed and rational form. Apart from this difference—and it is a great difference—Marxianism and Hegelianism both repeat the idea of the unified Society-State which is already apparent in the Greek *polis* and has continued to recur through subsequent ages. Marxianism, or Leninism, as it confronts us today, presents again the picture of an omnicompetent Society-State which embraces the whole of life; and just as Plato would have had his 'republic' control theology and aesthetics, as well as economics, so the Union of Socialist Soviet Republics aims at providing a new form of faith and a new style of worker's art and literature, in addition to regulating all economic life, agricultural as well as industrial.

§ 11. FRENCH SYNDICALISM AND ITS TREND

THE theory of French syndicalism[1] has generally followed a different line. Here there has been a genuine revolt against the

---

[1] The French *syndicat*, like the Italian *sindacato*, may be defined as a group formed for the defence of common *economic* interests. The *syndicat* accordingly differs from the *association*. While, in the words of the Waldeck-Rousseau law of 1884, 'les syndicats professionnels ont exclusivement pour objet l'étude des intérêts économiques, industriels, commerciaux et agricoles', the essence of an *association* is the pursuit of a disinterested object, or, in the words of the law of 1901 (also associated with the name of Waldeck-Rousseau), 'l'association est la convention par laquelle deux ou plusieurs personnes mettent en commun d'une façon permanente leurs connaissances ou leur activité dans un but autre que de partager des bénéfices'.

The distinction between *syndicats* and *associations* is a matter of importance. It revolutionary doctrine of 1789—the doctrine of the national State, entirely controlled by a single *souveraineté nationale*, as the one organization and sole organizer of life. It is true that a form of syndicalist theory first appeared in England, during the period of the Reform Bill of 1832; partly in the pacific teaching of Robert Owen, who advocated the organization of trades in associations and the union of these associations, through their representatives, in a central national council; and partly in the more militant doctrine of William Benbow and other extremists, who preached a general strike or 'holiday month' and founded (but failed to establish) a Grand National Consolidated Trades Union for the purpose. But the general theory of syndicalism, in the course of its development, became specifically French; and its first clear prophet, who may also be said to have remained the chief of its prophets, was Proudhon (1809–65).

A printer and proof-reader by profession, but turning also in his later years to the career of a journalist and author, Proudhon expounded the doctrine, first that the economic order was anterior in time and superior in importance to the political, and secondly that *droit économique*, based upon and constituted by the principle of *mutualité*, was similarly anterior and superior to *droit politique*, which ought to be deduced from, and should be a reflection of, the economic principle of mutuality. The essence of the economic order, in his view (as that view was expounded in his work *Du Principe fédératif* of 1863), was a federal essence: the order, he held, was by its nature *une fédération mutualiste*, composed of occupational groups freely formed for the purpose of production and exchange and freely cohering in virtue of their mutual service and benefit. (Proudhon was thus attracted to the idea of the social contract, which, he wrote, 'should become in reality, and not merely in Rousseauist abstraction, the basis of society'.) Such an economic order— federative and 'mutualist'—issued by its nature in an economic

may be added (1) that as *syndicats* are defined as having 'exclusively' for their object the study of economic interests, they would seem to be debarred from political objects, and (2) that even *associations*, with their wider scope, are null and void, under the law of 1901, if they are founded for a cause, or with a view to an object, 'qui aurait pour but de porter atteinte à l'intégrité du territoire national et à la forme républicaine du gouvernement'. This is the legal framework within which syndicalism arose—from which it derives its origin, but against which it is also a protest.

rule of right, or *droit économique*, of reciprocal service and proportionate exchange between its constituent groups; and it was, with its correlative rule of right, the major substance and inner core of human interest. True, indeed, there had also developed, in the course of time, a political order, which represented 'the social body in its unity and in its relations with the world outside': true, again, this political order had its own *droit politique*, or political rule of right, for the regulation of the social body in its unity and its relations. But the functions of the political order were subordinate, and might even be called sub-functions; and the political rule of right should be derived from, and should correspond to, the principles of the economic rule—with the citizens of the political order voting according to their occupational divisions, and with a system of political federation (here Proudhon thought in terms of 'autonomous' communes and 'sovereign' provinces) as the proper corollary of the natural and spontaneous federalism of the economic order.

This is all a clear reaction against the revolutionary principle of a single and indivisible France. A division is made between the economic order and the political: the political is relegated to a lower plane, in which it is a reflection of and a derivation from the economic; and within both orders a plural system of federalism is enthroned. But the simple and cardinal principle of Proudhon is the division between the economic and the political order. He makes things 'two and two, one against another': he sets the economic order and its *droit économique* over against the political order and its *droit politique*. The later theory of syndicalism, as it has since developed in France from the seed sown by Proudhon, and as it appears in the polemics of Georges Sorel's *Réflexions sur la Violence* (1908) and the legal argument of Duguit's *Traité de droit constitutionnel* (1911), has proceeded, consciously or unconsciously, on the lines already traced by Proudhon in his doctrine of the economic order and its *droit économique*. The syndicalists, opposing themselves to the revolutionary idea of the single and sovereign nation, have preferred and championed the idea of a prior and higher economic society; and they have conceived this society not, like the German Marxists, in terms of colliding classes, but in terms of occupational groups, complementary to one another and knit together in a federal union by the fact of mutual need and the bond of mutual service. Syndicalists and Marxists might have the same goal: Proudhon might speak of *une souveraineté effective des masses travailleuses*, as Marx and his followers spoke of a proletarian dictatorship; and French syndicalists of the twentieth century (repeating Benbow's scheme of 1834) might proclaim the 'myth', or even embrace the policy, of the general strike, as the Marxists embraced a similar policy of revolution. But there is still a world of difference between the general climate of syndicalism and the general climate of Marxianism—the difference between a federal society of complementary occupations and a warring society (which is *not* a society) of colliding classes. The difference shows itself clearly when we turn to the notion of *droit économique* propounded by Proudhon and elaborated by Duguit. The very word *droit* is significant: there is right in question as well as the might of conflicting opposites; and the theory of syndicalism—the theory of *mutualité*, with each autonomous group of producers freely exchanging its products for those of other groups on a just basis of reciprocal equality—has been an influence in the development of juridical thought in France.

There remains, however, a dualism, or more exactly a scheme of dyarchy, at the root of syndicalist theory. The political order and its *droit politique* stand by the side of the economic order and its system of *droit économique* with no clear delimitation. It is easy to begin with the simple postulate of 'two and two, one against another'. On the one hand, you assume a federal economic order of *syndicats ouvriers*, based on a primary *droit économique*, and you suppose that in this order each of the units will be autonomous, though you also suppose the existence of some central federal organ—even if it be only a statistical committee—competent to suggest how much each unit is to produce, and for how much of the product of other units it should exchange its product. On the other hand you assume a political order (also federal, as far as possible—but you admit that the degree of federalism will be less than it is in the economic order), based on the secondary *droit politique*, and dealing with the same society of men regarded as a *corps social* or unity; and you suppose that the agents of this order will handle the things which belong to unity, such as education within and foreign relations without. But what is to follow on this beginning? Some may wish to move boldly ahead; to extend the range of economic federalism almost to the extinction of the unitary State, or indeed of any form of State; to urge, as the great means of that extension, the preaching and the waging of a general strike for the paralysis of the political order. Their policy will be, 'Let the coercive machinery of the State be made to disappear, and let its place be taken by the mutual and freely co-operating services of workers, traders, teachers, and the rest'. Others, less radical or more cautious, may refuse even to preach, and still more to practice, the general strike; and instead of seeking to extinguish the State in favour of a self-acting society of services, they may content themselves with an attempt to reconcile and unite the political order with the economic. Their policy will be, 'Let us introduce elements from the economic order into the political; let us base the political parliament on electorates composed of *syndicats ouvriers*, or at any rate let us institute an economic parliament (which may conveniently be called an economic council, and be vested at the least with consultative powers) by the side of the political parliament'.

But whatever its forms and its oscillations, the ideas and trends of French Syndicalism have exerted an influence not only in France but also in England and Italy. Distinguishing the economic order from the political, and emphasizing its federal nature and the autonomy of its federated units, syndicalism has partly challenged, and partly even modified, the rigours of Marxian Socialism. In England the syndicalist leaven may be said to have had two effects. One, which has now disappeared, was the philosophy of 'Guild Socialism'—a sort of Franco-German mixture: German in its 'socialism', and in vesting the State with the ownership of the means of production; French in remitting to the 'Guild', or rather to a number of guilds, the management of those means, and French again, though with some modifications, in its theory of the two Parliaments, an economic parliament based on guilds for the affairs of economic society, and a political parliament based on local constituencies for the affairs of the State. The other effect—if indeed it be an effect, and not a native and independent development (we have to remember that syndicalist ideas appeared in England as early as 1834, and that an organized system of powerful trade unions is an old and indigenous growth)—is the crossing and modification of the Socialist or Labour party and programme by ideas and policies of a syndicalist character. The Socialist or Labour party is largely based on the adherence and subscriptions of trade unions: by its side stands the Trades Union Congress as a central federal organ, economic in character, but also interested in politics (just as, conversely, the Labour party is political in character, but also interested, and deeply interested, in economics); and there is thus a criss-cross and interfusion which is confusing in theory and yet works in practice. As with the party, so with the programme. The programme has been, and still remains, a programme of the nationalization of industries and their final control by representatives of the community; but it has also been, and still is, a programme of the association of the various grades of the workers, both managerial and manual, in the conduct and the administration of their respective industries. There is thus accommodation and compromise—there is even what may be called a 'margin of impression'—in the English adjustment between socialism and syndicalism.

The influence of syndicalism in Italy has been of a different character. It may be said to have followed two main directions, affecting, on the one hand, the Vatican and the policy of the Papacy, and, on the other, the Quirinal and the policy of the Italian State from 1922 to 1939. The two directions differed: indeed they differed profoundly; but they were united by one common feature. Alike in the Papal Encyclical *Quadragesimo Anno* (1931) and in the various and multifarious secular laws of the Fascist period there is a common use of the idea of 'corporativism'. Corporativism may be defined as syndicalism writ double. It is a philosophy of the economic group as consisting not only of workers, but also of employers, both of them acting together, in a double organization which is somehow also single, to render the service and enjoy the benefits of their particular branch of economic activity. As such a philosophy it has pitted itself against the two extremes of *laissez-faire* individualism and 'regulatory socialism'. But corporativism itself has its own extremes and oppositions. At one end of the scale is the *ordo* of the Papal Encyclical, with the employers and employed of each *ordo* freely collaborating in the production of goods and the rendering of services, and with all the *ordines* freely joined in concord for the promotion of the common good; and here the keynote is freedom—freedom for the members of each *ordo* to choose whatever form they prefer; freedom, too, tor the whole society to recover the riches of an articulated system of social groups, *per diversi generis consociationes composite evoluta*, which in 'an earlier age' (apparently the Middle Ages) was interposed between the individual and the State, easing and smoothing their relations and contacts. At the other end of the scale is—or was—the *corporazione* of the Fascist system: an institution, it is true, which similarly embraced employers and employed, but an institution created by the State, controlled by the State, and intended, by definition, to serve as 'an organ of the administration of the State'. The corporativism of the Fascist régime was a pseudo-syndicalist stucco hastily applied and superficially attached to a structure of *étatisme*; and all its paraphernalia of vocational groups and vocational representation, Proudhonist as it might appear, was at the antipodes from Proudhon. The history of ideas may be a history of their degradation. Few ideas, in any country, have been so degraded as the idea of syndicalism was in Fascist Italy.

In itself, and apart from its 'corporative' transformations whether Catholic or Fascist, syndicalism has made its contribution to the development of human thought. It has been a force which has made for the disengaging of the concept of Society from the concept of the State. But it has also done more—or less—and this in two ways. In the first place, it has tended to confine the idea of Society to one of its aspects or fields, and to make it essentially, or even solely, a matter of economics. Society is wider than that. It *is* a matter of economics; but it is also a matter of religion, of education, science, and culture, of charity in its broadest sense, of the play of the faculties in amusement or the enjoyment of leisure, and of all the activities which the mind of man proposes for the various purposes of its own free exercise. In the second place, syndicalism has sometimes tended, in its extremer forms, to push its conception of Society almost to the length of denying and destroying the State. There is room for both State and Society; and as long as human nature remains the same, and men are men, the State will always be with us. The political order has its necessity: it is at least as natural as the economic; and it may even be said to be prior, in the sense that it is the necessary condition of the existence of any form of economic order. There were States before there were guilds: and there could not have been any guilds—or, for that matter, any property, or any production, or any exchange—unless there had been a rule-making State in terms of whose rules such things could develop.

BOOK II

STATE AND SOCIETY

A General View of their Relations

§ I. THE DISTINCTION BETWEEN SOCIETY AND THE STATE

TURNING from this historical retrospect back to the ideas of today, as they were summarily described in the beginning of the argument,[1] we may now proceed to develop and amplify that description, with a special reference to English conditions and the general structure of English life. We start from the primary fact of the existence of national society. The nation, one in itself and always retaining the same identical body of members, confronts us, none the less, in a double aspect. This double aspect may be seen from three different points of view.

The first point of view is that of purpose or function. On the one hand, the nation, legally organized and assuming the aspect of a single legal association, acts in the terms and under the 'articles' by which that association is constituted (that is to say, in the terms and under the rules of the 'constitution') for the single legal purpose of making and enforcing a permanent system of law and order. On the other hand, the nation, socially organized (within the framework, but not by the act, of the legal association), and assuming the aspect of a plurality of associations (owing to the number and variety of the different social impulses), acts for a variety of purposes other than the legal purpose; purposes religious, moral, intellectual, aesthetic, economic, and recreational. (The Football Association and the Marylebone Cricket Club must also be counted among 'associations'.) In personal composition the legal association and the social organization—or in other words the State and Society—are one: they both include the same body of persons. In purpose they are different: the State exists for one great, but single, purpose; Society exists for a number of purposes, some great and some small, but all, in their aggregate, deep as well as broad.

[1] In Book I, § 2.

The second point of view from which the nation may be seen in its double aspect is that of organization or structure. Function determines structure; and the difference of purpose or function just noted necessarily involves (as indeed the argument has already implied) a difference of organization or structure. As organized legally, in the terms and under the rules of the one legal purpose, the members of a nation belong to one organization only, the State; though that one organization, if it be federal, may be a State composed of sub-states, and even if it be unitary may still (at any rate where local self-government is practised) be a State composed of units cherishing and practising some measure of 'autonomy' and thus, as that term implies, 'making laws on their own account'. As organized socially, in the terms and under the impulse of their many social purposes, the members of a nation belong to many organizations; though these all combine and coalesce in the general complex of Society. Yet the multiplicity of Society still remains in spite of such combination; and it shows itself twice over. In the first place, there is not only economic society, as the radical economist too readily assumes: there is also the society of religion, the society of moral conscience and of the virtue of charity, the society of art and aesthetic taste, the society of education and culture, and still other forms of society as numerous and as various as the needs of the human mind. Man belongs to some form of society for every purpose he can conceive, since every purpose can be advanced by social action, and none can be far or fully advanced without such action. In the second place, it is well to remember that even economic society itself is various, plural, and even multiple. There is no one economic society, unless or until we attain an undifferentiated workers' society. There is a wide-flung range of economic groups, from the simplest partnership or shop to the greatest of federations or the largest of amalgamations; and in all this wide-flung range, so long as there are still two sides to the economic process (a side of the employers and a side of the employed), the groups are 'two and two, one against another'.

The third point of view from which we may see the double aspect of the nation is that of method. The State employs the method of coercion or compulsion: its purpose of declaring and enforcing a scheme of law and order makes the method necessary; and the unity of its organization makes the method possible. Society uses the method of voluntary action and the process of persuasion: the nature of its purposes can be satisfied, and is best satisfied, by that method; and the multiplicity of its organization, which enables men to choose and relinquish freely their membership of its various and alternative groups, enables them also to escape coercion by any group if coercion should be attempted. But we have to admit that this distinction between the method of the State and the method of Society, if true in the main, is not always true. Economic forms of association begin to acquire a power of coercion when trade unions become organizations which a man must enter, and cannot relinquish, if he wishes to get or to keep employment. Distinctions of thought are always clearer than differences of fact. In fact, and in actual life, there is always a 'margin of imprecision'. The State, if it is coercive, has also a voluntary aspect, at any rate under a democratic system of government by virtue of which each citizen lays his mind alongside of other minds in a voluntary process of common debate and mutual persuasion. Conversely, social groups, though voluntary in their nature, may assume coercive power, as churches no less than trade unions have done in the course of history.

§ 2. THE STATE AS A LEGAL ASSOCIATION, AND THE SCOPE OF ITS LEGAL PURPOSE

IT has just been said that the State exists for the great, but single, purpose of law. The question may be asked, 'But what of the idea, as old as the age of Aristotle, that the State exists for the sake of the general good life of its members?' The further question may also be asked, 'Does not the State, apart from ideas, and as a plain matter of fact, actually regulate issues other than legal issues?' A review of history is sufficient to show that the State in its time has touched many issues and played many parts; and it still continues today to be multifarious in its activity. It has acted in the religious field, by measures ranging from the establishment of a State-Church to the regulation of the trust deeds under which free churches own their property and manage their daily concerns. It has acted, and it acts increasingly, in the economic field: in our own history the long line of its acts runs from the Elizabethan Statute of Artificers (and even earlier statutes) to the contemporary statutes which 'nationalize' some of the staple industries. It has acted in the field of the intellect, by a succession of Education Acts: it has acted in the field of conscience, and in the name of social justice, by the institution of a system of public social services: it has acted in matters of the body, as well as in matters of the intellect and of conscience, and what it has done for public health and physical fitness is not the least of its doings. Can all these labours be comprehended under the rubric of law, or ascribed to a single 'legal purpose'?

The answer is that the term 'legal' does not denote a set of things in a separate compartment, comparable to but separable from other sets of things (religious or economic or intellectual or moral) in other similar compartments. Life is not only a matter of compartments: it is also a matter of modes. The term 'legal' connotes a mode, if it also serves to denote a compartment; and what it connotes is of more importance than what it denotes. Considered as a mode, the term 'legal' means a method or process of action, irrespective of the field of action or the content of the field. Legal action—we may also call it 'political', for, as it will be argued later, the political is also the legal, since the State is essentially law[1]—legal action is a mode of treating things in general, things of all sorts and descriptions, religious or moral or educational or economic or whatever they may be, *so far as they can be brought under a rule of law and thus made a matter of compulsory uniformity*. Law touches and treats *all* acts—so far as acts are amenable to its touch and treatment.

But it is only external acts which are amenable to such treatment. A rule of law is an order (ultimately issued, as we shall see later,[2] by the community itself, but immediately issued by some organ which declares and enforces the sense of the community), to do, or to abstain from doing, a defined and definite external act: an order enforced, in the last resort, by another external act of physical coercion. From this point of view the State may order its members, as it did in 1559 by the Elizabethan Act of Uniformity, 'all and every . . . to resort to their parish church . . . upon every Sunday and other . . . holy days . . . upon pain that every person so offending shall forfeit for every such offence twelvepence'. This is a legal order to perform an

---

[1] *Infra*, Book III, § 1.   [2] *Infra*, Book IV, § 6.

external act of physical attendance at public worship: an order enforced, in the event of contravention, by another external act of physical coercion which takes twelve pence from the pocket of the offender. In a sense this is not a regulation of the religious life, which is a matter of the inward mind: it is a regulation of external acts performed in connexion with religious life. But the crux of the matter lies in the word 'connexion'; and the enforcement by the authority of the State of an act so intimately connected with religious life as to be a symbol of inward conviction, and to be regarded in that light by the agent and enjoined with that intention by the authority, is something which is *ultra vires* and beyond the power of law. The long struggle and the ultimate triumph of English Nonconformity, vindicating the principle that 'in matters of the mind there is no compulsion', has recalled the State to its bounds. We recognize today that true religion is a matter of the mind, to be sought and found in voluntary co-operation with others of like mind, and therefore to be sought and found in the area of Society. But we also recognize that the State cannot be excluded wholly from the field of religion. Religion means organization as well as inward conviction. Organization involves financial and other external consequences; and those consequences come within the ambit of law, and therefore of the State. Wherever the legal mode is needed, that mode must necessarily enter. Wherever it cannot act—wherever, that is to say, compulsory uniformity is impossible—the mode is necessarily precluded.

The argument which applies to the religious field applies equally to the moral and the intellectual; it applies even to the economic. The economic process is indeed particularly immeshed in financial and other consequences of a legal order which bring it particularly and peculiarly within the ambit of law and the supervision of the State. But so far as it is a process which requires for its operation factors that cannot be 'reduced to the one'—the irreducible inward factors of spontaneity of individual initiative and free variety of individual experiment—so far, and to that extent, it escapes, and will always escape, the net of legal regulation. Here, as in every other field, the argument brings us to two conclusions. The first is that there is no set of things, and no compartment of issues, about which you can say to law and the State, 'You shall not enter; you have nothing to do with it: this is a reserved compartment'. The second is that for every set, and in every compartment, all that law and the State can do is to secure external acts of obedience under the sanction of otherwise applying external acts of coercion.

The first conclusion will lead us to say that the State and its law exist for the sake of the general good life. The second will lead us to say that all they can do for the general good life is to secure, by the ultimate sanction of force, the uniform doing of external acts, and to erect thereby an external framework for the inward movement of a good life which proceeds by its own proper motion. There is no salvation in the State: there is only a sovereign safeguard. Salvation lies in ourselves, and we have to win it ourselves—in the shelter of the sovereign safeguard. We may dream of a State which itself is an institute of salvation. We only dream; and our dream is one which denatures the State and unspheres law. The State of reality is by its nature a sovereign safeguard—no more, but also no less; and the sphere of law is obligatory rules of external action—no more, but also no less. Even if we ourselves, as members of the legal association, are makers and motors of the safeguard, it is only a safeguard, and not an institute of salvation, that we make and move, *in that capacity of ourselves*. Even if we ourselves, acting directly or through an organ appointed by us for the purpose, are the declarers and enforcers of law, it is only law—a set of compulsory uniform rules of external action—which we declare and enforce.

There remains a large sphere of activity which lies outside the State. It is the sphere, in a word, of the inward movement of the good life. That movement is not only a matter of the 'individual', acting as an individual. It *is* a matter of 'individuals': but how much, and how often, do individuals act *in* groups, or *as* groups—in families (the innermost cells of our life), in schools (which are free societies of the mind in their inward operation, whatever their external framework may be), in churches and chapels, in professions and occupations, in 'clubs', 'societies', and 'associations' of every sort and description? The inward movement of the good life is at least as much social as individual; and voluntary social co-operation is one of its greatest channels. Nor is such co-operation limited to the inward life. It has also helped, and it still helps, in making the external framework, and securing the external conditions, necessary for a good life. The State is indeed the sovereign maker of the external framework; but it is not the only maker. There has always been, and there still remains, a space for social activity in the provision of the framework. In the first place, the State will always be, as it were, behind in the provision which it makes. There will be external conditions which it has not, as yet, secured, because there is not, as yet, a general conviction of their necessity; and the laboratory of social invention, engaged in pioneer's work, has to go ahead in planning and contriving voluntary expedients, and even systems, which at a later stage may be generally adopted and incorporated in the general framework. Secondly, even when the State has itself secured external conditions in this or in that field, it has only secured them (it can do no more by its very nature) in the shape of a uniform rule, which is the same for all indifferently and without respect of persons. But persons are different; and some of them will need their special conditions, over and above, or diverging from, the conditions secured by a uniform rule. Here social activity enters once more, not as a pioneer going on ahead, but as a 'mate' or collaborator standing by the side of the State to make some necessary adjustment or to add some necessary complement. The State, for example, may give unemployment benefit, and even add to it public assistance, by uniform rule; but there will still be special cases, and there will still be room for social action to meet such cases.

§ 3. THE PLACE AND FUNCTION OF SOCIETY IN THE COURSE OF ENGLISH DEVELOPMENT

IF we consider the relation of the State and Society in point of time, we shall find it hard to assign any priority or to say which precedes the other. On the one hand, it may be argued, there must have been society of some sort—some voluntary habit of living together and 'sticking together'—before men could develop a system of conscious self-organization in terms of law. From this point of view Society is anterior to the State: the naturally given fact of Society precedes, if it does not produce, the consciously created fact of the State. From this point of view, and on this assumption that Society is a naturally given fact, we may also say that it is wrong to speak of a 'social' contract, as if a conscious contract had created Society—though it may well be right to speak of a 'political' contract, wherever at any rate we can detect a conscious agreement creating (or recreating) the State, as we can, for instance, in North America in 1787. (There is a note of Lord Acton, among his manuscripts, 'Rousseau's error was in affirming that society comes from contract: Burke denied that the State itself comes from it—also wrong.'[1] The antithesis is hardly fair, either to Rousseau or to Burke; but the idea behind the antithesis is just.) On the other hand, it may also be argued that there is a sense in which the State precedes Society. When the State is once there, with its scheme of law and order, it provides a general security in whose shelter social formations can easily grow. From this point of view it is possible to regard Society as growing round the State —surrounding it, indeed, with growths—and yet leaving it always as the core.[2] From this point of view, too, we may even say that the State is anterior to Society, or at any rate prior to the great bulk of the voluntary social formations which constitute Society.

It is perhaps idle to discuss priorities, and it is simplest to say that, at any rate in historic times, the State and Society have been concomitants, either acting in turn on the other. In England, at any rate, the interaction has been mutually beneficial; and in particular the presence of a settled State, which we have enjoyed since the Revolution of 1688 (and even that was an agreed transaction rather than a 'revolution'), has been favourable, on the whole, to the existence and action of voluntary social formations, ranging from voluntary hospitals, voluntary educational societies, and voluntary companies (whether or no they are called companies) such as Lloyd's and the Stock Exchange, to free churches, trade unions, and even political parties, which, as has already been noticed and must be noticed again at a later stage of the argument,[3] are really 'social' rather than political in their nature. . . . Indeed it was sometimes suggested in a phase of opinion current at the beginning of this century,

---

[1] Quoted by Dr. Cobban, in *Rousseau and the Modern State*, p. 232.
[2] *Supra*, Book I, § 9, *ad finem*.
[3] *Supra*, Book I, § 9, *ad finem*; *infra*, Book V, § 4.

that we English were progressing, and ought to progress still further, by way of a regression back to the epoch of the Middle Ages—that paradise of voluntary groups and Eden of pure society. But there is a great difference, in this respect, between the Middle Ages and our own age. Groups flourished in the Middle Ages in the absence of an effective State and an operative scheme of law and order; but the price paid for their flourishing was so heavy that men turned by preference to an effective State and sacrificed groups on its altar. Groups flourish today, if with less luxuriance, in the presence and under the shelter of an effective State; and for us to go back to the Middle Ages, in the sense of abandoning an effective State, might mean a sacrifice of the groups we have for groups we should hardly like to have—on such conditions and at such a price.

It we take a just view of our actual mercies, we shall recognize that the development of England since 1688, and not least in the course of the nineteenth century, has been marked by two characteristics. One of them has been the parallel growth of Society and the State, of voluntary co-operation and political regulation, with one of them sometimes gaining on the other (as at present, and under conditions of emergency, the State would seem to be gaining), but with both still moving and both still active. The other characteristic has been the interconnexion of the two growths—not divided into compartments, but mutually interfused and reciprocally interacting. The latter of these characteristics is particularly notable. On the one hand, as Bosanquet remarked,[1] voluntary social groups, acting first in lieu of the State and then acting upon the State, can do an initial work of social experimentation which will afterwards, if it is successful enough to merit general adoption, be 'endorsed' or 'taken over' by the legislation of the State, as an 'adopted' road is incorporated into the road system of a town. Here Society serves as a laboratory for the State; and here we may cite the history of primary education, which was first conducted by two voluntary societies (one Anglican and one Nonconformist, but both founded about 1810), and then 'endorsed' and 'adopted' by the State in 1870 and afterwards. Here, too, it is to be noted that the State, in endorsing and adopting the results of volun-

---

[1] Introduction to the second edition of *The Philosophical Theory of the State*, p. xxxiii.

tary initiative, may still respect and preserve the original initiative, as it has done, for example, by the retention of 'voluntary schools' in the general framework of its own system. Again, and on the other hand, just as social action aids the State, so the State in turn may aid social action. It may subsidize approved societies in the conduct of their voluntary work, as it did when a grant of £20,000 (afterwards made annual) was voted in 1833 for the building of school houses and distributed for that purpose between the two voluntary educational societies. In one way or the other—whether through the stimulus applied to the State by social action, or through the aid given to social action by the State—it may be said (as it was said by Mr. Sidney Webb, some forty years ago) that in the course of the nineteenth century 'voluntary association and government action have always gone on side by side, the one apparently always inspiring, facilitating, and procuring successive developments of the other'.[1]

Two factors in English life have contributed to the ready germination of voluntary societies and to easy relations between these societies and the State. One of them may be called, in a term coined by Dr. Johnson, the 'clubable' character of the English genius: its taste for founding and managing clubs and companies, from the East India Company, which governed an empire, to the village cricket club. The club and the committee are part of the general grain.[2] They proliferate equally on allotments and in Pall Mall: in the 'combination' rooms of colleges and in 'combinations' of employers or workers: in 'an assembly of good fellows meeting under certain conditions' (Dr. Johnson's definition of a club), and in the assembly of national representatives, meeting as a Parliament at Westminster, but becoming in process of time a club as well as a Parliament. By itself this proliferation of societies and combinations might have embarrassed the State: indeed at times it has done so; and the State has occasionally stretched out a hand

---

[1] In the *Cambridge Modern History*, vol. xii, p. 747.

[2] Two examples may be cited. One is 'the Club' (the club *par excellence*, with no other distinctive name), founded by Dr. Johnson at the end of 1783, which met at the 'Essex Head' in Essex Street, off the Strand. It still survives. Another is the Green Ribbon Club, founded in 1675 with Shaftesbury as its president, which met (not many yards away from Essex Street) at the King's Head Tavern, where Chancery Lane abuts on Fleet Street. As long as there is a Whig or Liberal party in England, that club, too, still survives.

against 'corresponding societies' and against 'conspiracies' in restraint of trade. But a second factor in English life has come to the rescue, and relieved or removed the embarrassment. This second factor is the peculiar character of the English State and of English law. The English State itself has had some of the qualities of a club, and it has thus had a fellow feeling for clubs which has made it generally kind. Not only is the House of Commons something in the nature of a club: political parties, as has already been noticed, have long combined the character of social formations with the activity of political forces; and in the area of local self-government, during the two centuries which followed the Revolution of 1688, the Quarter Sessions of the Justices of the Peace were a sort of county club, which might meet in a county hotel (as the Berkshire justices did when they passed 'the Speenhamland Act' of 1795) to settle issues of county policy. Similarly, English law may be regarded as largely the product of a club, or rather of a group of clubs, the Inns of Court with their barrister members from whom the judges are drawn; and it is certain that in one of its elements, its peculiar law of trusts, English law has provided a shelter and shield for voluntary society. Under the law of trusts a society need not confront the State directly as a property-owning body vested with a corporate capacity which makes it amenable to visitation and liable to dissolution. The property of the society may be vested in trustees—individual persons who hold it for the benefit of the society: who alone are recognized by the State as the holders of the property, so that the society remains in the background; but whom none the less, in case of need, the State will compel to discharge the trust incumbent on the property, with the result that the society in the background has a charmed and protected existence. Free churches, trade unions, and all sorts of societies have flourished under the shelter of the trust, 'so wide', as Maitland has said, 'was that blessed back stair', and so great was the latitude which it gave to 'social experimentation'.[1]

---

[1] 'The blessed back stair' is a phrase used by Maitland in his introduction to Gierke's *Political Theories of the Middle Age*, p. xxxi. That the trust 'has been a most powerful instrument of social experimentation' is a phrase used in an essay on 'The Unincorporate Body' in Maitland's *Collected Papers*, vol. iii, p. 298.

§ 4. NATIONAL SOCIETY AND THE
NATIONAL STATE

THE argument may now proceed to a statement of some conclusions involved or implied in its previous course.

(*a*) Under modern conditions, and as a result of the historic process by which they have been created, the basic form of human community, which we may call the community *par excellence*, is the nation—an inclusive all-purposes body of persons, covering a territorial area or *patria*, and containing within itself a variety of particular-purpose societies.[1] More fully defined, the nation may be said to be a body of persons, inhabiting a definite territory and thus united by the primary fact of contiguity, who physiologically, and in respect of the blood in their veins, are generally drawn from a number of different races or breeds brought by time and their own wanderings into the territory, but who psychologically, and in respect of the content of their minds, have been led by a life of contiguity to develop two forms of mental sympathy. The first is a common capital of thoughts and feelings acquired and transmitted in the course of a common past history: a common capital, or tradition, which includes as a rule a common language, a common religion (which may, however, assume a number of different forms), and a common culture variously expressed in art and architecture, in literature, in social habits, and otherwise. The second is a common will to live together for the future, freely and independently increasing the common capital of thoughts and feelings, and thus exercising a right at the very least of social, but possibly also of political self-determination.

A reflection may be added to this definition of the nature of a nation. When nations became self-conscious, as they did in the nineteenth century and have progressively done in the twentieth, they seek to express and interpret—but they may only succeed

[1] In regard to the terms 'community' and 'society', both used in this sentence, it may be noted that etymologically there is little reason for any distinction. 'Community' connotes a sharing in services or functions (*munera*); 'Society' a sharing in the activity of partnership with other *socii* similarly engaged in a common undertaking. 'Community' is perhaps more general, and 'society' more special. When we speak, as we often do, of the 'community' (with the definite article), we are thinking of the genus; when we speak of 'society' (without any article, definite or indefinite), we are thinking of something which, though much the same, is narrower and more special in the sense that while 'the community' generally implies the presence of a State as well as that of societies, 'society' simply implies the presences of societies.

in distorting—what may be called the 'idea of the Nation'. The
term 'nation' may thus acquire different senses among different
nations, and even at different periods of the history of the same
nation. In Germany under the National Socialists the nation
became, in an interpretation which was also a distortion of its
nature, a racial structure built on the basis of an assumed con-
sanguinity or common Aryan blood which was supposed to
carry in its corpuscles a psychological treasure (as if time and
tradition were not the main makers of such treasure), and
which was to be kept pure from any admixture in order that the
treasure might also be pure. In Italy, again, the nation became,
in another interpretation which was also a visionary distortion,
a metaphysical super-person: not a body of persons united by
the psychological bonds of a common tradition and purpose,
but a person above that body of persons, 'with a being, ends, and
means of action' (so it was expressed in a document curiously
entitled the Charter of Labour) 'superior to those of the individuals, separate or grouped, of whom it is composed'. It is
a relief to turn from such interpretations to the simplicity of
France, even if France may be said to have exaggerated the
moi and the sovereignty of the nation. The French conception,
based, in its present form, on the Revolution of 1789, is neither
racial nor metaphysical. The sovereign nation is simply the
population of the territory of France, one and indivisible in
the strength of the natural frontiers by which it is enclosed,
and united together internally by the bond of a common
amour du pays natal. In a word, the nation is something rooted in
the soil of France—in its sun, its wine, its speech, its social
habits, its general culture and way of life. . . . But however the
nation may be conceived, and however its unity may be interpreted, the fact of the unity of the national community is the
primary fact—except in the philosophy of Communist Russia,
which is, or was (for even here the nation *will* recur),[1] based

[1] It would seem to be significant that the Constitution of the U.S.S.R. adopted in
1937 twice uses, if not the term 'nation', at any rate the term *patria* or fatherland—
in Russian *otechestvo*. In one section there is a reference to socialist property as 'the
source of the wealth and might of the fatherland'; in another 'the defence of the
fatherland' is made the sacred duty of every citizen of the U.S.S.R. (The Russian
word which corresponds to 'nation' is *narod*, which literally means 'growth over',
and suggests the spreading of the stock or breed over the wide space of the Russian
fatherland or *otechestvo*.)

faith of the Scottish people')[1] and also with the added legal right
of separate Scottish courts and some measure, though a diminishing measure, of separate Scottish rules of law. But it is
seldom easy for a national minority to be content to exist simply
as a *social group*. On the one hand the State, mainly based on the
national majority, may seek to insist that the right of a national
minority to use its own language does not extend into the area
of State institutions, such as the schools and courts of the State;
and it may thus raise legal issues which carry the national
minority out of the social sphere into that of the legal association and its compulsory rules. On the other hand a national
minority may itself raise legal issues, and challenge the legal
rights of the State: it may, for example, claim a separate legal
position (some form of autonomy or 'home rule') within the
legal association; or it may even claim that it ought to be a
separate and independent legal association and is therefore
entitled to secede and assume the position of a sovereign State.
To distinguish between the 'social' and the 'legal' sphere is no
solution to the problem of national minorities, unless they on
their side are willing to recognize and observe the distinction,
and unless the majority nation on which the State is predominantly based is equally willing to recognize and observe the
same distinction.

A third and last addition to the argument is necessary in
order to explain the place of the constitution in the structure
of the modern State. By the terms of the definition suggested,
a modern State is a territorial nation organized as a legal association by its own action in creating a constitution. On this
showing the constitution is a bridge, made by a nation, which
spans the interval and maintains the connexion between the
nation and the State. Such a view may readily be challenged.
Do all nations, as a matter of fact, create a constitution by their
own act, in order thereby to constitute themselves States? It
may be argued that constitutions generally are not made, but
grow: *nascuntur, non fiunt*. Hegel may be cited in evidence:
'What is called making a constitution is a thing that has never

---

[1] The Schedule to the Church of Scotland Act, 1921, Article III: see also
Article IV, where it is recited that 'this Church . . . receives . . . from its Divine
King and Head, and from Him alone, the right and power subject to no civil
authority to legislate, and to adjudicate finally, in all matters of doctrine, worship,
government and discipline in the Church'.

happened in history: a constitution only develops from the national spirit identically with that spirit's own development.'[1] Short of that, it may well be argued that there are at any rate *some* constitutions, such as the English, which have not been made, but have grown historically; and it may thus be contended that the English nation has never created a constitution —but is nevertheless a State.

Two answers may be made to this contention. The first is that almost every modern State (alike in Europe, in America, and in Asia) has come into existence in its present form, and as what it now is, through the creation of a constitution which is the constituent charter of its being. Either there has been a break in the national life, a revolution, followed by a national act reorganizing the nation as a new legal association under a new constitution (this happened in France in 1789, and has happened again and again in different countries since); or there has been some act of separation from a larger whole and some consequent reconstruction of the separated unit or units (as the North American colonies separated from Great Britain in 1776 and then proceeded to reconstruct their life under new constitutions of their own making); or, conversely, there has been some union of parts hitherto separate in a new federal body, and this union has been accompanied, and indeed made, by the creation of a federal constitution, such as the American constitution of 1787, or the Canadian of 1867, or the Australian of 1900. In one or another of these ways, or in some way similar to these, almost every State of the modern world has been organized in its present form, and as what it now actually is, by an act creating a constitution; and this act has generally been the overt act of a nation, expressing itself in and through an assembly of national representatives,[2] though sometimes

---

[1] *Philosophy of Mind*, § 540.

[2] Again and again we may trace the idea of national creation in modern constitutions. 'We, the people of the United States,' so runs the beginning of the American federal constitution of 1787, 'do ordain and establish this constitution.' 'We, the undersigned, representatives of the kingdom of Norway,' it is stated at the end of the Norwegian constitution of 1814, 'hereby declare this constitution, as adopted by the National Assembly, to be the Fundamental Law of the Kingdom of Norway, to which each and every one must conform.' Similarly, more than a century later, the preamble to the constitutional charter of the Czechoslovak Republic declares that 'We, the Czechoslovak nation, . . . have in our National Assembly this 29th day of February, 1920, adopted the following constitution.' The same form of

the form of the act may have been that of a royal grant (or *octroi*) in deference to the national will, or again of a parliamentary grant made to a dominion or colony in pursuance of its desires. These are the facts of the modern world; and when we are constructing a theory of the nature of the modern State, we have to adjust our theory to those facts.

But there is also a second answer to the argument that constitutions are historical growths, and not acts of creation. Even when a constitution has not been created at a point of time, but has been developed through the centuries along a line of time: even where a nation, during those centuries, may seem, at any rate in form, to have had little or nothing to do with constitution-making: even then, and even there, the formation of the constitution has been at each step an act of will and creation, and the whole of the constitution, as it now stands, is a nationally endorsed scheme of rules (not necessarily written, but none the less effective) which makes the State what it is today, controlling its operation and constituting its character. From this point of view the distinction between written and unwritten constitutions—or, more exactly, the distinction between constitutions created *uno ictu* and constitutions developed by a long and continuous process (*both* containing unwritten as well as written elements, though the proportion of the written to the unwritten may be larger in the former than it is in the latter)—is more a distinction of form than a distinction of substance. Both are alike memoranda of the association of the State; and both constitute it equally as the legal association which it is.

§ 5. A PRELIMINARY VIEW OF SOVEREIGNTY

In this connexion we may attempt a preliminary account of the notion of sovereignty.[1] There *must* exist in the State, as a legal association, a power of final legal adjustment of all legal issues which arise in its ambit. The legal association will not be

---

preamble ('We, the people of Eire, . . . do hereby adopt, enact, and give to ourselves this constitution') appears at the beginning of the Irish constitution of 1937; and though there is no such preamble or formula of creation in the Russian constitution adopted in 1937 (which may be regarded as a constitution based on an *octroi* or grant made by the leaders of the Communist Party), the draft of the constitution was at any rate laid before the people of the U.S.S.R. with a formal request for suggestions and amendments.

[1] For a further and fuller account the reader is referred to Book V, § 5.

a single unit, and law will not be a unity, unless there is some-where *one* authority to which crucial differences ultimately come, and which gives, as the authority of last resort, the ulti-mate and final decision. Different social groups may press different views of what is, or ought to be, law; it is even possible that different departments of the State may hold, and seek to enforce, different notions of what is legally right; there *must* be a final adjustment-centre. That final adjustment-centre is the sovereign, the topmost rung of the ladder, the *superanus* or *sovrano*, the 'authority of the last word'. Sovereignty is not the same as general State-authority, or *puissance publique*: it is the particular sort of State-authority which is the power, and the right, of ultimate decision.

In one sense sovereignty is unlimited—unlimited and illimi-table. There is no question arising in the legal association, and belonging to the sphere of its operation, which may not come up to the sovereign, and which will not be finally decided by the sovereign if it so comes up to the topmost rung. The adjust-ment-centre must be competent to adjust *every* issue, without exception, which may stand in need of adjustment. But there are other considerations also to be noticed; and these will show us that sovereignty, if it is not limited to particular questions and definite objects (limited, that is to say, in regard to the *things* which it handles), is none the less limited and defined by its own *nature* and its own *mode of action*.

In the first place, and as regards its *nature*, sovereignty is the authority of the last word. Only questions of the last resort will therefore be brought to the sovereign. Much will be settled in the lower ranges and in the ordinary course of the action of general State-authority. In the second place, and as regards its *mode of action*, the sovereign is a part and an organ of the legal association. Nothing will therefore come to the sovereign which does not belong to the nature and operation of the legal associa-tion, *as such*. Sovereignty moves within the circle of the legal association, and only within that circle; it decides upon ques-tions of a legal order, and only upon those questions. Moving within that circle, and deciding upon those questions, sove-reignty will only make legal pronouncements, and it will make them according to regular rules of legal procedure. It is not a capricious power of doing anything in any way: it is a legal power of settling finally legal questions in a legal way. Upon this it follows that sovereignty, confined by its nature to the sphere of the legal association, will not enter or seek to control the sphere of society, unless questions arise in that sphere (such as the interpretation of a trust deed or of the articles of association of some form of voluntary society) which invite a legal decision and are amenable to such a decision. There are areas of social action which cannot be entered by law or brought under legal control. Sovereignty, being by its nature legal, does not impinge on these areas.[1]

Who, then, or what, is the sovereign, in the sense of being the final adjustment-centre of the legal association?

(*a*) Ultimately, and in the very last resort, the sovereign is the constitution itself—the constitution which is the efficient and formal cause of the association; which brings it into being; which forms and defines the organs and methods of its operation, and may also form and define (if the constitution either contains or is accompanied by a 'declaration of rights') the purposes of its operation. It may be objected to this view that the sovereign is a body of living persons, and not an impersonal scheme; and that ultimate sovereignty must accordingly be ascribed, not to the constitution, but to the constitution-making body behind it which can alter and amend its provisions. But there is an answer to that objection. The impersonal scheme of the constitution is permanently present, day by day, and year by year; it acts continuously, and without interruption, as the permanent control of the whole operation of the State. The body of persons which can alter and amend the constitution (and which, by the way, can act only under the constitution, and in virtue of the constitution) is a body which acts only at moments of interruption, and therefore at rare intervals. The continuous control may more properly be termed sovereign than the occasional interruption; and we may accordingly say that the constitution itself, in virtue of being such a control, is the ultimate sovereign.

(*b*) Secondarily, however, and subject to the *ultimate* sovereignty of the constitution, we may say that the body which makes ordinary law, in the sense of issuing the day-to-day and the year-by-year rules of legal conduct, is the *immediate* sovereign. That body may be differently composed in different

[1] The reader is referred to § 2, above, and § 6, below, of this Book.

political systems. In the United States, for example, it is composed of Congress and President acting independently (though with mutual checks and reciprocal powers of overriding one another's authority) on a system of co-ordination. In the United Kingdom it is composed of Parliament and His Majesty's Ministers acting interdependently, and with a mutual give and take (though here too there are mutual checks, and Parliament can dismiss the Ministers by an adverse vote as vice versa they can dismiss Parliament by advising His Majesty to use his power of dissolution), on a system which is one of connexion rather than co-ordination. However composed, the body which makes the ordinary law of the land is the immediate sovereign, which issues final legal pronouncements on ordinary current questions to the extent and by the methods authorized under the constitution. The immediate sovereign which makes the ordinary law in the United Kingdom is authorized by the constitution to a greater extent of action, and to action by easier and speedier methods, than the immediate sovereign which makes the ordinary law in the United States; but in either case the immediate sovereign is a body authorized by the constitution, acting and able to act because it is so authorized.[1]

On the argument which is here advanced the constitution is the *ultimate* sovereign, in virtue of being the permanent scheme, or standing expression, of what may be called the primary law

[1] It is an illustration of the greater extent of the authorization given to Parliament and His Majesty's Ministers in the United Kingdom that they can make and amend the constitution itself by much the same process as they make and amend ordinary law; whereas in the United States the body which makes and amends the constitution is a different body from that which makes and amends ordinary law. The extent of the authorization thus given in the United Kingdom may seem to be so great as to abrogate any distinction between the ultimate sovereignty of the constitution and the immediate sovereignty of the body which makes the ordinary laws of the land. But reflection will show that this is not really the case. Parliament and His Majesty's Ministers act under the constitution, and subject to the constitution, even in the act of amending the constitution. It is true that, with an unwritten constitution, men may not be clear what it is, or may disagree about what it is. But it is also true that with a written constitution, men may not be clear what its written terms actually mean, or may disagree about what they mean. Neither the power of Parliament and His Majesty's Ministers to alter the constitution, nor the vagueness of the constitution, impairs the ultimate sovereignty of the constitution of the United Kingdom. The simple proof of that sovereignty is that the United Kingdom has undergone more than one 'peaceful revolution' since the Revolution (also peaceful) of 1688. Revolutions are not peaceful unless the constitution is admitted to be finally sovereign.

of the political association; and the law- and rule-making body is the *immediate* sovereign, in virtue of being the constant source and perennially active fountain of what may be called the secondary law of the land. Two difficulties confront the argument, one of them largely formal, but the other more substantial. The first and largely formal difficulty is that it would appear to be inconsistent to begin by ascribing ultimate sovereignty to the constitution rather than to the constitution-making body, and then to proceed to ascribe immediate sovereignty to the law- and rule-making body rather than to the law. Does not consistency demand either that both sovereigns should be impersonal systems, or that both should be personal bodies; either that the ultimate sovereign should be 'the rule of the constitution' and the immediate sovereign 'the rule of law', or that the ultimate sovereign should be the constitution-making body and the immediate the law- and rule-making body? We may answer that inconsistency is inherent in the nature of the case. The position of the primary law of the State is different from that of the secondary law. In the sphere of the primary law, which is in its nature permanent, it is the law itself, as a constant control, which matters more than the body of persons who occasionally vary and change the control. In the sphere of secondary law, which is in its nature constantly changing with the change of circumstances and situations, it is the body of men constantly making the changes, and always at the helm, that matters most in the eyes of men and is accordingly felt and acknowledged to be the immediate sovereign.

The second and more substantial difficulty raises deeper considerations. It has been said, in the argument here advanced, that the law- and rule-making body acts and is able to act because it is authorized by the constitution. But may it not also be said, and should it not rather be said, that the law- and rule-making body acts, and is able to act, because it is authorized by the nation, or short of that by national opinion, or, simpler still, by the electorate and its vote? And if that may be said, is it possible to ascribe any immediate sovereignty to that body, and should not such sovereignty be rather ascribed either (1) to the nation, or alternatively (2) to the thought of the nation, as expressed in the form of public opinion, or even (3) to the action of the electorate (as the organ *par excellence* of the nation), in electing—and thereby, in some sense, also authorizing and even 'instructing'—the body which makes the laws and issues the rules of legal conduct?

Three ideas are involved in the considerations which have just been raised—the idea of the sovereignty of the nation, or 'national sovereignty' (in the sense in which the term is current among French thinkers): the idea (which some English and American thinkers have cherished) of 'the sovereignty of public opinion'; and the idea of 'the sovereignty of the electorate', which in practice, in a number of continental countries, has been often interpreted to mean the sovereignty of the party or combination of parties which has secured a majority of electoral votes. The most serious of these three ideas—all akin to one another, but rivals as well as kin—is the idea of the sovereignty of public opinion. We may therefore begin with that idea: we may then proceed to the idea of the sovereignty of the electorate; and we may end by examining the idea of 'national sovereignty' in the French sense of that term.

(*a*) By the side of the State—so our argument has run— national Society continues to exist; to pursue a process of general thought in the form of national discussion; and to act for a variety of social purposes through a variety of social organs also engaged in a process of thought (they could not otherwise act) which pours itself into the general pool of the thought of the whole society. By the exercise of this process of thought in the form of discussion national Society precipitates a body of opinion, which we may call indifferently by the name of national or public opinion.[1] This body of opinion will affect and qualify the action of the law-making body. *Legally*, that body still remains the immediate sovereign, and it therefore remains unlimited and illimitable, except by the constitution: *actually*, it has its ear to the ground of public opinion, and although it may do *de jure* whatever it wills to do within the limits of the constitution, it moves *de facto* within the limits (necessarily, by their nature, elastic) of an encompassing body of

---

[1] The difficulty of the term 'public', derived from the Latin *populus*, is that it suggests the organized legal community or *respublica*, and thus imports the idea of the State. It is not the State, but national society, which is the area of opinion. But 'public opinion', although it is a term which may offend the purist anxious for words of clean significance, is consecrated by usage, the final master and arbiter of terms.

opinion precipitated by the nation. Some have made this fact of the relation of public opinion to the law-making body the ground of a distinction between two kinds of sovereignty—political sovereignty, regarded as resident in public opinion, and legal sovereignty, regarded as resident in the law-making body. But the difficulty of this distinction is that all sovereignty is essentially legal, and you cannot divide what is essentially legal into the legal and the other-than-legal. (It is a different matter to make a distinction between two *grades* of legal sovereignty, the higher and ultimate grade of the sovereignty of the constitution, and the lower and immediate grade of the sovereignty of the law-making body: the difference there is a difference of hierarchy and degree in one and the same kind of sovereignty, and not a difference of two kinds.) We shall do well to cling to the idea of the one immediate legal sovereignty of the law-making body, admitting (or rather contending), as we do so, that in operation and practice this sovereignty acts with regard and respect—though not in legal subjection or any legal relation—to the general body of national thought and the weight of its opinion. That, however, is true not only of the law-making body and of the immediate legal sovereignty which it exercises, but also of the whole of government and of State-authority in all its range. Executive officials are particularly bound to act on the ground of law; and yet even they will be wise to remember in the course of their executive action that opinion must count as well as law. The law-making body is particularly able, in virtue of its representative character, and therefore particularly bound (though never legally bound), to remember and regard the existence of public opinion.

(*b*) The idea of the sovereignty of the electorate is one of a different order from that of the sovereignty of public opinion. The electorate is not the national society, however great its numbers may be; and the verdict it passes, at a given time, on the programmes and candidates submitted to its choice is something different from the constant play of national thought. The electorate is a legal organ of the legal association: it is part and parcel of the State. Normally, as its name suggests, it exists and acts for the single purpose of choosing the law-making body. It may, however, be authorized by the terms of the constitution to act on occasion for the further purpose of concurring in the passage of law, through the institution of the referendum: it may even be authorized by the constitution to act for the still further purpose of joining, upon occasion, in the first motion of law, through the institution of the initiative. In either of these events, or both, the law-making body is not the legislature[1] only, but the legislature and the electorate acting in conjunction; or rather it is the latter on the occasions when the institutions of the initiative and the referendum are employed, and it is the former, and only the former, on the occasions when they are not. (The oscillation is somewhat perplexing; and that is one of the reasons why the referendum and the initiative have never attained a general vogue.) But it is one thing to hold that the electorate may, in certain circumstances—that is to say, on some particular occasion—become a part of the immediate sovereign: it is another thing to hold that the electorate should, in all circumstances, be regarded as the whole of the immediate sovereign. To profess a belief in the sovereignty of the electorate is to subscribe to this latter view.

But it is difficult, and indeed impossible, to subscribe to the view that the electorate, in and by itself, can ever be regarded as the immediate sovereign. There are, indeed, arguments which may be advanced in support of the view. One of them is the argument that the electorate, merely by the fact, and in virtue of the act, of electing the law-making body is super-sovereign over that body. In itself that argument carries no weight: the electorate which chooses the immediate sovereign does not become an authority over it by virtue of its choice, any more than the electors who choose a professor become an authority over him by virtue of their choice. Another argument may seem to carry more weight. This is the argument that the electorate not only elects the law-making body, but also 'instructs' it at the time of election, and that therefore the body so instructed must act, during its term of office, according to its instructions. There *is* a sense in which the result of a general election is a sort of general instruction to the law-making body. But this general instruction is, at the most, a general expectation that the

[1] It is perhaps unnecessary to repeat, but it may be wise to do so in the interest of clarity and consistency, that the law-making body is never merely the legislature, but the legislature and the ministers acting in conjunction. That has already been noted in a previous passage of this section. Here the term 'legislature' is employed as a shorthand term for that conjunction, which is always present.

majority of the persons elected will seek to carry into effect the programme on which they have been elected—subject, however, to the march of events and new conjunctures of circumstance, and subject, above all, to free discussion with the minority (who have also been elected and have also their rights and functions) and to the achievement of some compromise based upon such discussion. Such a general expectation, so qualified and so circumscribed, imposes no legal obligation upon the persons elected: it does not make the electorate a legal adjustment-centre: it does not diminish—it even increases—the duty of the body of elected persons to act as such a centre, and to make the actual adjustments to the best of their ability and by the use of their discretion.

There is a further remark to be added. The idea of the sovereignty of the electorate, when we pursue it to its inmost recesses, is really a cover or outwork for the idea of the sovereignty of party. The name of the electorate may grace the measure, but party is the real flame. The majority party pleads the verdict and instruction of the electorate—that is to say, of the majority of the electorate, for there is also a minority which has also given a verdict and instruction—in order to cover its partisan claim to make adjustments in its own sense and on its own motion. Party has a great and legitimate function in a democratic system of government; the function of formulating choices for the electorate, the function of arraying sides in the legislature, the function of cementing the Cabinet (and also the anti-cabinet, or Leaders of the Opposition) in the sympathy of a common loyalty. But if it is ubiquitous, it is never sovereign; and if it contributes to adjustments, it is not their maker. The hidden notion of the sovereignty of party is something more dangerous than the open idea of the sovereignty of the electorate. The electorate is intermittent: party is always there. The electorate is a legal organ, acting in public and by methods publicly prescribed. Party is partly public, but it is partly also private; it is partly a matter of the State, but it is partly also a matter of Society and voluntary social arrangements. The sovereignty of party, however it might be veiled under the name of the electorate, would be a sovereignty always acting but often acting obscurely and sometimes deviously. There is all the more reason for refusing to accept the idea of the sovereignty of the electorate when we reflect on the nature of the actual sovereign which that idea might be used to veil.

(*c*) The idea of the sovereignty of the nation (*souveraineté nationale*) is an idea which has had a large vogue in France. It is already indicated in one of the articles of the Declaration of the Rights of Men and Citizens of the year 1791: 'le principe de toute souveraineté réside essentiellement dans la nation.' If, however, we analyse the term 'nation', in so far as it bears on the idea of sovereignty, we shall see that it must mean one of two things. It may mean, in the first place, the whole population of a national territory, considered as the source of public opinion; and in that case what has already been said of the idea of the sovereignty of public opinion must also be said of the idea of national sovereignty. It may mean, in the second place, that part of the population which constitutes the electorate; and in that case what has already been said of the sovereignty of the electorate must also be said of the idea of national sovereignty.

We may therefore conclude that immediate sovereignty cannot be ascribed to the nation, any more than it can be ascribed to the electorate or to public opinion, but must be ascribed to the law-making body, and to that body only. It is that body, and only that body, which makes the actual adjustments of questions under debate; and it is the adjustments made by that body, and only those adjustments, which are binding and obligatory on the members of the State. It is true that the sovereignty of the law-making body is limited: indeed it is doubly limited— legally limited, by the need of keeping within the constitution and acting under the constitution; practically limited, by the need of keeping in harmony with the opinion of national society and acting in conformity with its general trend. The fact that the constitution is a legal limit on the immediate sovereign makes the constitution super-sovereign; the final sovereign; the ultimate sovereign. But the fact that the public opinion of Society is a practical limit on the immediate sovereignty of the law-making body does not make that opinion in any sense sovereign. The term sovereign belongs to the legal sphere, and to that sphere only. The constitution belongs to that sphere: public opinion does not. To vest sovereignty in the public opinion of national Society is both illogical and dangerous. It is illogical, because sovereignty does not belong to the social sphere in which opinion moves, but only to the legal sphere in which the State moves and has its being. Again it is dangerous, for the simple reason that it magnifies unduly the nature and scope of sovereignty. If we say that public opinion, and the nation which forms that opinion, is sovereign, we tie ourselves to an undefined and unlimited sovereign, which can do what it will and will do what it can. The pure legal sovereignty of a law-making body which confines itself to adjusting legal issues, by legal methods, in legal subjection to the constitution, and also, at the same time, in some degree of practical subjection to the trend of national opinion—such sovereignty, so confined, is a definite and limited thing.[1]

§ 6. THE SOCIAL AREA AND THE NATURE OF SOCIAL GROUPS

IF we hold fast to the conception of the State as a legal association, acting under an ultimately sovereign constitution, through an immediately sovereign law-making body, we shall recognize that there is a large area of social life which the State will not touch, or, rather, will touch only at those points where the 'social' spills, as it were, over into the 'legal', and thus trends to legal consequences. The State, for instance, will not touch religion, so far as religion is a matter of internal and spiritual activity, though it may be compelled to touch it at points where the existence and action of religious bodies raises legal issues such as the interpretation and the administration of trusts; and the reason why it will not touch religion is the fact that law, through which by its nature the State always acts, is essentially a matter of uniform rules, for the control of external actions, which are irrelevant and inapplicable to the inner nature of religious activity. Similarly, the State will not touch economics, so far as economics is a matter of the internal and mental activities of original decision at the point where a problem arises and original experiment for its solution by the method of trial and error; though it may, and will, be compelled to touch economics where the existence and action of economic bodies and groups raises legal issues of the rights and duties of persons who are immediately concerned or indirectly affected. It is impossible to

[1] For a further discussion of the nature of sovereignty see below, Book V, § 6.

convert the general operation of economic activity, with its multitudinous problems of particular decision and its manifold requirements of particular adaptation, into a system of uniform legal rules. But it is also impossible not to create a system of such rules, in a field of action which may be called one of 'supervision',[1] rather than 'operation', for the mass of similar problems, involving general issues of the rights and duties of persons, which the activity of economics always presents and which become increasingly pressing as public opinion becomes increasingly aware of their presence.

There is a difference in this matter, as we shall have occasion to notice later, between religion and economics; and the cause of religious liberty is a different cause, at any rate in degree, from that of economic liberty. Economic activity raises legal issues, and is therefore drawn into the area of the State, to a vastly greater degree than the activity of religious life. But the two liberties, even if they differ, have been, and may be, defended together by the same general argument. There are two possible lines on which they may thus be defended. One line of defence, which has just been suggested, is directed to the nature or quality of the subject-matter involved; the other is directed to the nature or quality of the agents which handle the subject-matter. On the first line of defence, the argument advanced in favour of religious and economic liberty is that the subject-matter involved, or in other words the activity in question, is an internal activity, a motion of the mind, which as such and by its own nature must be free from legal compulsion. On the second line, the argument is that the agents which handle the subject-matter, or conduct the activity, are living groups, of the nature of persons, which as such and by their own nature must possess and enjoy the liberty inherent in all personality.

The latter line of defence has often been employed by English thinkers since the beginning of the century. The foundations were laid by Professor Maitland, as long ago as 1900, in the introduction to his translation of a section of Gierke's work on *Das deutsche Genossenschaftsrecht*, which was published under the title of *Political Theories of the Middle Age*. The subsequent development of events—particularly the judgement of the House of Lords, in the year 1904, in the Free Church of Scotland case,

[1] On the notion of 'supervision' see below, Book VI, § 5.

and the Osborne judgement of the same House, in the year 1909, in a case concerning the rights of trade unions—led to further building on these foundations; and a general theory began to be advanced of the general rights of groups, both religious and economic, in the system of the modern State. The gist of this theory was (1) that a group, such as a Church or a trade union, is a real person, a group person, with its own group mind, its own group will, and the general attributes of personality; (2) that groups of this order come into existence, and continue to grow, as such real persons, not in virtue of a legal act outside themselves, such as parliamentary authorization, but in virtue of their own motion and by their own spontaneous action; and (3) that being real persons, which have come spontaneously into existence and continue to grow spontaneously, these groups have rights of acting freely for their own purposes, which the State is bound to respect (as it is generally bound to respect all rights of personality), so long as they are not exercised for purposes inimical to its own purpose of maintaining a scheme of law and order.

We may begin by noting that this general theory is double-edged. If it is applied to groups other than the State, it fosters syndicalism, or a general philosophy of the autonomy of groups (and particularly of economic groups) at the expense of the authority of the State. If, on the other hand, it is applied to the State, and if the State is regarded as a *personne morale* with a *volonté générale* transcending and reconciling individual wills, the theory fosters *étatisme*, and issues in a philosophy of the total and engulfing State whose will is the peace—and the tomb—of its members. If groups are to be the beneficiaries of this theory, the greatest group may well be the greatest, and even the only, beneficiary. We shall, therefore, be wise, before we turn groups into persons (and 'real' persons at that), to inquire what a person is, and in what sense, if any, a group may be called a person. Here we must draw a distinction between the moral world and the legal. In the moral world the only persons are individual human beings. It is they, and they alone, who have minds: they, and they alone, who have wills. In the moral world there are no group persons, no group minds, and no group wills. There are, of course, groups in the moral world. But these groups are not persons. They are bodies ('wholes', as Aristotle would have said)[1] composed of individual persons who hold common ideas and will common purposes, but hold them as individuals and will them as individuals: individual persons who, of course, interact, and are what they are because they interact, but who are still individual persons. The unity of a group, in the moral world, is not the unity of a common mind: it is the unity of a common content of many individual minds.[2]

We may now turn to the legal world. Here we have to notice that the word 'person' has a peculiar sense. A study of etymology will help us to understand this sense. Originally the word *persona* signified an actor's mask, and thence, by an easy transference, the character or *dramatis persona* who wore a particular mask. A further transference carried the word from the stage to the field of law; and *persona* became the legal mask worn, and the legal character sustained, by a legal actor or agent on the scene of the legal State. A still further transference carried the word in time from the legal sphere to the moral; and *persona* became a personage or person who sustained a character and played a part on the general scene of man's moral activity. The dramatic, the legal, and the moral senses of the word have each their own significance; and, in particular, the legal sense has a peculiar significance of its own which must be distinguished from that of the moral. In the legal sense individuals—that is to say men and women who are already persons in the moral sense and agents in the moral world—are further conceived as wearing legal masks; as each sustaining a legal character; as being legal actors or agents who play their part in the 'drama' or action of the legal State; in a word, as being 'persons at law'. But this is not all. In the legal sense, and in the view of the law, a group of individuals, which as a group is not a person in the moral sense or in the moral world, may also wear a legal mask, sustain a legal character, and be a person at law. This is what happens when a group becomes 'corporate' or embodied, and when, as such, it is 'legally authorized to act as a single individual'. It may then hold property, sue and be sued, make and break

[1] On Aristotle's conception of the nature of a 'whole' (*holon*) see the writer's translation of the *Politics*, and the note at the end of Book III, c. I.

[2] We sometimes speak of the 'mind' of a meeting, or the 'sense' of a meeting. We do not mean that the meeting, as such, is a being with mind and sense. We only mean that there is a common *content* of the many minds, and the many senses, which are present and active in the meeting.

contracts, suffer and inflict torts, and generally behave and be treated as a quasi-individual. But it remains a quasi-individual, and does not become an individual: it remains in the legal sphere, but it does not enter the moral: it is a person only in the legal, and not in the moral, sense.

How are these quasi-individuals, these purely legal persons, admitted to their position? Obviously, if they exist as persons only within the legal area, they must be admitted into that area by an act of the legal association, or in other words of the State. This is not to say that the act of the legal association—which may take the form of executive warrant or charter, or of legislative authorization, or of judicial decision[1]—is an act of creation. It is an act of recognition. The group is already there as a fact before it achieves recognition as a person; and groups may continue to remain as facts without being recognized as persons. In the whole of the area of legal personality the State is an organ of selection and recognition. This is true, in a measure, of individuals, as well as of groups. The State makes some sort of selection even among individuals; it determines which of them it will recognize—or, more exactly, which of them it will *not* recognize—as legal persons in its legal scheme. In England, for instance, an 'idiot' is not a legal person, and in France a person punished with civil death (*mort civile*) forfeits all legal personality. Similarly the State selects among groups, determining which it will accept as legal persons in its scheme; but here—more concerned with positive selection than with negative—it picks and chooses not those which it will not recognize, but those which it *will*. Individuals are legal persons unless they are excepted; groups are legal persons only if they are accepted. No groups, therefore, are legal persons in the absence of specific authority in their favour—authority proceeding from the executive or legislative or judicial organ of the State.

We may now draw the argument to a conclusion, and bring the conclusion to a point by taking a particular example. The conclusion is, on the one hand, that no groups are real persons, possessing real minds and wills of their own apart from the minds and wills of their members; it is also, on the other hand,

---

[1] The judicial decision proceeds by analogy, and recognizes as a legal person any group analogous in its nature and action to a group already recognized as such a person by an executive charter or by legislative authorization.

that some groups are legal persons, vested with legal capacities of acting in the sphere of the State as though they were individuals, and vested accordingly with the consequent position or status of quasi-individuals. Trade unions may serve us as an example. A trade union is not a real person, acting in the moral world. It is not even one of those groups which are legal persons, entitled to act in the legal world as quasi-individuals; for it is not in the eye of the law (though some judicial decisions in the past have tended in this direction) 'corporate' or embodied, and therefore it is not a person at law. But if a trade union is neither a real person nor a legal person, then there is little to be gained from discussing its rights, or the measure of liberty which it should enjoy, or its general relation to the State, *in terms of persons and personality*. If we wish to defend the rights and the liberty of trade unions, we shall do better to adopt the line of defence which starts from the subject-matter of their action and the nature of their activity; which looks pragmatically to what they do, and not metaphysically to what they are. The real question, in any discussion of the relation of trade unions to the State, is not the question whether they are persons, of whatever sort or character. It is the simple question whether the State, in determining its attitude to a group of individuals acting together on the basis of common ideas for the realization of a common purpose, should leave their activity to operate freely in the voluntary area of social initiative and social experiment, or should draw it into the involuntary area of legal control and legal uniformity. The 'being' of the group (person or not-person? and, if a person, which sort of person, the moral or the legal?) is irrelevant to that question: the one thing relevant is what the group does, what its activity is, and whether that activity can, and should, be regulated by law.

On this basis it may be argued that, as the activity of a trade union is multiple (partly charitable or educational, partly political, and partly—indeed mainly—economic), different considerations will come into play in each different field of activity. So far as the activity of a trade union is charitable or educational, it should, in principle, be left free to operate in the voluntary area, because it is an internal or spiritual activity, a free motion of the mind, which belongs by its nature to that area. So far as the activity is, directly or indirectly, political—so far as it consists in raising political funds to support a political party, or in promoting a strike intended or likely to affect the government of the community by pressure or the community itself by privation and hardship—the activity may, in principle, be brought under legal control and made subject to legal rules. (This is not to deny that, in practice, the State may be wise in abstaining as far as possible from the policy of legal control, and in preferring to trust to voluntary good sense and the voluntary action of public opinion.) Midway between these two activities—the charitable or educational activity, and the activity which is directly or indirectly political—there is the main and general activity of trade unions, the economic activity, which consists in collective bargaining (backed by the power of the strike) about the wages and conditions of labour. Here, if we follow the principle that original decision, at the point where a problem arises, and original experiment for its solution, by the method of trial and error, are the cardinal factors which ought to be respected in the field of economics, the activity of trade unions will be left, as far as possible, to operate freely in the voluntary area. It cannot, indeed, be left utterly free. On the one hand the State is bound to protect the rights of persons, if and so far as they are adversely affected by particular acts of trade unions (such as acts of intimidation) in the course of the general activity of conducting a strike: on the other hand it is bound to ensure the efficient and continuous operation of its own administrative agencies (post office, police, and the general civil service), and it must thus impose some measures of restriction on trade unions formed by its own employees. Generally, however, and apart from such exceptions, the presumption remains in favour of the freedom of the economic activity of trade unions. But it must again be repeated that that presumption is not based on any 'personality' of trade unions, or the nature of that 'personality'. It is based entirely on their activity and the nature of that activity.

Because it is activities that matter, and because one and the same group may have, and indeed is likely to have, different orders of activity at the same time—activity of the voluntary order in the social sphere, and activity of the controlled order in the legal—it follows that the same group may belong, and indeed is likely to belong, to both spheres simultaneously. A group moves in two worlds, or at any rate shows two faces: it is, as a general rule, both a voluntary group acting freely in the social sphere and a state-regulated group acting under law in the legal. A Free Church lives and moves almost altogether outside the legal sphere: but even a Free Church—or rather the trustees who hold its funds on its behalf—will come into the courts, and be drawn into the legal sphere, if a question arises about the application of its funds and its property. The same may also be said of trade unions: indeed, it may be said even more, because a trade union may not only come into the courts on a question of the proper application of its trust funds, but also on a question of the effect of its acts, or the acts of its representative agents, on the rights of persons whom they may affect. But if we connect we must also distinguish the status of the religious group and the status of the economic. Both move in two worlds; but the one moves more in both than the other. When a religious group has vindicated the position of a Free Church, and established itself and its life in the area of Society, it remains in that area untroubled (unless some rare issue of funds or the like should draw it out into the legal sphere), because its main activity is a practice of spiritual conviction which does not affect other persons—at any rate in ways of which the State can, or will, take cognizance. No economic group can escape so entirely, or remain so untroubled; for the main activity of economic groups consists in the doing of external acts which may affect other persons adversely. It is true that a trade union has, at its roots, the same sort of desire as a Free Church to defend and maintain a set of inward convictions; but the convictions themselves, even when they reach their highest point of a genuine passion for moral principles, are convictions of a different order from those of a religious society, and the means of their maintenance and defence are mainly material means. The theorists who have connected the cause of religious liberty with that of economic liberty have sometimes forgotten that there is a difference which divides, as well as an analogy which connects, the two causes.[1]

[1] It may seem, at first sight, that the system of an established church such as the Church of England—a church 'by law established', and controlled by the State even in the field of ritual and liturgy—is directly opposed to the course of the argument, since it draws such a church almost wholly into the legal sphere, and thus runs counter to the idea that religious activity belongs to the voluntary area of

§ 7. THE IDEA OF A SOCIAL PARLIAMENT

A DISTINCTION has been drawn, in the general course of the argument, between national Society and the national State. The State, we have said, is legal—specifically and essentially legal—and just because it is legal, and therefore also compulsory, it must leave room and scope for the action of voluntary Society, being in its nature 'unable to satisfy the pressure of the varied currents of economic, religious, cultural aspirations by its exclusive action'.[1] At the same time, we have also said, the State is the one and only form of legal organization, and the only vehicle of legal action. The State is only the agent of law, but it is also the only agent of law; and whenever a legal question arises in any field whatsoever, or a legal rule has to be made on anything whatsoever, it is the State alone which acts and which alone can make the rule.

A question, however, has been raised whether there ought not to be some central organization of Society: some social parliament, or even some general system of social parliaments, which might be added to the political parliament of the State, and might stand by its side in some sort of relation, whether subordinate and advisory or co-ordinate and concurrent. Hitherto

society untouched by the legal rules of the State. But two propositions may be advanced. The first is that the Church of England exists freely in the voluntary area, in so far as it develops freely its different shades of doctrine—Evangelical, Catholic, and Modernist—and freely expresses and seeks to spread its opinions on great current issues of general national life, both domestic and international. The second is that if the Church has been drawn to an exceptional extent into the legal area, there are two sides to that matter. On the one hand, the Church has exceptional legal privileges: the Head of the State, for example, must 'join in communion with the Church of England as by law established'. On the other hand, and as the price of such exceptional legal privileges, the Church incurs exceptional legal obligations: the ritual and liturgy of the society with which the King must join in communion cannot be altered without the consent of the King in Parliament. The privileges and the obligations may be said to balance and cancel one another. But it must be admitted that the system of the Church of England, as by law established, is a survival of the sixteenth-century notion of a single Society-State which was everything rolled into one—a Church as well as a State, and the one and only vehicle of the whole common life of the nation. Whether the survival ought now to be sloughed is another matter. In one sense it is an anachronism. In another it is an antidote. The peculiar English connexion between the establishing State and the established Church prevents the State from becoming purely secular and the Church from becoming predominantly clerical. An anachronism which possesses the quality of an antidote both to secularism and to clericalism is hardly even an anachronism.

[1] *Supra*, Book II, § 4, p. 56.

(so the argument runs) there has been only a single mirror—the political mirror—the political parliament which reflects, or as we say 'represents', the legal association as such: ought we not also to have another mirror, or even a set of other mirrors, reflecting some one great aspect of Society as such, or even several of its different aspects?

The suggestion most commonly made is of a single social mirror, an economic council (or economic 'parliament', or economic 'sub-parliament') reflecting the one great aspect of Society implied in the adjective 'economic'. That suggestion acquired vogue, and even seemed likely to be translated into fact, at the close of the war of 1914–18. In Great Britain an industrial conference, convened by the Prime Minister in 1919, proposed the institution of a National Industrial Council, to be elected by the workers and employers in each industry separately, and to be vested with the general power of advising the Government on industrial legislation. The proposal, however, was left in abeyance and Great Britain has remained content with a single political parliament. On the Continent more was attempted, but little, in the issue, achieved. Germany instituted in 1920 a National Economic Council, by the side of the Reichstag, for the purpose of advising the Government on social and economic legislation; but the Council soon dissolved into committees which advised the Government directly, and eventually even the committees ceased to be asked for advice. France instituted in 1926 a National Economic Council, which (after 1936) included 173 members representing economic groups and interests, to study economic problems, to report on them to the Government, and to advise the Government on all economic measures proposed in Parliament. In a different setting the French Economic Council still remains, and its powers have been confirmed and expanded by the new French Constitution of 1946; but it is not clear that it plays any role of importance, or that it has relieved the political Parliament of any part of its burden. Italy, under its Fascist régime, instituted from 1930 onwards a National Council of Corporations, containing representatives of employers and employed and empowered 'to formulate rules for the general co-ordination of the national economy'.[1] The National Council of Corporations

[1] The phrase is vague and grandiose, but so was the general vocabulary of

stood by the side of the Senate and the Chamber of Deputies
(with the latter of which it was eventually merged in 1938), but
like so much else in Italian Fascism it served rather as a theatri-
cal property than as an actual institution.

If, as has just been said, Great Britain has in practice remained
content with a political Parliament, the idea of a social parliament has continued to be mooted among us in theory. The
Guild Socialists, in the early years of the century, advocated the
institution of two parliaments—an economic parliament, based
on guilds, for economic affairs, and a political parliament,
based on local constituencies, for the business of the State.[1] In
1920 the Webbs, in a work entitled *A Constitution for the Socialist
Commonwealth of Great Britain*, similarly advocated a plurality of
parliaments. Pleading the hypertrophy of a single parliament
and—even more—its 'vicious mixture' of functions separate in
their nature, they suggested that the old political parliament
should henceforth be confined to its proper and original functions of the conduct of external relations and the maintenance
of internal law and order. A new social parliament, they proposed, should then be instituted by its side to take over the
more modern functions of the management of social policy and
the general development of a 'way of life' or 'type of civilization'. In their ingenious and carefully constructed scheme of
parliamentary dyarchy both of these parliaments were to be
elected (though not simultaneously, or by the same method)
on the basis of geographical constituencies.[2] Both were to co-
operate by a system of joint committees; and in the event of a
clash a joint session of both was to make the final decision. But
as the control of the budget and the power of the purse were
to be vested in the social parliament, it would appear that the
social parliament was to be the greater of the two. This was
an extreme and dubious plan—the more so as it was never
made clear how the maintenance of law, entrusted to the
political parliament, could be divided from the management

Italian Fascism. The functions of the Council were never clearly defined. In any
case, its functions were of a 'pre-legislative' or preparatory character; it could only
offer advice.

[1] *Supra*, Book I, § 11, p. 38.

[2] It is notable that the Webbs proposed a social parliament which was *not* based
on social groups and the principle of social vocation, but on geographical constituencies and the territorial principle of neighbourhood.

of social policy (and from all the making and maintenance of law involved in that management) which was assigned to the social parliament.

Dr. Temple, afterwards Archbishop of Canterbury, was at once more moderate and more extreme in the proposals he made in 1928 in a work on *Christianity and the State*. Pleading the example of the National Assembly of the Church of England (an ecclesiastical parliament competent, under its enabling act of 1919, to deliberate on and make provision for all matters concerning the Church, subject to the consent of both Houses of Parliament in such matters as by the law of the land require parliamentary sanction), he proposed, in addition, (1) an industrial parliament, based on voluntary associations, which should legislate in its own department subject to the veto of the political parliament, and (2) an educational parliament, based on voluntary bodies of teachers and also on local education authorities, which should legislate in its own sphere 'subject', as he wrote, 'in one way or another to parliamentary veto'. This was consequently a proposal for what may be called a set of social parliaments—an ecclesiastical, an industrial, and an educational parliament. In that sense it went beyond the proposal of the Webbs. But Dr. Temple also suggested that the political parliament should impose a limit or veto on the acts of these several social parliaments, and in this respect his proposal was more moderate than that of the Webbs.

Mr. Churchill, in a Romanes lecture delivered at Oxford in 1930, confined himself to industry, and followed in the track of the policy proposed by the industrial conference of 1919. He suggested a House of Industry (but a House on a different level of power from the two existing Houses of Parliament) empowered to prepare and recommend solutions of industrial problems. This would be an advisory body—parallel, let us say, to the French advisory Economic Council. Of late Mr. Amery, in his *Thoughts on the Constitution* of the year 1947, has adopted and expanded Mr. Churchill's suggestion. Pleading, like Dr. Temple, the analogy of the functions and powers of the National Assembly of the Church of England, he proposes a third 'House', or 'sub-parliament', which might frame measures altering or amplifying Acts of Parliament, subject to the consent of the two existing Houses. This third House would be based on trade unions and employers' associations, possibly with the addition of representatives of consumers nominated by the Government. It would have the advantage, he argues, of enabling the new principle of 'functional' representation to be tried without destroying the existing geographical principle.

There is here a variety of counsellors, and a multiplicity of counsels. In structure, most of the counsellors suggest a social parliament of a new type, based on the functional principle, and representing vocations: the Webbs are perhaps alone in arguing for a social parliament based, like the political, on the principle of local or geographical constituencies. In function, some would vest the social parliament only with the power of advising the political parliament or, alternatively, the executive government: the Webbs, however, would make it a concurrent or even a superior legislature; others, again, would attempt a *via media* and give to the social parliament the position of a subordinate legislature, competent indeed to enact laws but only with the assent of the political parliament. On one issue all would seem to be agreed. They would all institute the social parliament— whatever the basis of its composition, or whatever the extent of its function—by an act of State and by way of a formal amendment of the constitution. They do not consider the possibility that a social parliament may possibly be evolved by an act of Society; that it may, as it were, grow of itself; that it may begin and end in Society, as a purely social organ, simply and solely expressive of social opinions and aspirations.

Nothing need here be said, at any rate for the moment, about the composition of a social parliament. There is a prior question of greater importance—that of its powers. Should it have the powers of a concurrent parliament, or should it have only advisory powers? The first alternative has commended itself to a succession of thinkers, which began with the Guild Socialists, was continued by the Webbs, and may still be traced in the theories and suggestions of Dr. Temple and Mr. Amery.[1] The basis of this first alternative is the policy of functional devolu-

[1] Strictly, indeed, the suggestions of Dr. Temple and Mr. Amery are not in favour of a concurrent parliament (or set of parliaments), but only in favour of a new House (or Houses) to frame and to submit measures to the existing Houses. But a new House which framed and submitted measures of economic policy to the two existing Houses, and which was styled by the name of a third House, would come near to being concurrent.

tion: the policy of sorting out and separating functions at present combined (or, as the argument goes, 'viciously mixed') in a single parliament, and of remitting some of the functions so sorted out and separated to a new body or bodies. Such a policy raises a grave but also simple issue. What would be left to the old 'political' parliament, if a system were adopted of functional devolution upon another 'social' parliament or set of 'social' parliaments? It is possible to answer that question by saying that law would remain: that though economics and education (the general management of social policy and the general development of a 'way of life' or 'type of civilization') would be lost to the political parliament, the maintenance of law (along with the conduct of external relations and the control of a system of defence) would be left. But what is law?

Law is not a separate or separable *set* of things in an isolated compartment. It is, as we have already seen,[1] a general *mode of action.* It is a mode of dealing, by uniform rules, with things in general—with things economic and educational, and with all other sorts and sets of things which are capable of being brought under and regulated by a uniform rule or system of rules. Law, in a word, is a general mode of action which ranges over all places where a uniform rule is possible, and which touches, as it ranges, every sort of thing; but if it is general it is also single, and must proceed from a single source. Being general, and ranging everywhere, it ranges over the field of economics. One cannot distinguish law from economics, or say that law belongs to one sort of parliament and economics to another.[2] Being, on the other hand, a single mode, law has a single organ for its making or declaration. The State, in the shape of the political parliament through which it acts, is the only organ and maker of law. The State, on the theory here assumed, is only a legal association; but, by the same token, it is also the only legal association. Because it is that, its political parliament is the one adjustment-centre. There cannot be a plurality of adjustment-centres. If there were, they would themselves need to be adjusted. There must be some one, single, final adjustment-

---

[1] *Supra*, § 2 of this Book.

[2] It is a logical fallacy to distinguish law, which is a general mode of action, from economics, which is simply a special set of things. The 'vicious mixture' which makes law penetrate everywhere is inherent in the nature of law.

centre; and that adjustment-centre is necessarily compelled by its nature not only to adjust finally all sovereign issues (issues, that is to say, which demand the exercise of sovereignty),[1] but also to take the initiative in formulating their adjustment. A magnetic attraction draws such issues directly to the one final authority. Men will always seek to go straight to it, and the institution of other instances will not defeat or deflect the attraction. That attraction will be especially strong in the field of economics. Economic issues, in these troubled days, are the issues which specially demand adjustment. They are swept particularly, and swept directly, to the final adjustment-centre; and that centre is accordingly compelled, both by its own nature and by their urgency, to take the initiative in their adjustment, and to act with an original efficiency as well as a formal finality.

The powers of a social parliament will not therefore be powers of legislation. They will, at the most, be powers of advice to the one and only legislative authority—or, more exactly, for even 'advice' is too strong a term, they will be powers of expressing social opinion and formulating social aspiration at the bar of that authority. Now a State-created body, acting in the framework and as a part of the State, is not the natural or logical vehicle for the exercise of those powers. Society is something different from the State, and the formulation of social opinion is something different from the formulation of legal rules. If Society is the area of voluntary formations and voluntary action, we should naturally expect a social parliament (or a complex of social parliaments, corresponding to the complexity of society) to form itself voluntarily, and not to be formed by an act of State-creation. We should also expect it, when it is formed, to move in the area of Society and to proceed by the method of social action: to express social opinion and aspiration, and to serve as an indication of the trend of thought in general Society. It will thus be a new form (and yet, perhaps, by no means so new as its advocates think) of that play of national or public opinion which, as we have seen,[2] is always at work behind the political parliament, and which is always affecting and qualifying the action of that parliament.

We must not exaggerate the peculiarity or the novelty of the

[1] *Supra*, § 5, pp. 59–61.   [2] *Supra*, § 5, pp. 64–5.

idea of a social parliament. It is an idea which is neither so peculiar nor so novel as many are inclined to think. There already exists, and has long existed among us, a whole complex of what may be called 'social parliaments'. There are the 'social parliaments' of the organized professions (though there is as yet no federal parliament of all the professions); there is the 'social parliament' of the occupations, in the shape of the Trades Union Congress; there are the 'social parliaments' of the employers in the shape of their federations and unions; there are the 'social parliaments' of the different churches; there are a number of 'social parliaments' (partly professional, but some of a wider scope) in the field of education. The novelty of the idea of a social parliament, in the form in which it has become recently current, consists in the suggestion of a new *joint* social parliament in the field of industrial production, representing both workers and employers, and drawing together the separate 'social parliaments' in which the two sides have hitherto acted. This would, indeed, be something new, though there have been tentative movements towards it during the last thirty years. But the question is whether such a new joint social parliament cannot form itself, and is not likely to form itself, by the method of voluntary action. We may safely answer that the fertility of social invention is not exhausted; that the idea of the voluntary formation of such a new joint body has already been mooted between workers and employers; and that in the new conditions of production and the new social temper of our time the idea may thrive to fruition. We have already formed a number of specialized social parliaments for ourselves by the method of voluntary action. There is no reason, in the nature of things, why we should not form for ourselves, by the same voluntary method, a new social parliament, of a greater scope and of wider dimensions, in the shape of a joint industrial parliament.

But such a new social parliament, so formed, will be a parliament of Society (otherwise it will not be a 'social parliament'): it will not be a parliament of the State, or a 'third House', or anything else which is *in pari materia* with the organs and organization of the legal community. It will be simply an organ, larger and more catholic in its scope than the previous organs, but not different from them in its nature, for the expression of social opinions and social aspirations. We must beware of importing into our thought about social parliaments any idea of a policy of devolution; any idea that the State should remit to social organs its own specific and inalienable political function of preparing, formulating, and enunciating all the rules of law. Devolution is a current word. It is the reverse side of the word 'congestion', which is often applied to the parliament and the general government of the State. It is possible that there *is* congestion of the State; but if there is the remedy has to be found within the State. Devolution of the legal powers of the territorial State, if it should be attempted, will naturally be territorial devolution—devolution, that is to say, on the territorial sub-divisions of the State, which are of the same nature as itself. It will be devolution on national areas, if such areas are contained in the State. It will be devolution on provincial, regional, and local areas of one order or other—in a word, on areas of neighbourhood. (Neighbourhood is the great bond of men, uniting people of all sorts, for purposes of all sorts, in common areas of residence which are the areas of those general contacts and general relations that really need adjustment.) But even devolution of this order, devolution of the territorial order, logical as it may seem, may not be practicable in a country such as Great Britain. Here a large population is massed together, upon a small soil, in a system of relations so inextricably interwoven, from one end of the country to the other, that any legal rule must always be a rule which also runs from end to end. It is difficult, after all, to think even of a system of provincial or regional sub-legislatures in the conditions of such a texture.

How much more difficult, then, will it be to think of a system of social sub-legislatures, or to advocate a policy of functional devolution—devolution, that is to say, on social-economic groups pursuing social and economic aims in the area of Society. Here we cannot even plead the claims of logic in our favour, as we can for territorial devolution. On the contrary, we are involved in a confusion of ideas. Social groups belong to the area of Society; they are not subdivisions of the State. No social group, and no assembly representing such a group or a number of such groups, is fitted by its nature to act as an organ of the legal and rule-making association which we call the State. It is true that the opinion of a social group, or of an assembly representing such a group, may properly affect the State, because it is a part and a form of that encompassing body of general social opinion which is always playing upon, always affecting, and always qualifying the action of the legal association. But it is also true that a social group in itself, and any assembly representing such a group or a number of such groups, is not, and is not by its nature fitted to be, a law-making, or even a law-formulating, or indeed in any sense a legal body, as all organs of the legal association must be.

There is not only a confusion of ideas, and a defect of logic, in the idea of functional devolution of the powers of the State. There are also grave practical difficulties. One of these practical difficulties is the difficulty of space. The members of social groups (doctors, miners, teachers, transport-workers, lawyers, agricultural workers) are necessarily scattered in space, and separated by interstices. But the State, and each division of the State, is by its nature a territorial continuum. It is based on contiguity in space, and on the fact and feeling of neighbourhood. To combine in a single scheme the functional and the territorial would be to mix and confound the discrete and the continuous. There is a second and greater difficulty—a difficulty not of material space, but of mental sentiment and moral solidarity. Functions, when they are complementary and are consciously felt to be complementary, *may* serve to draw men together in the sense of a common need and the feeling of mutual dependence. But it is also true, and even more true, that they also serve to divide, and that each industry, trade, occupation, and profession develops its own special interest, its own peculiar bias, and its own exclusive group-interest. It would be far from easy for the State to devolve upon such bodies the performance of any of the common duties which it owes to the whole territorial community. The essence of the State, and equally of the divisions of the State, is a common territorial citizenship, which unites the residents in a common area for the common handling of the common questions that concern them all in their common capacity as neighbours.

But while there is reason to doubt the idea that the State should devolve any part of its powers upon social groups, there is little reason for doubting that the modern State owes a large and generous measure of respect to such group in the exercise of their own intrinsic and native powers. It would not show that respect—indeed it would do the opposite—if it sought to incorporate social groups in its own organization, and to make them part of its own legal system. There are other and more generous methods which the State can adopt. In the first place, it can recognize frankly that there is a whole area of social action parallel to, if different from, its own area of legal action: an area of voluntary action, of tentative non-official effort, of many-sided initiative and manifold experiment. In other words, it can recognize that it is not only concerned with individuals ('the State and the Individual' is not the whole of the matter), but also with societies: it can admit that it is in its nature not only an association composed of individuals, but also an association composed of associations (*consociatio consociationum*). Accordingly it can respect and protect the liberty and the rights of groups, as well as the liberty and the rights of individuals. In the second place, and as a part of such respect and protection, it can develop a general law of associations and their rights, side by side with its private law of persons and the rights of persons. It can construct, as a modern jurist has said, a system of 'public law on the lines of a comprehensive treatment of the rights and duties of various social organizations— . . .ecclesiastical, professional, educational, literary—that have stepped in between the individual and the State and are daily growing in importance in their task of organizing scattered individuals into conscious and powerful groups'.[1] In the third place, and as a still farther extension of its respect for and its protection of the life of voluntary societies, it may even give positive aid and encouragement to their activities. Just as the modern State increasingly aids and encourages the development of individuals by the provision of what are called public social services, so it can also aid and encourage the development of societies, when they are doing good work for the benefit of the general community, by fostering their expansion and even by giving them financial aid. The policy of financial subsidies adopted by the British Government during the last thirty years towards the

[1] Vinogradoff, *Outlines of Historical Jurisprudence* (London, 1920), vol. i, p. 97. The argument of Vinogradoff may be compared with that of Whitehead, in the essay entitled 'Aspects of Freedom' in his *Adventures of Ideas* (see below, Book VI, § 7, p. 277).

societies, called universities, that serve the advancement of learning and the general promotion of higher education, may be cited as a notable example of the respect which the modern State can show, and the encouragement it can give, to societies which render voluntary service, in their own way, for the benefit of the general community.

BOOK III

THE PURPOSE OF THE STATE
AND THE IDEA OF JUSTICE

§ I. THE STATE AND LAW

IN the two previous books of this treatise the State and Society have both been in question; and the aim of the argument has been to study and define their relations, first in historical terms, and then in terms of contemporary life. The future course of the argument will be directed purely to the State: to the purpose which it serves, and the idea of justice on which it is based; to the rights which it secures, the principles of their distribution, and the methods of their declaration and enforcement; to the grounds of the obligation which it imposes on its members, and the limits of that obligation; to the nature of the functions which its government exercises, and the relation of those functions to the rights of individuals.

The State, on the conception here adopted, is a legal association: a 'juridically organized nation, or a nation organized for action under legal rules'.[1] It exists *for* law: it exists *in* and through law: we may even say that it exists *as* law, if by law we mean not only a sum of legal rules, but also, and in addition, an operative system of effective rules which are actually valid and regularly enforced. The essence of the State is a living body of effective rules; and in that sense the State is law.

To understand better the terms 'State' and 'law' we shall do well to study their etymology and history: to discover their original sense, and to trace the connotations and associations which they have gradually acquired in the course of time. The English word 'State' comes from the Latin *status*, which has had a curious and chequered history during the centuries of its development. (Words too have their growth and their evolution; and they too may go through curious mutations.) In classical Latin, the word *status* meant generally the 'standing'—that is to say, the position—of a person or body of persons: but by Cicero's time it had come to be specially applied to the 'standing' or

[1] *Supra*, Book II, § 4.

D

position of the whole community, and Cicero accordingly speaks of the *status civitatis*, or the *status reipublicae*, in the general sense of the constitution and institutions by which, and in which, the *civitas* or *respublica* stands.[1] Travelling through late Latin (in which, like many other words beginning with similar double consonants, it acquired an initial *i* and became *i-status*), and then through the Romance languages, the Latin *status* gave us eventually three English words—(1) 'estate', in the sense of a standing or position in regard to some form of property (a 'real estate' in land, or a 'personal estate' in movables); (2) 'Estate', as when we speak of the three Estates of the realm, using the word in the primary sense of a grade or rank in the system of social standing or position, and thence in the derivative sense of the body of persons belonging to such grade or rank; and, finally, (3) 'State'. This last derivative, it is important to notice, was not originally used in the Ciceronian sense of *status civitatis* or *status reipublicae*; nor did it mean, as those phrases had meant, the general standing, position, or 'polity' of the whole community and all its members. It had another and different connotation, which long persisted and may still be traced in modern usage. The word 'State', when it came into use in England during the sixteenth century, brought with it from Italy the idea of a high 'State' or stateliness (*stato*) vested in some one person or some one body of persons. It meant primarily a peculiar standing, of a kind which was political, and of a degree in that kind which was superior or supreme; and thence, by an easy extension, it came to be used derivatively of the person or body of persons invested with such standing. This was the usage down to 1789, and even later: the 'State' meant primarily the position of being the superior or supreme political authority, and thence it came to be applied derivatively to the person or body enjoying that position. It was thus a term very similar to, and practically identical with, the terms 'sovereignty' and 'sovereign', similarly derived from the Latin (in the late Latin form *superanus*) and similarly transmitted to England through Romance derivatives from the Latin (and especially through the Italian *sovrano*).

[1] It may be noted accordingly that in classical Latin the word *status*, in itself a colourless word, only acquires a political colour when it is followed by another word which gives it that colour, such as *civitas* or *respublica*. By itself, and alone, it has no political significance.

Bacon, in the beginning of the seventeenth century, uses 'State' as a term synonymous with or parallel to 'King', as when he speaks of 'Kings and States' consulting judges. Louis XIV, in the middle of the seventeenth century, must have thought that he was stating a truism, and not attempting a paradox, when he exclaimed *L'État, c'est moi!* Was he not in his own view, as in that of his subjects, the person who enjoyed the 'state' and position of being the supreme political authority, and was he not therefore 'the State'?

So far, and so long as these views prevailed, the notion of authority, of a position or 'standing' of supreme authority, and of the person or body placed in that position and having that 'standing'—this was what formed the connotation of the word 'State'. Such a connotation belongs to a graded and hierarchical society, in which there are different states or 'Estates' (or sorts and conditions of men) arranged in ascending degrees, and one of these states or 'Estates' is *the* State *par excellence*.[1] But this connotation begins to disappear—or rather to be overlaid—when a graded and hierarchical society yields to a society of equals. After the end of the eighteenth century it may be said, *L'État, c'est nous!* The State is now the whole community: the whole legal association; the whole of the juridical organization. This is democracy, or a result of democracy: we must henceforth think of the State as ourselves (or as the juridical organization which we have given to ourselves, or the legal association into which we have formed ourselves); and we must henceforth give the name of 'Government' to the authority—before called 'State'—which is now seen as exercising on our behalf the powers which it had hitherto claimed as its own. But language is slow in adapting itself to changes of thought; and words may long continue to carry the associations of a vanished past. We still use the term 'State' with the connotation—only overlaid, and not yet erased—of earlier centuries. We regard the State still as some sort of being, somehow distinct from ourselves, which still interferes with us (thus we speak of 'State-interference'), and against which we still must defend the cause of individualism in

[1] The words 'State' and 'estate', which are etymologically the same word, flow easily into one another. From this point of view it was no great error, in the days of monarchy, to think of the King as a State (or Estate) of the realm. He *was* a State; the highest of 'Estates'; in fact, *the* State.

the war (as Spencer called it) of 'The Man versus the State'. It is a sad complication of thinking that we so often think with obsolete words, or rather with words whose connotation, in the sense in which we still use them, is obsolete or obsolescent.

From the etymology and history of the term 'State' we may now turn to those of the term 'law'. The term appears to have been borrowed by the English, about the year 1000, from their Scandinavian invaders: it came to them not from the Latin (the Latin terms *lex* and *legalis* are not cognate in origin or connotation),[1] but from a Teutonic root meaning to 'lay', to place, or to set. Law is thus etymologically something *positum*, or, as we should say, 'imposed': it is something laid down or set, as one sets a task or lays down a rule; and it is accordingly defined in the *Oxford English Dictionary* as 'a rule of conduct imposed by authority'. If this definition be accepted, we are carried back to the notion of the State as being, in its nature, a superior or supreme authority: we are led to regard law as a rule, or a body of rules, imposed by that authority; and we are driven in the issue to conclude that the command of the State, regarded as a supreme authority, is *ipso facto* the law for its members, regarded as the 'subjects' of that authority. This indeed is a view which long prevailed. It may be called the Austinian view of law. It is expressed by Austin in the propositions that 'law is a command which obliges a person or persons'; that 'the term "superiority" ... is implied by the term "command"'', and that accordingly 'every law simply and strictly so called is set by a sovereign person or ... body of persons to a member or members of the independent political society wherein that person or body is superior or supreme'.[2]

Upon this view, then, the State is regarded as being in its nature authority—the superior or supreme authority—and law as being a body of commands set by that authority to all the persons who are its subjects. The view has some historical justification, or at any rate explanation; but it does not square with the facts and ideas of contemporary life. We have already seen

[1] *Lex* is generally referred by philologists to a Latin root meaning to gather and, derivatively, to read: it is thus connected with words such as 'collection', 'lectionary', and 'lecture'.

[2] The passages come from Jethro Brown's *The Austinian Theory of Law*, in § 59, § 70, and § 219. On the notion of law as a command or set of commands, see also below, Book IV, § 6.

that the word 'State' no longer suggests to our minds the idea of authority, or presents them with a picture of the high 'state' and the sovereign status of a person or body of persons enjoying and exercising a right of command over subjects. It rather suggests to our minds the idea of association; it presents them with the image of an associated group, as wide and as multitudinous as the whole of a nation, which lives together by virtue of a constitution which it has made, and lives by the rules of law made for it and on its behalf by a law-making agency which acts as its organ under that constitution. The State is now—though that was not the sense of the word when it was adopted into our language—the *status reipublicae*, the standing or condition of the whole of the legally organized community. It is, in its primary and abstract sense, the status or position, common to us all, of being the members of a legal association: it is, in its derivative and concrete sense, the members themselves—the whole of the members—when regarded as holding, and holding in common, such status or position. Upon this conception of the State there follows a correlative conception of law. Law ceases to be the product of the authority of a person or body of persons conceived as being superior or supreme in the political society in which they act. It becomes the product of the whole of the association, primarily in the form of the constitutive memorandum of association (or, as it is generally termed, the 'constitution') made, or at any rate ratified, in the general usage of modern States, by the action of the members themselves,[1] and secondarily in the form of a current system of legal rules made by a body, or bodies (for, as we shall see, there may be more than one body concerned), representative of the members and acting on their behalf under the constitution and in virtue of the authority conferred by the constitution.

That is the line we may follow if we think in terms of the present. But even if we go back to the past, and consider the source and the growth of law in terms of the past, we may find that we are driven to the conclusion that law has always been something more than the simple command of a single person or body of persons possessing authority over all others. That conclusion emerges when we ask and endeavour to answer two questions. The first concerns the way in which the general

[1] See above, Book II, § 4.

body of law has been imposed and made binding on a political society. Has it been the way of command, or the way of something other than command? The second question concerns the origin of the various branches of law which go to form the general body. Have they all proceeded from a *single* source; or have some come from one source and some from another, and are there thus *several* sources of law?

The development of Roman law will help us to answer these questions. The Latin word for the general body of law is *jus*, which is something broader and more comprehensive than *lex*, though *lex* is one of its elements. How is this *jus* imposed? Before we return an answer, we shall do well to study the etymology of the word. *Jus* is not connected with the verb *jubeo*: it does not mean what is commanded by authority, or *quod jussum est*. That may be true of *lex*, which has some connotation of command, and which is defined by the Roman jurists as '*quod populus* jubet *et constituit*'. But *jus* has a different connotation, and is associated with different ideas. It seems to be connected with the Latin word *jungere*: it means primarily a joining or fitting, a bond or tie;[1] and it readily glides into the sense of binding or obliging. We may define *jus*, in its original form, as 'what is fitting' and therefore also 'binding'; or in more detail, we may say that 'it conveys . . . the idea of valid custom [i.e. the deposited common tradition of the 'fitting'], to which any citizen can appeal, and which is recognized and can be enforced by a human authority'.[2] We may then go on to think of *jus*, in its developed form, as a body of binding or obliging rules which—however they have been made, whether by the growth of valid custom or by legislative enactment or otherwise[3]—the courts recognize as binding, and not only recognize but also enforce. We must notice here the importance of the courts. The Romans—at any rate in the period of the Republic—thought less of State-authority, making law by command, than they did of the authority of the courts, giving effect to law (however made) by recognition and enforcement of its rules and remedies. It is significant that the same

---

[1] The Romans accordingly spoke of the *jus amicitiae* and the *jus necessitudinis*—the bond of friendship and the bond of relationship.

[2] A. H. J. Greenidge, Historical Introduction to the fourth edition of Poste's *Gaius*, p. xvi.

[3] 'Otherwise' includes, as is explained below, both the action of the judicature and the pronouncements of jurisconsults skilled in the law.

word *jus* is used to denote both the body of law and the courts which enforce that body. We may therefore say that what imposed the whole body of law and made it binding on the members of the Roman community, was not the command of a law-giver (though that, as we shall presently see, played some part and made some contribution) : it was rather the recognition given, and the enforcement applied, by a law-court. It is the law-court, and not the law-giver, which is summoned to the mind by the notion of *jus*; and we may say of the Roman people, what a modern writer has said of the English-speaking peoples, that 'to them, whether lawyers or not, law means a body of rules enforced by the courts'.[1]

That, for the Romans, was the criterion of law, and that is an answer which may be given to the question, 'How and in what way has the general body of law been imposed and made binding on a political society?' We now come to the other question, 'What is the origin of the various elements or branches of law which go to form the general body?' Here we have to inquire into the various sources of *jus*, and to consider how its different elements emerged and acquired definition. Custom, or unwritten law, or the *jus consensu receptum*, was one of the sources, and it is still mentioned as such in the *Institutes* of Justinian after a thousand years of legal development. (The *Digest* of Justinian has even preserved a passage of the jurist Julianus, approved and translated by Blackstone in the Introduction to his *Commentaries*, which puts custom on a level with, and bases it on the same foundation as, the declared rules of the written law. 'For since the written law binds us for no other reason but because it is approved by the judgment of the people, therefore those laws which the people have approved without writing ought also to bind everybody. For where is the difference whether the people declare their assent to a law by suffrage, or by a uniform course of acting accordingly?')[2] Apart from custom, the two main sources of *jus* (the two sources which formed the *jus scriptum*) were legislative declaration and legal formulation. Legislative declaration itself in turn flowed from a number of different

---

[1] A. L. Lowell, *The Government of England*, vol. ii, p. 473. 'The essential point', he adds, 'is that what the courts recognise and enforce is law, and what they refuse to recognise is not law.'

[2] *Digest*, L. 32, pr., § I D. The translation is that of Blackstone, in § 3 of his Introduction.

springs: one spring, the original, was the Roman people, from which proceeded *leges*; another spring, of a later date, was the Roman Senate, from which proceeded 'senatusconsults'—or senatorial decrees and ordinances hardly to be distinguished from *leges*; still a third, of a still later date, was the Roman *princeps* or emperor, from whom proceeded 'constitutions', in a variety of forms (decrees, rescripts, and the like), all possessing *legis vigorem*. If legislative declaration was thus triple, legal formulation was double: it consisted partly of the edicts of the magistrates who sat in the courts (edicts at first issued annually, as each new magistrate took office, but becoming in process of time continuous and traditional), and partly of the 'responses' of private persons 'skilled in the laws' (*jurisconsulti* or *jurisprudentes*) who gave their opinion as it were 'in chambers' when they were consulted, and to some extent represented the view of the legal profession.[1] The whole of this process of legal formulation was a great source of Roman law. The judges, and the legal profession behind them, played no small part in the making of *jus*. We may thus conclude that the sources of Roman law were multiple, and not single. We may also conclude that the judges not only imposed the whole body of law, in the sense that gave it legal effect by recognizing its validity. They, and the jurisconsults behind them, were also the *makers*, or at any rate the original declarers, of much of the law they imposed.

Two results emerge from this summary review of the development of Roman law. In the first place, the 'imposing' of law by the State is seen to be, in effect, the recognizing and enforcing of it by the courts. In the second place, the source of the law thus recognized and enforced is seen to be at least twofold, even apart from custom, and to consist not only of legislative declaration, but also of legal formulation by the double agency of the courts and the jurisconsults. The same, or very similar, results emerge from a consideration of the development of

[1] In the strict sense of the word, the *jurisprudentes* were not a profession, or comparable to the members of the English Bar. They were not organized, at any rate till the days of Augustus; and some of them were statesmen rather than professed or practising lawyers. But from the middle of the second century B.C. they developed a system of scientific jurisprudence: in process of time they became teachers of law: they published treatises or commentaries based upon their 'responses'; and by their general activity they affected and even guided the decisions of the magistrates who sat in the courts of law.

English law. In England, too, as well as in Rome, law is the general body of rules recognized and enforced, and in that sense imposed, by the courts. In England, too, as well as in Rome, the sources of law are twofold: in part the judges, with the members of the legal profession behind them, who have made, and continue to make, the 'common law'; in part the legislature, which enacts statutes and is thus the maker of statute law, and which, being the immediate sovereign and sitting in constant session, can at any time alter or annul the rules of the 'common law' in virtue of such sovereignty. From England, therefore, as well as Rome, we may learn the lessons (1) that the action of making law may proceed from more than one agent, and may involve a number of forces or sources, and (2) that over and above the action of making, and at least as important as that action, there is also the action of imposing the whole of the system of law (however its different parts may be made) by a continuous process of recognition and enforcement applied in and by the courts. But when once it is made, by whatever bodies, and when in addition it is steadily imposed by the recognition and enforcement of the courts, law possesses the attribute of validity and produces the effect of obligation. *Valet*—its injunction avails and prevails: *obligat*—it binds men to an engagement of performing what is enjoined.

§ 2. LAW AND JUSTICE

THE law which has hitherto been in question is positive law: law which is declared and 'set' (*positum*): law which is recognized by the courts and actively enforced by their action (*impositum*). Positive law is a large term, which embraces many divisions. If you look at its origin, asking yourself how it came to be and in what ways it was made, you will say that some of it is common law and some of it statute law. If you look at the matters with which it deals, and examine its content, you will say that some of it is primary or constitutional law and some of it secondary or ordinary law; and dividing the latter again, according to its subject-matter and content, you will go on to say that some of it is criminal and some of it civil law. But all the divisions, taken together, are one body of positive law, in the sense of a body of legal rules actually 'set' and actively enforced.

But is that the whole of the matter? Is the notion of law

exhausted by the conception of positive law? Here we are faced by the question whether there does not exist, side by side with the positive law which contains and expresses actual validities, another law which contains and expresses ideal values (values, possibly, none the less real for being ideal): a law which we may call 'natural', because it corresponds 'to the nature of things'[1] or to the nature of man (as a rational being living, or intended to live, in harmony with the rational nature of things): a law founded on what is right in itself, on what is just everywhere and at all times, on what is valuable whether or not it be valid. The question is as old as the *Antigone* of Sophocles; and Aristotle, in a passage of the *Rhetoric*,[2] already supplied an answer. Distinguishing between 'particular law', which is 'the law defined and declared by each community for its own members', and the 'universal law' of all mankind, he notes that the latter is 'the law of nature; for there really exists, as all of us in some measure divine, a natural form of the just and unjust which is common to all men, even when there is no community or contract to bind them to one another'. He cites the lines of Sophocles:

> Not of today or yesterday its force:
> It springs eternal: no man knows its birth.

The answer thus suggested by Aristotle was further developed by the Stoic philosopher Zeno and the Stoic school which he founded; and it passed from the philosophy of the Stoics into the jurisprudence of Rome. By the side of the positive law, the *jus civile*, recognized and enforced on Romans by the courts of the *civitas Romana*, the Roman jurists, in process of time, set the conception of *jus naturale*. This *jus naturale* may be defined as a 'law imposed on mankind by common human nature, that is by reason in response to human needs and instincts'.[3] But it is not 'imposed' in the sense that it is an actual body of law, recognized as such and enforced as such in the Roman courts of law. It is a spirit rather than a letter: a spirit of 'humane interpretation', present in the minds of jurists and judges, which affects the law that is actually enforced, but does so without being actual law in the strict sense of the word. Yet the fact remains that the

---

[1] Montesquieu, in the beginning of *De l'Esprit des Lois*, defines laws as 'les rapports nécessaires qui dérivent de la nature des choses'.

[2] Book I, c. xiii, § 2.

[3] Professor de Zulueta, in *The Legacy of Rome*, p. 204.

Romans cherished the conception of a law distinct from the positive law of the State (even if it was a spirit rather than a written and visible letter); that they regarded this law as universal, because it came from man's common nature and extended its range to all mankind; and that they gave it the name of 'natural' in contradistinction to the positive law which was the 'artifact' of the civic community.

The distinction drawn by the Roman jurists was sharpened and hardened in the course of the ages. Natural law became something more than a spirit of humane interpretation, subtly penetrating and quietly affecting the administration of positive law. It became a separate and almost rival body of law, claiming recognition and demanding enforcement by itself and in its own virtue. Two different, and indeed opposed, forces, acting at different times, conspired to produce this consummation. On the one hand, the Catholic Church espoused the conception of natural law; and the force of religious faith added majesty to a law which the Church interpreted as drawing its origin, through man's divine faculty of reason, from the very being of God. On the other hand, and at a later date, the secular spirit of rational enlightenment equally adopted the conception; and during the seventeenth and eighteenth centuries the secular force of rationalism, expressed in what may be called the secular school of natural law, brought the principles of philosophy (Cartesian or Leibnitzian) and the resources of logic to impress a new stamp of science on a law which was now interpreted in terms of reason and not of faith. Under such different auspices the natural law of mankind was made to confront the positive law of the State as something separate from it, something which might be opposed to it, and something which, in the event of such opposition, ought to be deemed superior to it.[1] Laws became 'two and two,

---

[1] The development was more marked, and went much farther, on the Continent than it ever did in England. Perhaps this was partly due to differences in the method and system of the teaching of law. On the Continent, and particularly in Germany, the teaching of law was largely a matter for the universities, and the fertility of academic speculation ran easily in the channels of natural law: in England the teaching of law was mainly a matter for the legal profession, which clung to its own traditional law. But the greater vogue of natural law on the Continent may also have been due, in some small measure, to differences of vocabulary. (Words are the instruments used in thinking; but the nature of the instruments used may affect the character of the thought produced.) Many of the languages of the Continent employ two different words where the English language uses one and the same

one against another'; there was a natural law and a positive law, and the two might fail to meet.

We thus seem driven to ask ourselves, 'Are there two separate laws, and is one of them "against the other"?' To put the question in that way, and to attempt to think in those terms, is to run at once into heavy weather and to steer a difficult course. If the State is a legal association, it must have one law as the condition of being one legal association or State. If there were two laws, there would be two States; or at any rate every member of the State would be torn in two by the question, 'Which law am I to obey?' Any theory of two separate laws is at once face to face with the possibility of a conflict between the two, and is thus confronted by the problem of finding a solution of the conflict. Theorists who gave their adhesion to the school of natural law were ready with their answer: in any case of conflict, natural law carried the day. Blackstone himself, in a passage of the Introduction to his *Commentaries* in which he is following, and even copying, a contemporary Swiss theorist of the school of natural law, can lay it down that 'the law of nature . . . is of course superior in obligation to any other . . . no human laws are of any validity if contrary to this'. The difficulty of such an answer was that there was no certain and known body of natural law; and even if there had been, there was no established system of courts to give it recognition and enforcement. In practice two things happened, which themselves conflicted with one another. In normal times it was allowed that positive law, as being known and enforceable, must necessarily

word 'law'. Germany, for instance, has *Recht* as well as *Gesetz*: France has *droit* as well as *loi*. *Gesetz* and *loi* are enacted law—the rule set up or laid down: *Recht* and *droit* both signify 'right'—the straight or direct line (*droit* comes from the Latin *directum*)—and they primarily imply what is right in itself and *should* be enforced, rather than what is laid down and actually enforced. In current usage, it is true, both *Recht* and *droit* have come to denote the whole general body of positive law, including (but also extending beyond) its enacted part: *droit*, for instance, is defined in the French dictionary as 'Ensemble des lois et dispositions qui règlent obligatoirement les rapports de société'. But the connotation of intrinsic right still lingers in both words: and if a prefix or adjective be added, and we speak of *Naturrecht* or *droit naturel*, that connotation returns in force. Our one English word 'law' is more pragmatic and positive than either *Recht* or *droit*: it is less readily patient of the addition of any prefix or adjective; and if either be added, the result is felt to be something of a contradiction in terms. We pay a price, in some cramping of thought and a certain check upon speculation, for being restricted to the one word 'law'.

prevail. In revolutionary times, as for instance during the American Revolution and the issue of the Declaration of Independence, an appeal was made from positive law to the 'evident truths' contained in 'the laws of Nature and of Nature's God'; and popular resistance was used to enforce the appeal to these truths. But a law (or laws) which operates only in revolutionary times, and operates then to overturn the State, can hardly be law in any real sense of the word. Real law must be constantly operative, and it must at once sustain the State and be sustained by the State.

We may therefore put the question which confronts us in a different form. Instead of asking whether there are two laws, 'one against another', we may begin by assuming that there is only one law, in any real sense of the word, and that this is the positive law which is actually imposed upon us, as members of a State, by the definite declaration and specific recognition of the organs of that State, legislative and judicial, and by the process of continuous enforcement which they apply. But having made that assumption we may then proceed to ask whether there are not two sources of this one law—(1) the personal source of a human authority (which may, in the last analysis, be the authority of the community itself, acting through organs evolved by it for the purpose of declaring, recognizing, and enforcing its own sense of the necessary rules of its common life),[1] and (2) the impersonal source of an inherent rightness or justice, which adds to a law proceeding from the personal source of a human authority the further strength of a sense that it is right and just in itself, apart from, and over and above, the fact of its being declared to be law. If we make this distinction, we may say that authority gives validity to law, and justice gives it value. A law has validity, and I am legally obliged to obey it, if it is declared, recognized, and enforced as law by the authority of the legally organized community, acting in its capacity of a State. A law has value, and I am bound to obey it not only legally, and not only by an outward compulsion, but also morally and by an inward force, if it has the inherent quality of justice. Ideally law ought to have both validity and value. We may even say that it is only because law, *as a whole and in its general nature*, possesses both attributes, that it actually operates and is actually effective.

[1] *Infra*, Book IV, § 6.

At the same time we must recognize that, for the purposes of the legal association, it is sufficient that a law has validity, and we are legally bound to obey it if only it has that attribute. Though law as a whole, and in its general nature, has both validity and value, any particular law may have only validity. But that is enough to involve an absolute *legal* obligation.

§ 3. THE MEANING AND ORIGIN OF THE IDEA OF JUSTICE

IT has already been noted that the root idea of the word *jus*, and therefore also of the words *justus* and *justitia*, is the idea of joining or fitting, the idea of a bond or tie.[1] Primarily, the joining or fitting implied in this root idea is that between *man and man* in an organized system of human relations. But we may also conceive of the 'just' and 'justice' as connected with, and expressed in, a joining or fitting between *value and value* in a general sum and synthesis of values. We recognize a number of different values as necessary to an organized system of human relations. There is the value of liberty: there is the value of equality: there is the value of fraternity, or (as it may also be called, and is perhaps better called) co-operation.[2] All these values are present in any system of law; but they are present in different degrees at different periods of time, and there is a constant process of adjustment and readjustment between their claims. The claims of liberty have to be adjusted to those of equality; and the claims of both have also to be adjusted to those of co-operation. From this point of view the function of justice may be said to be that of adjusting, joining, or fitting the different political values. Justice is the reconciler and the synthesis of political values: it is their union in an adjusted and integrated whole: it is, in Aristotle's words, 'What answers to the whole of goodness . . . being the exercise of goodness as a whole . . . towards one's neighbour'.[3] We must presently inquire into each of the values. But before we can do so, it is necessary to inquire into the origin and nature of the general notion of justice—the notion of the 'first' or 'total' value in which the others are all combined; by which they are all controlled; and in virtue of which their different claims (if and so far as a conflict arises) are reconciled and adjusted.

[1] *Supra*, § 1 of this Book.   [2] *Infra*, Book IV, § 4.
[3] *Ethics*, Book V, c. ii, § 10 (1130[b] 18–19).

How do we discover, and from what source do we draw, the total notion of justice—the general and controlling idea of the right and the just—which we feel that the law of the State should express? We acknowledge that justice will justify law to us; we admit that, in virtue of this justification, it finally ties and obliges us to law. But what is the source of its justifying grace and obliging power? Four different answers may be given to that question. The first is that the source of justice and of its power is religion. The second is that the source is nature. A third is that the source is economics. The fourth is that the source is ethics. We may now proceed to examine each of these answers in turn.

§ 4. RELIGION AS THE ORIGIN OF THE IDEA OF JUSTICE

THE medieval Church held, and the Roman Catholic Church (following the philosophy of the medieval schoolmen) still holds today, that it is God Who gives through His Church the notion of Justice, or idea of the rule of right, which is the impersonal source of law and the sustainer of the State in its task of declaring and recognizing law. This is plainly expressed in the theory of St. Thomas Aquinas. God Himself is always acting under an inflexible general rule of right (the *lex aeterna*) in the order of the universe which He has created and always continues to move. In addition, He has also expressed (1) a particular rule of right for mankind (the *lex divina*) in the revelation of the Scriptures, and (2) a more general rule of right for mankind (the *lex naturalis*) in the disclosure of His own being which He makes continually to the innate faculty of reason implanted by Him in man. These rules of right which God has expressed are above and behind all man-made law. It follows therefore that positive law (the *lex humana*)—the law imposed by human authority, and valid because so imposed—must always derive its value, and its final cogency, from conformity with the principles of 'divine' and 'natural' law. St. Thomas adds to this theory of law a parallel theory of human authority which is calculated to show how this derivation is, or may be, actually achieved. Authority, he holds, involves three separate elements, the primordial element of its *principium*, or foundation; the formal element of its *modus*, or permanent constitution (monarchical, aristocratic, democratic, or 'mixed'); and the active element of its *exercitium*, or actual operation at this or that moment of time by this or that body of persons. It is the community, or people, that determines the *modus*: it is the community that confers—as it also controls and may even withdraw in the event of misuse—the *exercitium*;[1] but it is God Himself who bestows, or we may even say *is*, the *principium*. Human authority, in its ultimate foundation, is thus an effluence of the Power of God. Being of that nature, it will act on the principles of divine and natural law as revealed, or as disclosed to reason, by God; and it will accordingly make the positive law, which it imposes on the members of the community, in conformity with those principles.[2]

None of the Protestant churches—not even the Calvinist—has developed a theory so logical or so comprehensive as that of St. Thomas Aquinas. But again and again they have advanced the claim that religion supplies the standard of justice which should inspire and control the law of the State. Sometimes they have gone to the length of demanding puritanical legislation, which would translate their own religious convictions into prescriptions of law; sometimes, more modestly, they have sought to formulate the ideal of a 'Christian order of politics and economics', which should serve the general community as an expression of social opinion and social aspirations, and should affect and stimulate the development of law along with, and by the side of, other similar expressions. We may readily admit that so far as religion is a source of ethical principles, and so far as ethical principles are the source of our notion of justice (a question which we have still to consider), religion may be counted as an ultimate source of that notion. But this is not to say that religion is an immediate source, or, even less, to say that it is the one and only source. There are a number of considerations which run counter to any such view.

---

[1] St. Thomas here proves himself 'the first Whig' in his theory of the popular basis of the *modus* and *exercitium* of authority. In the same way, and in the same sense, he holds that the scheme of positive law proceeds from the people or from a competent authority acting on behalf of the people. (*Supra*, Book I, § 4.)

[2] Blackstone himself was a Thomist, without knowing it, when he wrote (in the passage of the Introduction to his *Commentaries* which is borrowed from Burlamaqui), that 'upon these two foundations, the law of nature and the law of revelation, depend all human laws: that is to say no human laws should be suffered to contradict these'.

For one thing, we have to remember that the State includes among its members persons who have no religious belief and do not feel or acknowledge the claims of religion to their allegiance, as well as persons who have such belief and who feel and acknowledge such claims. We need a principle of value behind the law of the State which will embrace and convince both sorts of persons. For another thing, we have also to remember that religious belief creates churches, and that churches are societies which develop, in the process of time, authorities of their own. If we make religion the foundation of justice and the origin of the rule of right which the law of the State should express, a Church-authority may claim to decide, in the last resort, whether a given law is based on the foundation of justice and expresses the rule of right; and in that case the State-authority will cease to be the final authority which declares and enforces law for the community. Something of this sort happened in the hey-day of the medieval Church, when the Papacy claimed, as the final instance of Church-authority, to interpret and enforce an idea of justice derived from God through His revelation in the Scriptures and His disclosure of His Being to the faculty of reason, and when, in the strength of this claim, it sought to challenge the positive law of the State. Finally, and above all, we have to remember that religious belief issues in the conduct of life by standards which are higher than those of law and involve a quality of behaviour (in charity, for instance, and in chastity and temperance) such as law could not secure even if it made the attempt. The standards of religion can only be applied in the area of voluntary life which lies outside the State; and the quality of behaviour which they involve can only be achieved if it is sought freely and without any shadow of legal compulsion. If the State attempts to draw religious standards, and the quality of behaviour which they involve, into the area of the legal association, and to enforce them as the prescriptions and by the sanctions of law, it simply fails. It may even encourage what it seeks to prevent: it may encourage, for instance, the appetite for alcohol by prohibiting its manufacture, sale, and transport. Nor is this all. By making laws which cannot be enforced, it may foster disobedience to other laws which, if they stood alone, could be, and would be, enforced without any question.

§ 5. 'NATURE' AS THE ORIGIN OF THE IDEA OF JUSTICE

WHEN 'nature' is adduced as the origin of the idea of justice, the suggestion is that law has value, or may be made to have value, by being in accordance, or by being brought into accordance, with *la nature des choses*, or the natural order of things. But what is this natural order? It is not the natural order investigated by the physicist: man is not inanimate matter. Nor is it the natural order investigated by the biologist, though the biologist includes man in his studies along with the rest of the animal world. The natural order of the biologist is an order consisting in the selection of the fittest achieved by the way of struggle and survival: it is a uniformity, or a series of uniformities, observed in the animal world; and it cannot be argued that human law will be the better for squaring with any such uniformity or series of uniformities, or that it can ever be held, *on that ground*, to be the expression of justice. It may be right that the positive law of a human society should include eugenic prescriptions, which encourage the survival of 'good' elements and discourage the survival of 'bad'; but such prescriptions will not be right for a human society because they square with a uniform rule, selecting the 'fit' and rejecting the 'unfit', which runs through the history of happenings in the animal world. The 'good' is not the same as the 'fit'; and a rule of happenings among animal groups cannot be the source, or the justification, of a rule of conduct in a human society. In any case the idea of nature, and of a natural order of things, as a source of justice, is an idea far older than any development of modern natural science. It is at least as old as the Stoics, and it goes back as far as the end of the fourth century B.C. or even farther.

The Stoic conception of nature, which was transmitted to the Roman jurists and eventually to the Christian Fathers, is a conception belonging to a mixed world of religious belief and moral philosophy. The word 'nature', as it was used in legal and political speculation from the age of the Stoic Zeno to the age of the school of Rousseau, was the keyword of a religious-ethical conception of what *should be* in the spiritual world, rather than a term of art denoting what actually *was* in the material world of substance and the flesh. It is true that the Stoics pursued the study of cosmology rather than that of pure theology: it is true that they regarded the Godhead itself as a fiery ether or form of matter, pervading and going through all things, in virtue of its fineness, but none the less material. But though Stoicism had a material basis, it was still a spiritual creed. What the Stoics understood by 'Nature' was 'that ruling principle in the Universe which was Reason and God'.[1] The 'Nature' identified with God and Reason might, indeed, be a subtle form of matter, but it was none the less a 'ruling principle': an imperative of, or consisting in, the Reason which man shared with God. The Stoic canon of living 'in agreement with nature' was, therefore, fundamentally a canon of living 'according to the norm which man ought to realize'.[2] We may even say, in a paradox, that Nature was man's art: it was man's conception, achieved in the course of a conscious effort to fit himself into the Universe, of an ideal by which he could judge the mere given facts of his life in the past, and by which he could shape his life for the future into its rational, God-intended, 'natural' form.

Nature thus supplied the Stoics not only, or mainly, with a view of the order of things in the material world, but also with a creed of the spiritual order of the human world, as seen in its relation to God and in the light of His all-pervading Reason. The creed, in the form in which it was developed by Zeno and his successors, was built on a single premiss, and issued in three conclusions. The premiss was that men, in their essential constitution and nature, were rational beings who were each *divinae particula aurae* (a 'fragment', as they said, or detached part of the cosmic reason), and who all together shared, if only as such 'particles', in the all-pervading Reason which was the constitution and nature of God. The first conclusion drawn from this premiss was that men, being rational in their nature, should all be regarded as free and self-governing in their actions. This was the conclusion of Liberty; and Stoicism was thus the philosophy which nerved the opponents of tyranny. The second conclusion was that man, being all in their nature rational (though some were wiser than others, and there was a distinction between the *sapiens* and the *stultus*), should all be regarded as equal in status. This was the conclusion of Equality: *natura omnes homines aequales sunt*; and Stoicism was thus an influence which made for the

[1] E. R. Bevan, *Stoics and Sceptics*, p. 55.   [2] Ibid., p. 61.

amelioration, if not the abolition, of slavery. The third conclusion was that men, being united to one another by the common factor of reason, should all be linked together in the solidarity of a world-society—a single 'city of Zeus'[1]—under the control of a common law in conformity with their common nature. This was the conclusion of Fraternity; and this, in the old Greek world of multitudinous city-states and multitudinous civic laws, was the most revolutionary of the three.[2]

The Stoic premiss and its three conclusions formed a current of thought which has flowed for 2,000 years or more, through ancient Rome and the Middle Ages, through the Age of Enlightenment and the French Revolution, and is still flowing in our own age. This current of thought carries in its course an idea of justice, professing and claiming to be drawn from nature, which is a synthesis of the three values of liberty, equality, and fraternity. The one question which arises here, in connexion with the course of the argument, is that of the source from which this idea of justice is actually drawn. The conception of nature on which it rests is not a conception of physical nature (though, as we have seen, there *was* a physical element in the philosophy of Zeno): it is a conception of the spiritual nature of God and man; or, more exactly, it may be said to be a religious or theological conception of the nature of God, and a corresponding ethical conception of

---

[1] The phrase is used in the *Meditations* of Marcus Aurelius.

[2] Plutarch, in a well-known passage of the *De Alexandri Fortuna* (i. 6), connects Zeno's idea of the world-state with the career of Alexander. The main point in Zeno's political system, he writes, is that 'we should not live in city-states, divided by separate systems of justice, but should regard all men as our fellow-citizens, with one life and order like that of a herd of cattle feeding together on one pasture under a common law'. 'But this', he adds, 'is what Zeno wrote as a dream or vision of good law and politics based on philosophy; and it was Alexander who gave reality to the idea.'

The suggestion of Plutarch is that Zeno dreamed dreams, and Alexander *acted* along the line of his dreams. Dr. Tarn, however, in his book on *Alexander the Great* (vol. ii, Appendix 25, on 'Brotherhood and Unity'), argues that Alexander himself first dreamed the dream of human fraternity, and that Zeno adopted his dream. Alexander was 'the first man known to us', Dr. Tarn writes, to state that 'all men are brothers', and to hold that 'all men, being brothers, should live together in Homonoia', or the spirit of unity and concord; 'Zeno's great city of the world was founded on Alexander's idea of a human brotherhood.' Perhaps it hardly matters whether Alexander or Zeno first expressed in *words* the idea of human fraternity. What is certain is that the achievements and policy of Alexander were prior to the teaching of Zeno (Alexander died in 323, and Zeno began to teach in Athens in 301 B.C.), and that Zeno's teaching must have been affected by Alexander's world-conquests and by his policy of the reconciliation of all the peoples in his realm.

the nature of man. Nature is not, in this context, a source of justice which is distinct from religion and from ethics: it is rather a combination and fusion of religion and ethics. In the Stoic theory of natural law, as in the theory held by the Christian Fathers and proclaimed by the schoolmen of the Middle Ages and the Jesuit thinkers of the Counter-Reformation, both of these sources are present. In the theory of the secular school of natural law, during the seventeenth and eighteenth centuries, the religious element loses its power, and the ethical element is predominant. When that school, therefore, appeals to nature as the source of justice, its real appeal is to a code of ethics conceived as proceeding purely and solely from human reason and as rationally calculated to promote the sum of human happiness. Blackstone, indeed, is prepared to identify ethics and natural law: the rational pursuit of happiness, in his view, 'is the foundation of what we call ethics *or "natural law"*'.

The course of the argument has gone to show that the conception of nature is not a separate and original source of the idea of justice, but a source which is linked with and derived from religious belief and moral philosophy. There was, however, a twist or skew of the conception of nature which made it appear a separate and original source of the idea of justice. 'Nature' was sometimes supposed to denote an historic fact: the actual condition of man in the golden innocence of his prime. Men spoke of a 'state of nature', and imagined that state as an age of the reign of a pure law of nature. This is a modern twist, which was unknown to the Stoics and foreign to the ideas of the Roman jurisconsults who followed the Stoics. Perhaps the twist was partly due to what may be called a verbal cause. Words, as has already been noted, are not only instruments of thought but also influences upon it; and the Latin word *natura*, when it was used to translate the Greek *physis*, carried with it associations of original birth and a primitive condition which were foreign to the Greek, and which, as they grew in force, made 'nature' a happy infancy and the 'law of nature' a law of early innocence.[1] Partly, again, the twist may also have been encouraged by Christian ideas of Eden and the state of primitive grace which

---

[1] On the influence exercised on later thought by the adoption of the Latin word *natura* to translate the Greek *physis* see Sir John Myres, *The Political Ideas of the Greeks*, pp. 237–40.

preceded the fall of man. In any case, and whatever its cause, the twist meant the slewing round of an idea proposed for man's future into a supposed condition of his past, with the added suggestion that the supposed condition of the past ought to be recovered and restored. (Men like to depict their revolutions and ventures into the future as restorations of an idealized past; and Paine, for instance, in advocating the Rights of Man, readily appeals to the time when man came with his rights from 'the hand of his Maker'.) If nature is thus made a fact of the past, it may be held to be a separate and independent source, an historical source, of the idea of justice. But this historical source is only an imagined source, since the fact of the past is only an imagined fact; and even if it were an actual fact at an actual point of time, no single fact or point of time in the process of secular human history can be an ideal, or the source of an ideal, though the whole of the facts of history, and all its succession of points of time, may help to suggest an ideal towards which the process is moving.

§ 6. ECONOMICS AS THE ORIGIN OF THE IDEA OF JUSTICE

WITH the development of modern industry, which began on the Continent in the nineteenth century, the theory began to be advanced, first by French and German thinkers, and then, from Bakunin onwards, by Russian thinkers and revolutionaries, that the origin of the idea of justice could and should be discovered in the area of economics. Upon this theory the idea of justice is derived from the facts, or deduced from the principles, of economics. In the theory of Marx, which is a fatalistic theory of the dominance of matter and the material conditions of man's economic activity, the idea is simply derived from the facts: indeed it can hardly be called an idea, and it is rather a fate imposed by the facts. The positive law of the State, in any given conjuncture of economic conditions, is imposed on its members by the personal authority of the class which is dominant under those conditions; and the impersonal source of the law is similarly the inevitable imperative imposed upon that class by its own economic interest in the given conjuncture. When the given conjuncture of conditions is a system of capitalistic production, the bourgeois class is dominant, and the bourgeois class, itself determined by the system, determines the law in a sense corresponding to its interest. When the mutations of matter produce a different conjuncture, and issue in a system of socialized production, controlled by the workers themselves, the proletariate or working class is dominant in its turn, and that class determines the law, as the bourgeois class did before, under the compulsion of its own system and for the promotion of its own interest. As long as there is a State and as long as there is law, the law of the State will be made in the interest of the strong, and the source of the notion of justice (if indeed we can speak of such a notion, or of any notion at all, in the Marxian world of material forces) will be the fact of economic strength, moving and acting as it must. Only when the State itself disappears, and when law disappears with the State, can a form of society be attained which is common and equal for all, and involves no subjection of class to class. That form of society is communism—communism in its purity—communism at its highest. But that society will be non-political and non-legal; and being without law it will be informed by a disembodied spirit of justice. That spirit has no economic origin, but consists in a sense of 'the elementary rules of social life, known for centuries, repeated for thousands of years in all sermons', and at the long last spontaneously obeyed as men 'become accustomed to their observance without force'.[1] This is the evocation of a *deus ex machina*, dormant hitherto though known for centuries, and inoperative hitherto although repeated for millennia from the pulpits. It follows that after all there is, and has been for centuries and millennia, a notion of justice based on something—whatever that something may be—other than economic strength. But this notion has never been a source of law in the past; and it will not be a source of law in the future, because the future will be without law. Its foundation remains in mist; and it is only mist itself.

The theory of Proudhon and his successors follows a very different line from that of Marx and the successors of Marx. Proudhon, it is true, drew the notion of justice from an economic source: he preached, as we have already noticed, the priority of *droit économique*. But he did not, like Marx, derive his notion of justice from economic *facts*: he deduced it from economic *principles*, and primarily from the great principle of

[1] Lenin, *The State and Revolution*, chap. v. 2.

mutualité.[1] We have already had reason to notice the general conclusions which may be drawn from this principle; and something has already been said of the general tendency of French syndicalism, basing its theory upon the principle, to think in terms not of warring and colliding classes, but of occupational groups complementary to one another and knit together by mutual need and the bond of mutual service. Upon this basis the notion of justice drawn from the source of economics will be a notion based on the interest not of a class of society but of the whole of society and of all its complementary groups. The legal philosophy of Duguit may be cited as an example of such a notion of justice, and of the general view of the State and its law to which that notion leads.[2]

Duguit assumes that a national society must primarily be regarded as an economic society, and studied accordingly in the light of its economic structure and economic activities. The basic fact of such a society is the existence of different occupational groups, producing different things, but bound to one another by mutual need of one another's products and by a consequent system of mutual exchange. The essential principle is therefore solidarity—a term which takes the place of Proudhon's *mutualité.* Solidarity has two forms. The first form is the mechanical, which is based on similarity; and here the members of one and the same group use similar capacities in order to produce in co-operation a considerably greater product than they could produce in isolation. The second form is the organic, which is based on difference; and here the members of different groups use different capacities, on a system of division of labour which entails still greater co-operation, in order to produce a vastly greater product than could otherwise be produced. It follows that the maximum of production—which is the essential aim of the society, because it brings the maximum of consumption and the maximum of enjoyment—entails the maximum of co-operation. This maximum of co-operation involves and supplies the principle of solidarity; and this principle of solidarity furnishes in turn the notion of justice, the notion of what is right in itself, the notion of value, which is the impersonal source of law. The

---

[1] *Supra,* Book I, § 11.

[2] The account which follows of Duguit's philosophy is based on the 1927 edition of his *Droit Constitutionnel.*

name which Duguit gives to this notion is that of *règle de droit*. This *règle de droit* is a conception similar to Proudhon's *droit économique*; and it issues for Duguit in two imperatives, one negative and the other positive: (1) do nothing contrary to the principle of solidarity; (2) co-operate as far as possible in the realization of that principle.

In developing his theory Duguit proceeds to attach so great a measure of importance to the impersonal source of law, and to the need of law being inherently right in virtue of its accordance with *la règle de droit*, that he almost seems to obliterate any personal source. It is the value inherent in law, rather than the validity stamped upon it by a declaratory authority, which is his concern. He may even be said to deny the existence of any real authority, and, with it, the existence of any real validity of the law declared by *so-called* authority. True, there are persons called governors (*gouvernants*); but they only exist *de facto* and they are not competent *de jure* to promulgate binding rules. They are indeed facts, but they are only facts of force; they issue pronouncements or commands, but those pronouncements are in themselves no more than the dictates of force, and they only acquire validity, or impose any obligation other than that of *force majeure*, when they square with 'the rule of right' deduced from solidarity.[1] It follows that the governors (a term which includes all holders of political authority in any of its forms, including the members of legislatures) must be brought under 'the rule of right', and made subject to its control, if their acts and pronouncements are to possess any real validity and to impose any true obligation. Indeed they must be doubly brought under the rule of right, by being made subject to *both* of the imperatives in which it issues. Under the first imperative, 'Do nothing contrary to the principle of solidarity', any rule which they make and seek to enforce in contravention of that principle,

---

[1] A diagram in the form of a genealogical table may illustrate, if only roughly, the process of Duguit's reasoning.

○ = solidarity; an economic fact turned into a value or first principle.

□ = *la règle de droit*; what is right in itself as being the issue of solidarity.

◇ = *loi*, which may or may not be the legitimate issue of the *règle de droit*. (There is a straight line of legitimate descent from solidarity to the *règle de droit*; there *may* be a bar sinister in the descent from the *règle de droit* to *loi*.)

being *ex hypothesi* invalid, must be made inoperative by the process of judicial disallowance,[1] or, failing that, by the process of general social negation in the ascending stages of passive, defensive, and aggressive resistance. Under the second imperative, 'Co-operate as far as possible in the realization of the principle of solidarity', which is interpreted as commanding the governors to provide public assistance for the destitute, education for the ignorant, and work for the unemployed, any failure on their part to make such provision and to render the service due, being *ex hypothesi* a neglect of duty, must equally be remedied by judicial redress or corrected by the process of social agitation and social pressure.[2]

In the upshot of his argument Duguit not only seeks to make economics, and its principle of solidarity, the one[3] impersonal source of law; he also seeks to make it the one and only source; and he eliminates, in effect, the personal source consisting in a human authority. The elimination, indeed, is not complete: authority remains as an obstinate fact of power, however illegitimate its acts and its pronouncements may be; and though it is confronted by a higher *règle de droit*, drawn from a sovereign principle of solidarity, we can hardly be sure that the fact of power will obey the rule of right, even when the rule is backed by judicial action and supported by social pressure. The weakness of Duguit's theory, at this point, is perhaps not so much that it tends to eliminate human authority as a source of law, as that it tends to leave a powerful but possibly (or even probably) illegitimate human authority confronting a wholly legitimate but possibly powerless rule of right. But it is not this weakness or dualism of Duguit's theory with which we are here concerned. The question for us is not that of the relation of the governors to a rule of right founded on economics; it is the prior question of

[1] Some French jurists have argued that judicial disallowance should be applied to laws in contravention of the Declaration of the Rights of Men and Citizens issued in 1789. Duguit is arguing along the same line—but in the opposite direction—when he seeks to apply judicial disallowance to any rule made in contravention, not of the rights of individual men, but of the principle of social solidarity.

[2] The modern State, Duguit accordingly writes, tends to become 'une fédération des services publics qu'administrent les détenteurs de la plus grande force ayant non plus le droit de commander, mais le devoir d'assurer le fonctionnement ininterrompu et productif de ces services'. *Droit Constitutionnel* (1927 edition), vol. i, p. 589.

[3] But see the last note at the end of this section, p. 116.

the relation between the rule of right itself and the principle of economics from which Duguit supposes it to be drawn. Is economics, or a principle of economics, or the sum of the principles of economics, the primary basis and origin of the notion of justice?

In seeking to answer that question we may be wise to begin by a summary view of the influence which economics has actually exerted, during the course of history, on the making of ordinary positive law. If economics has largely influenced, through the ages, the making of ordinary positive law, this will be a presumption in favour of turning to economics in order to discover a basis and origin for the idea of justice. Is there any such presumption? The evidence of the past would appear to suggest that law has determined the order of economics even more than it has itself been determined by that order. If economic factors and economic interests have partly determined the legal system of order and the legal framework of rules, it is even more true that law has furnished the whole general system of order, and the whole general framework of rules, within which, and under which, the factors and interests of economics have had to work. Positive law is a general scheme, which covers, as has already been noted,[1] many fields of life besides the economic. The lawyers and legislators who have built that scheme have no doubt been influenced, at some periods and in some parts of their building, by economic interests, but the whole scheme has been built for the simple general purpose of tidying human relations and making them ship-shape and sensible; and the shaping force of this purpose has reached out into economics. Even a rule which has originally been made under the influence of some special economic interest may come to be absorbed, in the process of time, by the shaping force of the general purpose, and may be used to protect quite other and very different interests. The English rule or method of trust is an example. Designed originally to protect the position and property of daughters and younger sons of the upper classes, it has been shaped into a system protecting free churches and trade unions, and made to serve, in Maitland's words, as 'the most powerful instrument of social experimentation'.[2]

If that is the relation of economics to positive law, we may

---

[1] *Supra*, Book II, § 2.   [2] *Supra*, Book II, § 3, *ad finem*.

fairly expect something similar to be true of the relation of economics to the idea of justice, and we may refuse to believe that economic principles can ever be *the* source (though they may be a contributory source) of our idea of what is inherently right. Take, for example, Duguit's principle of solidarity. It is, to begin with, an observation based on an economic fact—the fact that men increasingly co-operate as they increase production. The observation is turned into a principle: men *ought* to co-operate more and more in order to increase production still further; and that principle then becomes the source of the *règle de droit*. But even in the realm of economic facts solidarity is not the only thing. There are other things which also serve to increase production: there is, for instance, inventive skill, leading to the discovery of new and more fruitful methods of manufacture: there is also managerial ability, leading to the discovery of new and more effective ways of arranging co-operation; and both of these things suggest that individual initiative matters as well, and may even matter as much, as social solidarity, and that it too may turn into a principle which is a source of the rule of right. Solidarity, we begin to see, cannot be the whole source of our notion of justice: taken by itself, and in itself, it cannot produce or explain the notion. A beehive has solidarity; but just because it has only the one factor of solidarity, it lacks some other factors—such as liberty of personal development—which human beings have always considered essential to the notion of justice. Solidarity may be one value in the system of values which we call by the name of justice; and giving it the name of *fraternité*, as the thinkers of 1789 did, we may place it accordingly by the side of *liberté* and *egalité*. But whatever name we give it, it is not the whole of the system. The economic fact of solidarity, even when it is turned into a principle and regarded as a value, needs the complement of other values.[1] It also needs, along with them

----

[1] It should be noted that Duguit, in the third edition of his *Droit Constitutionnel* (1927), criticizes himself, in vol. i, p. 116, for not having given sufficient prominence, in his earlier writings, to an element other than solidarity, 'dont il est facile de dire ce qu'il n'est pas, plutôt que ce qu'il est'. This other element is what he calls justice. He therefore proceeds to argue that solidarity *and justice* are the two sources of the *règle de droit*. But what is this justice which is thus by an afterthought placed by the side of solidarity? It is not, of course, any system or synthesis of values: it is simply one value by the side of others—or rather, by the side of another, i.e. solidarity. It is the value of *autonomie individuelle*: or, more exactly, it is the psychological fact of man's *sentiment de son moi*, turned into a value, as solidarity is

and in common with them, some principle of unity and reconciliation which creates a system, gives each of the values its place in the system, and causes and explains their inclusion.

§ 7. ETHICS AS THE ORIGIN OF THE IDEA OF JUSTICE

CAN we find this principle in ethics? If we answer in the affirmative, the moral standard of the community, precipitated in and enforced by the general moral conscience, will be the source of a notion of justice, containing a system or synthesis of values, which will be in its turn the impersonal source of positive law. We shall accordingly hold that if law is to have value as well as validity—value all round, and not some single 'broken arc' of value called by the name of 'solidarity' or by some other such name—it must satisfy, in the last resort, the demands of the general moral conscience, issuing and expressed in a general all-round notion of what is just and right in the conduct of human relations. In order that law may be valid, it is enough that it should satisfy the canon of declaration, recognition, and enforcement by a constituted authority acting on behalf of the community. In order that it may have value, over and above validity, law must also satisfy—*as much as it can, and so far as its strength avails*—the canon of conformity to the demands of moral conscience as expressed in the general notion of justice. In other words, and in simpler terms, law will have value only if it expresses and realizes—*so far as it can and in such ways as it can*—a rule of right for human relations ultimately derived from ethics.

Here we touch a difficulty, which the provisos already stated are meant to meet in advance. Law is not ethics; and legality, or obedience to law, is not the same as morality. Law is concerned with external acts, and its demands are satisfied by such acts because they are all that its sanctions, themselves external acts of physical compulsion, can possibly secure. Ethics is concerned not only with external acts, but also with internal motive:

the economic fact of co-operation, similarly turned into a value. Justice, therefore, is just a 'prolongation' or extension of egoistic feeling (*sentiment égoïste*): it is the complement, counterpart, and corrective of solidarity. But is this justice at all? Is it not *liberty*—in the somewhat savage dress of the egoist? Duguit has, very properly, a feeling that solidarity needs a complement. But the complement which he provides is *not* what he calls it; nor is it reconciled, in any way, with what may be called, in a literal sense, its 'opposite number'.

its essence, as Aristotle said, is 'a state of character, concerned with choice', which is freely determined in its choice by its own internal motive; and the demands of ethics are not satisfied unless an internal motive is present as well as an external act. An act is legal, whatever its motive, so long as it is the act demanded by the law. An act is not moral, whatever its outward show may be, if it is not inspired by an internal motive and does not proceed from a 'state of a character concerned with choice'.

But though we must draw a distinction between the nature of ethics and the nature of law, it does not follow that such a distinction abolishes any relation. Law and ethics are both concerned with what should be, and they both speak in the imperative mood: they both deal, in the main, with identical areas of life—marriage and its sanctities, the keeping of faith and the honouring of pledges, the duty of consideration for others, and man's general duty to his neighbour. How shall we express their relation? We may attempt two alternative methods of expression, and seek to discover which of the two expresses the relation best.

The first method of expression is based on the fact that law is a uniform rule of action binding on all men alike. Men in general run through the whole gamut of the moral scale: some act on this, and some on that standard: one standard is lower, and another higher. What law does, it may be argued, is to establish a moral minimum which every man must attain. It establishes, as it were, a lowest common measure of conduct which all can compass and which can therefore be made a uniform rule of action for all. If law bids me attach and keep burning a rear light on my bicycle when I am riding it in the dark, that is a lowest common measure of consideration for others, and it may, as such, be legally imposed. If law proceeds to fine me for riding without a rear light, it stimulates me into a disposition to obey the moral minimum—a disposition which itself is not moral (even though it results in obedience to the moral rule of consideration for others) because it is based on the negative and non-moral factor of force, and not on the positive and moral factor of an inward motive of spontaneous consideration. Law, when it is so considered, may be regarded as a school-master to bring us to morality, through the enforcement of habits of action by the use of coercive discipline.

But there is an obvious objection to this view of law. A moral minimum, enforced by non-moral means, may have *some* relation to ethics; but it is not a relation which can stand the test of scrutiny, or prove itself to be anything more than a superficial relation. If law is connected with ethics in the sense that it is meant to enforce the rules of ethics on some sort of common standard, ought not the standard initially to be something higher than a mere minimum, and ought we not to be constantly engaged in screwing the strings tighter and tighter, in order to produce a fuller and truer note? And, even more, ought not the standard, whatever its pitch, to be enforced by means, such as reformatory punishment and moral education, which will themselves have a moral quality because they tend to promote a moral disposition? These questions suggest that if once we adopt the idea that law is a moral minimum, we shall soon be led to seek to obliterate any distinction between law and ethics, and to substitute law for ethics, with the result of eliminating ethics.

We may therefore turn to another method of expressing the relation between law and ethics. This second method, like the first, is based on the fact that law deals only with men in the mass, and is in its nature no more than a uniform rule of action binding equally on all alike. But the corollary which we now draw from that fact is that the only thing which law can get from man in the mass is external conduct, because the only thing which it can apply to men in the mass is external force. From this point of view, and bearing in mind the word 'external', we arrive at another method of expressing the relation between law and ethics. We conclude that law is related to ethics in the sense that it seeks to secure the set of external conditions necessary for moral action, or the general framework of external order in which the moral conscience can act and determine itself most easily and most freely. Law, from this point of view, is not the lowest common measure of ethics, or the lowest story in the house of ethics: it is rather the best and highest set of conditions, set round the house and forming, as it were, a fence for its protection, which has to be assembled, and firmly established, before moral action can find a free space for its play and in order that moral development may unfold its energies freely. All moral development is inevitably confronted by external obstacles or hindrances: it is the function of law 'to remove the obstacles' or 'hinder the hindrances'.

The law relating to education, as it has been gradually assembled and established in England since 1870, may be cited as an example. Moral development requires—the more as the world grows older, fuller of accumulated knowledge, and fuller, too, of complications alike in the social structure and the material environment of life—a period of initiation in the fund of accumulated knowledge, and a period of introduction to all the complications of structure and environment. This initiation and introduction is what we call education. But the process of education is confronted by possible obstacles. The State has sought by means of its law to remove those obstacles progressively. First, there is the obstacle that there may not be schools enough to provide education for all. The State, which had already been acting, through the law of the budget, to aid the establishment of voluntary schools, proceeded in 1870 to establish by law an additional and general system of schools provided entirely from its own funds. Next, there is the obstacle that parents may not be willing, if the matter is left to their choice, to send their children to school. The State, which had already enacted in 1870 that the 'school boards' charged with the establishment of schools might, if they wished, make attendance at schools compulsory in their area, proceeded by a law of 1880 to make attendance compulsory everywhere up to a given age. Here we may say, from one point of view (the point of view of the parents), that the law established a moral minimum, by making it the legal duty of parents to do for their children, for a prescribed period, what parents are morally bound to do as long as they possibly can; but from another point of view (the point of view of the children), which is the essence of the matter, we have to say that the law removed an obstacle, and hindered a hindrance, by clearing away from their path a hurdle which would have impeded, or even blocked, their development. Finally, there is the obstacle that parents may not have the means to pay for their children's education, even though they are under compulsion to send their children to school. The State, which had already enacted in 1870 that 'school boards' might remit fees in cases of poverty, proceeded in 1891 to make remission of fees the general rule, and thus to make the compulsory period of education free and gratuitous as well as compulsory. In effect, it pooled the payment of fees among all the members of the community; it removed the obstacle to a child's development arising from his parents' want of means by making it the legal duty of all to provide the means.

In the whole of this process the driving force and the ultimate purpose is thus the growth of the child, during and through a preliminary period of initiation and introduction, into the stature of a free and responsible moral agent. But if that is the ultimate purpose which is served by law, the fact remains that law serves the purpose only by removing obstacles, and only by securing, in virtue of such removal, the presence of the external conditions which make development possible. The development itself must proceed from within; it must be self-moved and spontaneous; otherwise it will not be moral development. We may thus say of education, when we consider it in its essence as a process of moral development in which teachers and children co-operate, that it lies outside the law and is free from the arm of the State. It is not the business of law, or of any legal authority, to control the inner life of the process of education. It is only the business of law, and of any legal authority (even if it be called an education authority), to secure the external conditions of a process which, in itself, is necessarily independent of law and legal authority.

It follows from the course of the argument that if we have to choose between two conceptions of law—the conception which makes the purpose of law consist in the provision of a moral minimum, and the conception which makes it consist in the maximum provision of the external conditions which make moral development possible—we are bound to choose the second, and we are bound to choose it for the simple reason that it connects law and ethics more intimately, and more truly, than the first can ever do. Law which is conceived as a moral minimum suffers itself from being viewed as a minimum; and it makes morality suffer, by appearing to provide in its place a sort of low-grade substitute. Law which is conceived as the maximum provision of the external conditions of morality gains itself by being viewed as a maximum; and it also makes morality gain because it opens a freer field for its exercise, making it able to do its own work with less hindrance and fewer obstacles. It may even be said, in a paradox, that we connect law and ethics the more closely, the more clearly we distinguish their provinces. We separate them clearly if we define the one as the province of voluntary self-determination, with innumerable springs of individual initiative, and the other as the province of obligatory action, governed by uniform rules flowing in their set channels from a single central source. But we also connect the provinces which we have begun by distinguishing, and we connect them closely and intimately, if we add that it is the business of the province of law to defend and extend the province of morality —to defend it, in the present, by providing the conditions now demanded for its free play; to extend it, for the future, by increasing the provision of those conditions as new demands arise both from the development of social structure and from changes of material environment. To stand outside in self-restraint, and yet to defend with power—to be separate and yet connected—such is the relation of law to morality.[1]

On this basis the law of the State will be careful not to diminish the area of moral autonomy in the process of extending the area of legal automatism. If the State attempts to increase the area of the compulsory action—the area of law and coercion —by bringing into it actions which might have been safely left to voluntary self-determination, it is offending against the nature of law and the true relation of law to morality. It is indeed a safe rule for the State that it should always command and enforce by law any act which ought so much to be done that it had better be done under coercion than not be done at all; but it is equally a safe rule for the State that it should not, in seeking to secure the conditions of goodness, diminish the area of goodness itself. On the contrary, an increase of compulsion at one point should always result in a more than proportionate increase of freedom at others; for an increase of freedom which was merely equivalent to the loss involved by the change would merely leave things as they were, and afford no justification for the change which was being made. The law of education may once more be cited in evidence. A law which makes the attendance of children at school compulsory brings their parents, in that respect, into the area of legal coercion, and diminishes, to that extent, the area of free goodness; but the education of the

[1] See above, Book II, § 2.

child is so vitally important a condition of his own moral development, and the total area of free goodness may be so much extended by the compulsory provision of the condition, that the price may safely be paid.

§ 8. INDIVIDUAL PERSONALITY AND SOCIAL ORGANIZATION

THE course of the argument has led to the conclusion that the idea of justice, which is the impersonal source of law, is an idea which itself has its source in ethics and ethical principles. But the foundation of ethics, and the source of all ethical principles, is the value and the worth of individual personality. The moral world is a world of individual persons, each intrinsically valuable, but all existing in time, and all accordingly subject to the conditions of a time-process. The intrinsic value of each personality is the basis of political thought, just as (and just because) it is the basis of moral thought; and worth of persons—individual persons; *all* individual persons—is the supreme worth in the State. Existing under, and subject to, the conditions of a time-process, these persons—not fixed substances, but so many *growing* nuclei—are engaged in a motion of development, which is the turning of capacity into energy or (as we may also say) of 'potency' into 'act'. The end of any national society is to foster and encourage, in and through partnership, the highest possible development of all the capacities of personality in all of its members; and this end is the justice, or 'right ordering', of such a society, and may accordingly be called by the name of social justice.[1] Similarly the end of any legal association or State, which is based and superimposed on a national society, is to assemble and establish the external conditions required by every citizen for the development of his capacities; and this end is the justice, or right ordering, of such a legal association, and may accordingly be called legal justice.

The formula here suggested—the highest possible develop-

[1] The term 'social justice', in common usage, tends to be applied only to economics, and to be used only to denote a just distribution of economic duties and rewards. Justice of this economic order is indeed a necessary part of 'social justice' in the larger sense of that term; for a just distribution of economic duties and rewards is a necessary means to the fostering and encouraging of general personal development. But social justice, in its broader sense, is a matter of something more than merely economic duties and rewards.

ment of all the capacities of personality in all the members of society—was foreshadowed in a formula of the eighteenth century. That formula, which would appear to have been invented by Francis Hutcheson,[1] sometime professor of moral philosophy in the University of Glasgow, but which was afterwards adopted and popularized by Bentham and his disciples, was 'the greatest happiness of the greatest number'. It is a shadow of the truth; but it is also a dangerous shadow. If happiness, as it readily may be, is identified with pleasure, and thus made to consist in a surplus of sensations of pleasure over sensations of pain, it becomes the end of Society and the State to secure for as many persons as possible, and in as great a degree as possible, the presence of a static condition of pleasurable sensation. This is the filling of a sieve with water. Owing to the law of satiety, which means that a continuing pleasure is a continually less pleasure, there will always be a leakage of pleasurable sensation; and the static condition will not even be static. In any case, and even if it were possible to prevent it from deteriorating and running backward,

In pejus ruere ac retro sublapsa referri,

a static condition is not in harmony with the conditions of the time-process to which man is subject; nor does the human faculty of judgement, which recognizes values and applies them *in foro conscientiae*, assign most value to the person most steadily enjoying most pleasure with the minimum of leakage. A personality dynamically developing all its capacities in a constant progression is a better answer to the process of time and a greater satisfaction to our sense of values; and our formula of social and legal justice, or the right ordering of Society and the State, will accordingly be the highest possible development of capacity in the greatest possible number of persons.

There is a sense of the word 'happiness'—a chameleon-like word, which can change its colour to match different environments—in which it may be, and has been, applied to such development. Happiness need not be identified with pleasure. It may be defined, as it was by Aristotle (though the Greek word which he uses is perhaps better rendered by our word 'felicity'),

---

[1] 'That Action is best, which procures the greatest Happiness for the greatest Numbers.' Hutcheson's *Inquiry into the Original of our Ideas of Beauty and Virtue* (1725), Treatise II, Sec. iii, § 8.

as consisting in the unhindered energy of the higher—because more rational—capacities of man's soul. Proceeding upon this basis Aristotle is even willing to allow that happiness of this order—the happiness of the soul of man freely exercising its energy in the full play of its higher capacities, both by contemplation and action—is attended by a 'supervening' pleasure, or added bloom of joy, which comes from the conscious sense of itself and its own existence and motion. We may therefore argue, if we follow Aristotle, that there is a form of happiness—a form of happiness attended by pleasure—which is, after all, the end of Societies and of States, and which supplies the formula for their right ordering. But that argument has its dangers, and it may lead us into quicksands. For one thing, the happiness of Aristotle's theory, even if we understand it in his own high sense, is a happiness which he reserves for the few, who have 'opportunity of leisure'. It may mean the highest possible development of capacity; but it does not mean such development in the greatest number of persons. For another thing, it is unlikely that happiness, if once we begin to use that term, will ever be understood (except by a few) in Aristotle's sense. It goes against the general grain, and the general use of language, to use the term in any other sense than that of a surplus of sensations of pleasure over sensations of pain. A few may rise to the height of Aristotle's conception of happiness; and those few may even transcend him in refusing to reserve for the few the high happiness which he conceived and described, but reserved as a prize for the few. That is not enough. We need a formula which is equally understood by all, without doubt or equivocation— just as it equally embraces all, without difference or respect of persons. No formula of 'happiness'—always an equivocal and shifting word—can satisfy that condition. The Benthamite formula has the merit of extension (the best words in it are 'the greatest number'); but it has also the grave defect of a low conception of the happiness thus to be extended and spread 'in widest commonalty' among the greatest number. A formula based on the philosophy of Aristotle may remedy the defect of quality in the Benthamite formula; but it is also likely, in the process, to lose the merit of extension which that formula possesses, and to encourage the thin satisfaction of a limited *élite*.

But if we abandon any formula of happiness, and content

ourselves with the notion of the highest possible development
of capacity in the greatest possible number of persons, we are
not yet out of the wood. The objection may be raised that a
notion which makes the end of Societies and States consist in
the maximum development of so many individual persons is a
notion which is anti-social, or at any rate a-social, even if the
number of such personalities is itself a maximum number and
is thus conterminous (or nearly conterminous) with the whole
range of national society and the national State. Such an
objection, if it be raised, can be pressed in a number of searching
questions. Do we not speak of the *commune bonum*, of the general
welfare, and of social well-being? When we use such terms, do
we not imply, by the fact of their use, the existence of a social
whole, which experiences or enjoys, with some sort of sentient
existence, this welfare or well-being? Must we not therefore
take into account the presence not only of individual personalities, but also of a social 'personality', or at any rate (if we reject
that term, and refuse to ascribe personality to any form of being
which is not individual) of a social 'organism'?

Something has already been said,[1] in a previous discussion
of the nature of social groups, in regard to the conception of
'social' or 'group' personality. In the course of the discussion a
distinction was drawn between 'moral' personality and 'legal'
personality; and the argument was advanced that while legal personality could be predicated of groups, moral personality could
be predicated only of individuals, and was an attribute peculiar
to individuals. If that argument be true we are precluded from
ascribing personality to the social whole.[2] The only form of
personality which can here be in question is *moral* personality
(that follows from the moral terms *commune bonum*, general welfare,
and social well-being which have been used); and this is exactly
the form of personality which the social whole, by its very
nature, cannot possess.[3]

---

[1] *Supra*, Book II, § 6.

[2] The term 'social whole' is here used in a sense which is intended to include both
Society and the State. Later in the argument, the metaphor of the organism, as a
description (or rather an illustration) of the nature of the 'social whole', is discussed
with a special reference to the State; later still, with a reference to the economic
or physical aspect of Society; and finally, with a reference to the moral or spiritual
aspect of Society.

[3] The State, as distinct from Society, may possess the legal form of personality:
that is to say, it may possess and exercise the capacity of suing and being sued in

But if we are thus precluded from regarding this whole—this Society to which we belong; this national Society which is also a national State—as a social personality, may we not, at the least, regard it as a social organism? We may begin by noting that the term 'social organism' is a metaphor, and only a metaphor: it is not a description or a definition. The question before us, therefore, is not a question whether the term 'social organism' is an accurate definition: it is a question whether the term is a useful metaphor—whether, in other words, it is a term of comparison which can profitably be used to throw light on the nature of the thing to which the comparison is applied.

Defining a metaphor as a term 'carried over', by a process of 'transference', from the thing which it immediately signifies to a thing supposed to be analogous, for the purpose of illustrating the nature of that thing, we may begin by asking what the term 'organism' immediately signifies, and then proceed to ask how far that term, with the addition of the adjective 'social', illustrates the nature of Society. In its own immediate significance the word 'organism' comes from an original Greek word meaning 'that with which one works', or, in other words, a tool or instrument; and even in our modern usage, which connects it with the science of biology and accordingly applies it to living structures (apparently remote from the notion of instruments or tools), the word still bears the impress of the original Greek. An organism is something animate which is a compound of parts serving one another, and serving thereby the whole which they collectively constitute, as instruments for the attainment of a

courts of law, as a legal person of the corporate order. Society, as distinct from the State, possesses neither the legal nor the moral form of personality. We speak indeed of national character, and the word 'character' may seem to involve the presence of personality. But national character is a shorthand term which is used to denote the common characteristics of the individual members of a nation—characteristics expressed in no single person, but in millions of persons succeeding one another generation by generation. The nation is a society of persons; but a society of persons is not a person.   It may seem to some that the State and Society are degraded by a refusal to regard them as moral persons; and the question may be raised whether their action would not be higher, if a higher view were taken of the nature of their existence. There is a twofold answer to the question. In the first place, even if good might come of it, it cannot be right to pretend the existence of the non-existent. In the second place, evil would be far more likely to come of it than good. A State or Society conceived as a super-person might well develop a super-morality which freed it from the rules of individual conduct, and liberated it for (or enslaved it to) the pure pursuit of its own super-good, which might well be no more than a corporate egoism.

common purpose; it is a composite living structure, in which the parts are 'organs' or tools, mutually instrumental to one another and collectively instrumental to the life-purpose of the whole. We may accordingly say that the essence of the animate organism, in the realm of biology, is the instrumentality of each part in relation to the life-purpose of the whole.

Can we carry that notion over from the realm of biology and transfer it to the realm of social and political theory? Is there enough analogy between the composite living structure which we describe as an organism, and the organized form of Society which we describe as a State, to justify us in speaking of the latter in terms borrowed from the former, and in seeking to illustrate the nature of the State by the use of the metaphor of organism? The State is certainly an organized society: in other words, it is an association constructed and articulated, by the action of its members, for the permanent purpose of declaring and enforcing a system of law directed to the attainment of justice. But to define the nature of the State in those terms (even if we use the word 'organized' in the process) is at once to see the differences between the State and an organism, rather than to detect an analogy. (This is not to say that we may not eventually discover *some sort* of analogy: it is only to say that it is difference which immediately leaps to the eye.) In the first place the State is a structure which is made by the action of its parts, and created by the volition of its members. We cannot say that the parts make the structure of the physical organism: if either makes the other, it is the organism which makes the parts. In the second place, the essence of the State may from one point of view be said to be the opposite of that of the physical organism. If the essence of the physical organism is the instrumentality of each part in relation to the life-purpose of the whole, the essence of the State is the instrumentality of the whole in relation to the life-purpose of each part. The State is a whole which is instrumental to its parts, in the sense that it exists to secure the conditions of the development of its members; it is a whole in which every part is final and independent, in the sense that each is a personality which as such is an end in itself and responsible for itself. Lastly, the purpose of the State is different in kind from that of the physical organism. The purpose of the physical organism is purely physical; it is that of maintaining in the present, and reproducing in the future, the physical life-force of the *whole* structure. The purpose of the State is indeed partly physical: it is, in part (though even here there is a difference between its purpose and that of the organism), a purpose of maintaining physical life—the physical life of its *individual* members—under healthy physical conditions and encouraging its reproduction under similar conditions. But the main and essential purpose of the State is something more than physical. Existing in the moral world, and resting on a moral basis, it has the primary purpose of maintaining—and not only maintaining, but also extending—the conditions under which each of its members, as a conscious moral agent, can freely and consciously develop the highest capacities of his nature. In a word, the life-force of the organism is that of the whole, and it is entirely physical in character: the life-force of the State (if we may speak of it as having a life-force) is that of its individual members, and it is predominantly moral in character.

The metaphor of the organism is thus a metaphor which cannot be easily, or without reservation, applied to the State, or used to illustrate its nature. It is the difference rather than the analogy between an organism and an organized society which leaps immediately to the eye. Yet there must be some analogy which later reflection is able to detect: otherwise the metaphor would not have been used, as it has been, for so many centuries. It is true that it acquired a fresh vogue with the progress of the study of biology in the nineteenth century; but the comparison of the 'body politic' to the physical body of man is as old as the Roman Republic, and was already being elaborated by the writers of the Middle Ages.[1] These elaborations are often fanciful; but sober reflection can still suggest reasons for a comparison between organized human society and the physical organism, and the progress of material civilization would seem to be adding more and more cogency to those reasons. It may well be argued today that the development of organized human society on its economic side produces an increasing analogy with the physical organism. For the purpose of subsistence, self-suffi-

[1] See Maitland's translation of Gierke's *Political Theories of the Middle Age*, notes 75 to 79 on pp. 131–2 (on the Body Mystical, Moral, Politic, and the Anthropomorphic conceits employed to illustrate its nature). The comparison is also elaborated by modern writers such as Grotius and Hobbes: see the writer's translation of Gierke's *Natural Law and the Theory of Society*, notes 92 to 101 on pp. 252–4.

ciency has long ceased to be the attribute of the family, or of the village, or even of the region: it is now possible only for a whole national society (if even for that), managing and maintaining itself as if it were a single body. In a highly differentiated system of the production of material necessities, all individuals become, in regard to that system and in so far as they are parts of its being, mutually instrumental to one another and collectively instrumental to the life-purpose of the whole. Whether or no 'we are all socialists now', we are all now socially interdependent—and thereby dependent upon the social whole which contains us—in respect of the satisfaction of our physical needs. That, so far as it goes, is a matter purely on the physical plane (though what we do, and are led to feel, on the physical plane may affect by a natural contagion of sympathy our acts and our feelings on other planes); it is, in itself, just a fact of economic life and livelihood. But this is the plane and these are the facts on which we are apt to fix our attention. Fixing his attention in that way, as has already been noted,[1] and paying an exclusive regard to the 'economic organism', Duguit arrives at the conclusion that the fact of the economic organism suggests a *principle* of solidarity (or, as we may also say, a *value* of 'mutuality') which is the final determinant of the whole State and all of its law. But this, as has also been noted already, is simply to make the economic organism all in all: to make it not only a fact, but also a source of principle and value—and indeed to make it *the* source, *the* one and only source, of principle and value. We may indeed admit that there is some analogy to an organism in the economic structure and operation of an organized national society. But to make that admission is not to allow that this 'economic organism', or, to speak more exactly, 'quasi-organism',[2] is the whole of organized national society (there are other sides which have to be considered), and still less to allow that it supplies a principle or value which should inform and control the whole.

None the less we may, and must, admit that the economic side of organized national society does, after all, provide some

[1] *Supra*, § 5 of this Book.

[2] If there is only some sort of analogy, we are bound to add the qualification 'quasi'. We are all the more bound to do so because, as has already been noted in § 5 of this Book, individual initiative, as well as organic solidarity, is a factor in the production of the maximum amount of material necessities.

sort of analogy to an organism. We may even carry our admission farther, and allow that on its spiritual, as well as its physical, side an organized national society has something of the character of an organism. It is true that individual personality is the final end, or the supreme value, in such a society: it is true that the final and supreme aim of such a society is to encourage the growth (by providing the conditions for its effort) of that *nisus* towards the development of capacity which is present in each individual. But we cannot stop there if we wish to get to the conclusion of the matter. We are all, in the course of our own personal development, and by the very nature of that develop-ment, profoundly interested in, as we are profoundly affected by, the development of others. There is no necessary clash between our separate and several developments. On the contrary, we are all, if in different ways and different degrees, mutually serviceable to one another and collectively serviceable to the common purpose of our whole society. I can only be at my highest by belonging to—by living, moving, and having my being in—the most richly and most generally developed society; by sharpening my mind on good minds wherever I turn (an argument, and not the least argument, for a rich and generous provision by the State of educational opportunities); by nerving my moral purpose in contact and co-operation with all others of a similar purpose wherever we gather together. In this spiritual sphere there is no clash of individual with individual, or of individuals with Society: we can say to one another

> My bounty is as boundless as the sea,
> My love as deep: the more I give to thee
> The more I have, for both are infinite.[1]

The analogy of the organism may thus be applied, after all, to the moral side of man's social existence, as well as to the physical or economic side. And if it can be applied to Society on its moral side, it can also be applied to the State. For the State, as we have already seen,[2] is simply Society, on its moral side, 'writ legal': it is Society turned into a legal association for the purpose of providing, in a legal form, the conditions needed by its members

---

[1] 'The greater the amount of each of the goods of the soul, the greater is its utility' (Aristotle, *Politics*, vii. 1, § 7). That utility is not only for ourselves. The good in us serves others) as the good in others serves us.

[2] *Supra*, Book II, § 4.

for the full development of all their capacities. As such an association it recognizes and guarantees, on the one hand, the legal right of each individual member to life, liberty, and the pursuit of personal development; but equally, and on the other hand, it also recognizes and enforces—in the very same act, and as the necessary complement to legal rights—the legal duties of all the members to do mutual service to one another and to render common and collective service to the whole body which they constitute.[1] From this point of view we may not only speak of a social organism, but also of a political organism: a political organism which is the consequence and issue of the social.

But though we may thus, when we reflect on the matter, discover a number of grounds for the use of the metaphor of organism—and that not only in the field of economics, but also in the social and in the political field—the fact remains that in all these fields, but especially in the social and political, the use of the metaphor is none the less dangerous. Words are good servants, but they can also, as has already been noted, be rebels; they can twist in our hands and turn round upon us. Just as the word 'happiness' can be a rebel against man's moral sense, so, too, the word 'organism' can be a rebel against his moral independence. There is no common good, or general welfare, or social well-being, which is anything other than the good, or welfare, or well-being, of actual and individual persons. To promote the common good is to promote the development, and increase the worth, of such persons; and there is nothing in our human world, other than actual and individual persons, which can experience and enjoy development or achieve an increase of worth. That is why the metaphor of the organism, if it be applied in the social and political field, may turn into a rebel or at any rate a false guide. The word 'organism' so easily suggests a super-existence beyond individual existence, with a life beyond individual lives, pursuing its own development and zealous for its own worth. When we use the word 'organism' freely, we begin to conjure with metaphor: we turn metaphor into myth, and myth into an idol, and we end by turning our human selves,

---

[1] The laws of taxation imposed and enforced by the State make us serve one another by our contributions in the cause of health and education, as they also make us serve the whole body in the cause of provision for its defence; and a law of military service makes us further serve the whole by a contribution of our persons as well as of our property.

which are ends in themselves, into means for the greater glory of the idol. This was the easy descent which was followed in Italy during the period of Fascist ascendancy; and it reached its height, or rather its depth, in the opening declaration of the 'Charter of Labour' of 1927—'The Italian nation, by its power and its duration, is an organism, with a being, ends, and means of action superior to those of the individuals, separate or grouped, of whom it is composed . . . a moral, political, and economic unity, integrally realized in the Fascist State.'[1]

When the idea of the organism can be put to such uses, we may well conclude that, even as a metaphor, it is a dangerous instrument of political thought. It twists in the hands too easily; and though 'it may appear to be attractive and to argue benevolence' (as Aristotle says of Plato's advocacy of his organic republic), we have to remember that it may also serve the malevolent ends of tyranny. There is indeed an attraction, and there is some suggestion of a genuine 'benevolence', in a term which carries the notions of mutual interdependence and common service to a common purpose; but there is also the opposite in a term which may also carry the notion that human beings are tools and human persons the servants of an inhuman super-person. It is better, after all, to think of organized Society not as an 'organism,' but rather as a 'scheme of organization': a scheme constructed by individual persons, and by nothing and nobody else: a scheme directed to the well-being of individual persons, and of nothing and nobody else. There is indeed a danger, it must be admitted, in thinking of organized Society merely and solely in those terms. We may easily run into a false individualism: we may forget that there is something more than construction (at any rate *conscious* construction) in the process of social and economic development: we may forget that no scheme of social organization can be directed only to the well-being of so many individuals as such (but how could it be *social* if it were?),

---

[1] Here, it will be noticed, the nation is defined as an organism. A little later in time, in the first part of *The Doctrine of Fascism* (published in 1932), the nation is relegated to a secondary position, and the State rushes to the front. Defining the nation as 'a multitude unified by one idea, which is a will for existence and power', the author of Part I of the *Doctrine* proceeds to lay it down that 'the nation is created by the State, which gives to the people . . . a will, and thus an effective existence'. It would thus appear that the nation, if it is indeed an organism, is an organism which owes its effective existence to the State. But an organism which is an artifact of the State has ceased to have even the semblance of an organism.

and that any scheme must necessarily be directed to the well-being of individuals as all members of one society, mutually connected with one another and mutually affected by one another. But if we choose—and choose we must—it is less dangerous to think of a 'scheme of organization' constructed by individuals and intended for their benefit than it is to think of an 'organism'. When we think and speak in such terms, we base ourselves on the firm foundation of individual responsibility: we start from the individual's power and duty of building a scheme of organized life by individual effort and building it for the purpose of individual betterment. When once that foundation is laid, we can safely add, as we are bound to add, that the effort must be concerted and the betterment must be shared. But even so we shall still remember that such a concerted effort, leading to such a shared betterment, is an effort of individual persons, leading to the betterment of individual persons.

This conception of a scheme of organization has its relevance in the economic field, as well as in the social and political. We may admit, as has already been admitted, that the development of Society on its economic side produces a growing analogy with the physical organism, by increasing the mutual interdependence of its members and their common dependence on the whole body. But if we accept the conception of a scheme of organization, based on the firm foundation of individual responsibility, we shall add a correction to that admission. We shall say that the supreme value of individual personality, of individual responsibility, and of individual development of capacity, has to be brought into, set above, and made to correct, the organic character of interdependence and solidarity which economics tends, by itself, increasingly to assume. Economic society tends to become an organism, and it must be rescued from that tendency. Economics cannot dictate to us what our scheme of organization should be and do: on the contrary our scheme of organization should dictate to economics (if there is to be any dictation, and so far as dictation is possible) what economics should be and do. It follows that the State, as the exponent and expression of a general scheme of organization, must be the controller of economics—not so much in the simple and superficial sense of nationalizing the means of production (that may indeed be *part* of the process of control, in this or that branch of production, but if it be made the *whole* it accentuates instead of correcting the organic tendency of economics), as in the deeper and broader sense of making the activity of production compatible with, and even serviceable to, individual personal development. The free person freely determining himself, in the greatest possible measure, even in the area of work, because he shares in determining the conditions of his work—this is the essence and the foundation of the scheme of organization which has to be superimposed on the economic organism, or, to speak more exactly, on the growing trend of economic society towards the nature of an organism.

BOOK IV

THE RIGHTS SECURED BY THE STATE

The Principles of their Allocation, and the Methods of their Declaration and Enforcement.

§ 1. THE NATURE OF RIGHTS, AND THE PRINCIPLES OF THEIR ALLOCATION TO PERSONS

THE argument of the previous section has led to the conclusion that the development of the capacities of personality in its members is the ultimate purpose served by the State and the final political value. It has also, and *pari passu*, led to the further conclusion that the law of the State is right, and possesses the quality of rightness or justice, in virtue of securing and guaranteeing, to the greatest possible number of persons, the external conditions necessary for the greatest possible development of the capacities of personality. These secured and guaranteed conditions are called by the name of rights. When it has framed a scheme of such rights, and proceeds to determine the distribution of the rights contained in the scheme, the State will act by general principles, which are generally and evenly applicable. Those principles have been called, since 1789, by the names of Liberty, Equality, and Fraternity. They were not, of course, an invention of the year 1789. They are as old as the Stoics, and as old as the State itself, however imperfectly they were applied for generation on generation. But the formula to which they were reduced in 1789 has now become their classic expression.

Two questions here arise for discussion. The first is that of the general nature of rights, and of the relation in which they stand both to their receivers and to their giver—if indeed the terms 'receiving' and 'giving' can properly be applied, and if we can rightly speak of the State and its law as giving or of its members as receiving. The second question is that of the general nature of the principles on which the State and its law proceed in determining the distribution of rights.

Rights in their nature are the result, and the embodiment in particular persons, of the general system of Right or Justice on which the State and its law are based. *Jura*, or rights, are parts and portions of *jus*, or Right, as distributed among, embodied in, and enjoyed by persons. I cannot have rights, in *any* sense of the term, apart from the notion of Right, and I cannot have secured and guaranteed rights, in the *legal* sense of the term, apart from the law which is based (though it may be imperfectly based) upon the notion of Right. My rights in general are my part and portion of a whole system of Right, as expressed and embodied in my particular person; and they cannot exist apart from the whole of which they are part and portion. Any particular right which I have is a capacity of enjoying some particular status, or employing some particular power of action, which has been secured and guaranteed to me by law, and has been so secured and guaranteed because it is my share, in this particular respect, of the general system of Right or Justice recognized and enforced as law by the State.[1] The sum of my rights is the whole of my capacity—my whole status and whole power of action—within the State and under its law: it is my general and total *persona*, or legal personality; it is my general position in the system of Right (in so far as that system is recognized by the State), and the whole of my share in that system.

We may therefore say that each individual is vested by law and the legal association to which he belongs with a legal *persona* or sum total of rights. We have then to add that he is so vested on two complementary grounds, the one immediate and the other ultimate. The immediate ground is that this sum total of rights is the expression for him, and in his case, of the system of Right on which the legal association is based. The ultimate ground is that this sum total of rights is the condition for him, and equally for all his fellows, of achieving the end which inspires and determines the whole of the system of Right—the end which consists in highest possible development of the capacities of personality, in the fullest sense of that term. Putting these

[1] It may be wise to repeat that the recognition may be imperfect and the enforcement therefore inadequate. In other words, law may fall short of Right; and my rights under the system of law may therefore fall short of my rights (my 'natural' or 'human' rights) under the system of Right. That is a difficulty which is bound to recur, in various forms, in the course of the argument.

two grounds together, we may say that our rights, which in their sum are our legal personality, are secured to us by law, and vested in us by law, because they are the conditions of the development of our moral personality.[1] I am given a *persona* or legal mask[2] (we may say in a paradox) in order to be my true moral self and show my true moral features. I am vested with a legal personality because I have, and in order that I may develop, a moral personality.

But though we may put together the two grounds on which my possession of rights is based, and treat them as mutual complements, there remains a distinction between them; and this distinction may produce a divergence and result in a conflict between two different conceptions of rights. On the one hand, I should not possess the complex of rights which is my legal personality unless I had a moral personality which is its ultimate source and cause. In that sense the origin of my rights is something in me, and my rights flow from the inherent fact of my own moral personality. If we stop at this point, we shall say that rights are 'natural' or 'human', meaning by the adjectives which we use that they come from the nature of man, in his own intrinsic being. (But even so, and even if rights are described as 'natural' or 'human', they cannot be conceived apart from a common human notion of Right, of which they are parts or portions embodied and expressed in each claimant.) We cannot, however, stop at this point. There is another side of the matter; and I should not possess the sum total of rights which is my legal personality unless it were vested in me by the State, which assigns it to me as the part which I play, and the *persona* which I sustain, in its 'drama' or scheme of legal action. In that sense the origin of my rights is something outside me, or at any rate something broader than I am (though I am a member, and an active member, of its being); and my rights flow from something more than my own personal nature in its own intrinsic being. This is simply to say that the State is the im-

[1] The word 'moral' is hardly adequate, unless we use it to include intellectual and aesthetic as well as specifically moral capacities—and indeed to include, in addition, capacities which in themselves may be termed physical rather than moral (such as bodily skills employed in the use of leisure), but which are none the less closely connected with the development of moral personality. Imperfect as it is, the word 'moral' may be allowed to serve for want of a better term.

[2] On the conception of *persona* see above, Book II, § 6.

mediate source of rights, and that rights, in any full sense of the word, without adjective or qualification, are never rights unless they proceed immediately from that source. Ideally a right will always be derived simultaneously from two sources, and will possess a double quality—(1) the source of individual personality, and the quality of being a condition of its development; (2) the source of the State and its law, and the quality of being secured and guaranteed by the action of that law. But in actual life we may find a sort of right, or a 'quasi-right', which is derived from one source only, and possesses only one quality. We may have a quasi-right which has only the source of individual personality and the quality of being a condition of its development, such as the right of a slave to personal liberty in a slave-owning State; and equally, and conversely, we may have a quasi-right which has only the source of the State and its law and the quality of being secured and guaranteed by the action of that law, such as the right of a slave-owner in a slave-owning State to the enjoyment of property in persons. All that we can say of such cases is that no actual State is ideal. There may be legal rights, legally valid, which ought not to be rights under the notion of Right which the nation in general (or, we may even say, mankind in general) has come to entertain; and conversely what ought to be rights under and in virtue of that notion may be denied by the law and have no legal existence. There will always be a gulf between the notion of Right and the prescriptions of law.[1]

From the general nature of rights, and the relation in which they stand to the State and the individual, we may now turn to consider the principles of their distribution. These principles may be called, if we use an Aristotelian term, the principles of distributive justice. They are the procedural rules which justice requires that law should follow in allocating and distributing rights among the members of the State. If justice be regarded (as it has been in the prévious argument)[2] as an order of society directed to the end of fostering and encouraging the highest possible development of all the capacities of personality in all its members, these procedural rules required by justice will be rules which follow from that order and are

[1] On law and its relation to Right or Justice see below, § 6 of this Book.
[2] *Supra*, Book III, § 8, pp. 123 sqq.

dictated by that end; and they will thus be ultimately derived from the ultimate value of personality and the development of its capacities. Again, if justice be regarded (as it has been in the previous argument) as the primary social and political value—though grounded itself on the ultimate moral value of personality and the development of its capacities—then the procedural rules required by justice may be considered as the secondary social and political values, and we may say, 'First Justice, and then the rules of Liberty, Equality, and Fraternity which follow on, and from, Justice'.

The procedural rule or principle of Liberty is in itself the simplest of the three, even though its application (as we shall have reason to note) is a matter of difficulty and complications. The principle means that the State treats each and every moral person as a free agent, capable of developing his own capacities in his own way, and therefore capable of enjoying and exercising the rights which are the conditions of such development. Accordingly it vests each person—each and every person who has reached what we call the age of discretion—with a recognized power of thinking and acting for himself, at his own discretion, and therefore on his own responsibility, in respect of the enjoyment and exercise of rights. Each person thus comes under, and all are covered by, a procedural rule of liberty which is also, at the same time, a rule of responsibility; for liberty is always also responsibility, and to be free to act is also to be responsible for action. Each person, again, comes under this rule, and all are covered by this rule, so far as concerns the enjoyment by each of rights—which is the same as to say, so far as concerns his enjoyment of his part or portion of the general system of Right recognized and enforced as law by the State. For not only is it true that liberty is also responsibility. It is also true that liberty is also, in its measure, legality; since the liberty of each is his legally recognized power of enjoying the rights which are his part and portion of law.

The procedural rule or principle of Equality means that the State treats all legal persons as equal in its presence or, as we say, 'in the eye of the law'. It will not assign higher and lower grades of legal personality. One moral personality matters as much as another; and the assignation of legal personality, which follows from and is based on the fact of moral personality, will reflect the fact on which it is based. Our Old English fore-fathers held that 'people and law went by ranks': today we recognize (though perhaps imperfectly even yet) that people and law must always go by the rule of equality. But this legal equality is by its nature something different from general or absolute equality. It is a legal equality of legal persons within the State. Outside the State, and outside the area of legal persons—that is to say, in the social or extra-legal sphere—there may still exist much inequality, alike in personal capacity, in social status, and in economic resources. How far the State can tolerate some of this inequality in the social or extra-legal sphere, and more especially how far it can tolerate inequality of economic resources, without offending against its own principle of the equality of legal persons within itself and in its own sphere, is a grave question of our times which leads to a clash of conflicting arguments. It is true, on the one hand, that the rule of Equality, as recognized and applied by the State, means equality only within the State, and therefore only with respect to the standing of legal persons in and under its scheme. It does not involve or mean equality in the social or extra-legal sphere: it is legal, and not social, equality; it is equality in terms of capacity for the enjoyment and exercise of rights, but not in terms of capacity for the enjoyment and exercise of all the multitudinous forms of social activity. On the other hand, it is also true that effective legal equality demands *some* measure of social equality. The State guarantees men equal rights in its polling-booths and its courts of law. But can those rights be effectively enjoyed on equal terms unless personal capacity is made *more* equal by an open system of State education; unless economic resources are made *more* equal by a further system of State regulation of the general national income; and unless general social position, so far as it depends on personal capacity and economic resources, is made *more* equal in and by the process of creating greater equality both in capacity and in resources? Yet *more* equality, in all these respects, is not the same as *total* equality; and any increase of equality in all these respects—personal capacity, economic resources, and social position—is only a means, and can be enforced by the State only in so far as it is a means, to the securing of effective legal equality. The increase (for example) of equality in respect of economic resources is not an end in itself, but a means to effective legal equality; and the amount of the increase imposed by the State, in the act of determining by how much resources are to be made *more* equal, will accordingly depend on the end which it is intended to serve.

The principle of Fraternity is a more difficult matter than the principles of Liberty and Equality. We may seek to formulate it by saying that the legal association, besides treating each individual member as a free agent in its scheme of law and an equal factor in the operation of that scheme, will also follow a third principle in distributing among its members the various rights which are the conditions of their personal development. This is the principle of providing for all and distributing among all the common equipment, material and mental (ranging from roads and sewers to libraries and museums) which is needed by all as the common background and common basis of their individual lives. All of us individually need liberty and equality for ourselves; all of us need collectively a common equipment for our common benefit. The usage of revolutionary France has given the name of Fraternity to the principle which leads to the distribution of this common equipment for common enjoyment.[1] Fraternity in its strict sense is an emotion rather than a principle, and in that sense it cannot be said to be *in pari materia* with the principles of liberty and equality. But it is a term which has been traditionally used in a broader sense, and it may perhaps be used provisionally to designate a principle, governing the distribution of rights, which might also be called by the name of 'co-operation' or 'solidarity'.[2] The liberty of each individual as a free legal agent; the equality of each as a legal factor in the legal association; and the fraternity of all in the common

---

[1] The fourth clause of the preamble to the constitution of 1848 contains a proclamation that the French Republic 'a pour principe la Liberté, l'Égalité et la Fraternité'. But it is not clear that the authors of the clause had any clear notion of what the last term meant. They made it a 'principle', but they did not define the principle. The cry of Liberty, Equality, Fraternity is older than 1848, and older even than 1789; though the first formal use of the phrase is said to occur in a motion carried by the Club of the Cordeliers, in June 1793, which ends with the words 'Liberté, Égalité, Fraternité — ou la mort'.

[2] If the last of these names be adopted, solidarity—discussed in an earlier stage of the argument, Book III, § 5, as a claimant for the position of the primary social and political value—returns again at this stage of the argument as one of the secondary values, derived and proceeding from the primary value of justice.

enjoyment of a common equipment provided by common and co-operative effort—these, in summary, are the three principles, long associated by an ancient tradition which goes back ultimately to a Greek origin, on which the State and its law proceed in determining the distribution of rights.

§ 2. THE PRINCIPLE OF LIBERTY

WE may start from the axiom of Kant, that 'rational nature exists as an end in itself'. Since man belongs to rational nature, this axiom leads to the practical imperative, 'Act so as to use humanity, whether in your own person or in the person of another, always as an end, never as merely a means'.[1] It follows that the State, in order to adjust itself to this moral axiom and its practical imperative, must be a State of free agents: it cannot include slaves.[2] The State is accordingly an association of free legal agents, and of nothing but such agents. Within that association, and under its system of law, there is room for nothing but the liberty of the free legal agent.

But the liberty of the free legal agent, acting in the sphere of the State, is not the only liberty. There is also the liberty of the free social agent in the sphere of Society. This social liberty is important: it has its own claims; and they need, and deserve, their own vindication. Social liberty may be menaced by the State, and curtailed in the name of the law and the defence of legal liberty. Invading the area of Society as a conqueror, but professing to be a liberator, the State may seek, for example, to bring religion into the area of its own legal rules, assimilating religious societies to legally incorporated companies, and determining the scope of religious liberty by the scope of the legal liberty enjoyed by such companies. This was long the tendency of revolutionary thought in France, from the days of the Civil Constitution of the Clergy in 1790 to the days of the Law of

---

[1] *Metaphysic of Morality*, § 277.

[2] Aristotle argued in favour of slavery on the ground that some human beings did not belong to rational nature—except in so far as they were rational enough to understand the commands of those who were more rational than themselves. He concluded that such men were intended by their nature to serve as 'merely a means', or, in his own phrase, as 'living tools'. His argument and conclusion were long accepted in European thought and practice. They disappeared in the course of the eighteenth and nineteenth centuries as the conviction gradually triumphed that 'a man's a man for a' that', and that all men belong to rational nature whatever the degree of their endowment.

Separation in 1905; and in our time it is again the tendency of Marxian thought, which may preach the ultimate 'withering away' of the State and State control, but which also exalts the power of the State, so long as it lasts, over all thought and the whole of life. But if social liberty, especially in that form or phase of its nature which we call by the name of religious liberty, can be menaced by the State, we have to admit that it may also be menaced by Society itself. The 'social stigma', as John Stuart Mill wrote in his Essay *On Liberty*, may be more dangerous to freedom of thought and discussion than legal penalties; and the social group, religious or occupational, may seek to subject the liberty of its individual members to a stringent control by itself and its own system of social discipline. In such a case the State may invade the area of Society not as a conqueror but as a genuine liberator. It may seek to limit the claim of a social group (for example a Church) to control the expression of thought and belief by its members, on the ground that the group is interfering with its own fundamental principle of the free agency of its citizens. Spinoza, for instance, in his *Tractatus Theologico-politicus* of 1670, demands that the State, as the organ of liberty formed to defend the free use of reason (*ut homines . . . libera Ratione utantur*), should rescue the cause of freedom of expression of thought and belief from the control of ecclesiastical authority. 'The untoward generation of metaphysical Article-makers'[1] against which he appealed has long disappeared; but new generations arise, in fields other than that of religion, and the liberating State is still needed—if only it can be found, and has not itself been enslaved to the dogmas of the 'Article-makers'.

We have seen that liberty is not only legal, but also social; and we have also seen that social liberty may on occasion be invaded, but may also (when social groups themselves become the enemies of such liberty) on occasion be defended, in the name of that legal liberty of which the State is the organ. Liberty is more than one: it is at any rate two; indeed we shall presently be led to suggest that it is even more than two, and that legal liberty itself—liberty within the State—is plural and has

---

[1] Matthew Arnold, quoted in Sir Frederic Pollock's *Spinoza*, p. 31, speaks of 'Spinoza's fervent appeal to the State to save us from the untoward generation of metaphysical Article-makers'.

several forms. Meanwhile, and before we move to that argument, we have to notice that legal liberty, just because it is legal, is not an absolute or unconditioned liberty. The truth that every man ought to be free has for its other side the complementary and consequential truth that no man can be absolutely free. The need of liberty for each is necessarily qualified and conditioned by the need of liberty for all; and the liberty of A will therefore be such liberty as he can enjoy concurrently with the enjoyment of similar *and equal* liberty by B and C and D. The liberty of the owner of capital to determine the conditions of work in the factory which he owns is a relative liberty which must be adjusted to the liberty of the worker to do his work under such conditions as leave him still a free agent and give him also a share in the determination of the conditions of work. Because the liberty of each is thus relative to that of others, and has to be adjusted to that of others, it must always be regulated; and indeed it would not exist unless it were regulated. Burke said with justice that 'abstract liberty, like other mere abstractions, is not to be found'; and if he wrote with a flourish when he said 'I love a manly, moral, regulated liberty as well as any gentleman', his adjectives have their truth. Liberty *is* regulated; and in the last resort it is regulated not only by the fact of relation between one man's liberty and that of others, but also by the fact that the liberty of all has a moral basis and must accordingly be what Burke calls 'moral liberty'. If regulation is already involved by the relation of agent to agent, it is further involved, and more deeply involved, by the intrinsic nature of the agent himself. If liberty be, as we have argued that it is, a derivative value, arising ultimately from the supreme value of the moral personality acting and developing its capacities as such, then the liberty which the State upholds, and makes a principle of its action, must be a liberty relative to, and therefore regulated by, the nature of such a personality. It is not the indefinite liberty of an undefined 'individual'; it is the definite liberty of a defined personality, seeking to realize specific capacities. Whether, therefore, we look at the relation of agent to agent, or whether we turn our view to the intrinsic nature of the agent, we come to the same conclusion: liberty in the State, or legal liberty, is never the absolute liberty of each, but always the qualified liberty of all. Liberty within the State is thus a relative and regulated liberty: it is the greatest common measure of liberty which is possible for all, as determined and defined (1) by the need of each to enjoy similar and equal liberty with others, and (2) by the need of all to enjoy the specific liberty of realizing specific capacities. But if it is thus conceived as relative and regulated, and regarded as a definite and determinate measure, liberty is not diminished in virtue of that conception. On the contrary it is increased. A relative and regulated liberty, actually operative and enjoyed, is a liberty greater in amount than absolute liberty could ever be—if indeed such liberty could ever exist, or ever amount to anything more than nothing at all.

There is no need, in the light of the previous argument, to speak of the relation of liberty to law. If liberty is one of the principles, or procedural rules, which justice requires that law should follow in distributing rights, then liberty is also law, or at any rate a part of law. (This is not to say that a particular law, or legal enactment, may not be a derogation from liberty: it is only to say that the general operation of law is also the operation and realization of liberty, as any one will recognize who studies the action of the English courts of law in vindicating, for centuries past, the cause of liberty in England.) But if liberty and law do not quarrel, liberty may quarrel with itself. Here we return to a theme which has already been suggested—the theme that liberty, even in the State, is plural; that there is more than one form of legal liberty; and, we may even add, that it is possible for one of these forms to quarrel with another. It is not only true that there is a liberty in the social area as well as the liberty in the area of the State: it is also true that there are different liberties, or forms of liberty, which coexist, and may even conflict, in the State's own area. We may distinguish three different forms of such liberty.

First, there is the liberty of a man in the capacity of an individual person—his personal liberty, or, as we may also say, his *civil* liberty. To Blackstone this civil liberty consisted in three articles—personal security, not only of life and health, but also of reputation; personal freedom, especially of movement; and personal property, or the free use, enjoyment, and disposal of all acquisitions. Today we might prefer to say that civil liberty consists in three somewhat differently expressed articles—physical freedom from injury or threat to the life, health, and movement of the body; intellectual freedom for the expression of thought and belief; and practical freedom for the play of will and the exercise of choice in the general field of contractual action and relations with other persons.[1]

Next to my civil liberty, there is my liberty in the capacity of a citizen: my liberty as a member of the public and a part of the legal association: my public or *political* liberty. To Blackstone this liberty is largely negative, and it seems to mean, in the main, the power of curbing government. One of its articles is, indeed, the constitution, powers, and privileges of Parliament; but the other four articles are limitation of the King's prerogative, application to the courts of justice for the redress of grievances, the power of petitioning government for redress, and the power of having and using arms for self-preservation and defence. Blackstone would thus appear to conceive government as something external, and to regard political liberty (apart from Parliament) as a sort of counterweight in me to a pull or thrust outside me. Today we have come to hold a different point of view. Government is not external: it is in us, or springs from us; and we regard political liberty as positive in its nature. It is a liberty not of curbing government, but of constituting and controlling it; constituting it by a general act of choice or election, in which we all freely share on the basis of universal suffrage; controlling it by a general and continuous process of discussion, in which we all freely share according to our capacities.

Besides the civil liberty which belongs to me in my capacity of an individual person, and the political liberty which belongs to me in my capacity of a citizen and a member of the public, there is also a third form of liberty in the area of the State. This is the *economic* liberty which belongs to me in my capacity of a worker, whether with hand or brain, engaged in some gainful occupation or service. The conception of this third form of liberty is comparatively recent; and it may be argued that the conception introduces an unnecessary distinction. Is not economic liberty implied in civil liberty, and is it not simply a part and parcel of the articles of civil liberty, especially the first and

---

[1] The third article is generally, and even vaguely, expressed. But personal property, in the sense of 'the free use, enjoyment and disposal of all acquisitions', is only one part of a much wider field; and some expansion of Blackstone's third article is obviously needed.

third, which have just been enumerated? And if we distinguish an economic form of liberty, are we not equally bound to distinguish a religious form, and to introduce also the further conception of religious liberty?

So far as religious liberty is concerned, we may answer that it mainly belongs to the social area, and that in so far as it enters into the area of the State, it finds its safeguard in the second article of civil liberty. (We may also remember that 'civil and religious liberty' was indissolubly one, and a single cry for the champions of liberty, in the eighteenth century.) But so far as economic liberty is concerned, we are bound to acknowledge that the field of economic relations presents special difficulties which warrant the conception of a special and separate form of liberty in relation to that field. It is true that liberty in that field is closely connected with civil liberty, and is largely included in that 'play of will and exercise of choice in the general field of contractual action and relations with other persons' which has just been mentioned as one of the articles of civil liberty. But it is also true that it is specially difficult to guarantee the play of will and the exercise of choice for all who move in the field of economic relations and contracts; and it is further true that this field is specially and particularly large. On this ground alone it may well be urged that the conception of a special and particular form of liberty is needed for this field. But this is not the only ground. If liberty in the economic field is closely connected with civil liberty, it is also closely connected with political; and we may argue, without any paradox, that since it is closely connected with both, it cannot be treated as being a part or department of either. It is not a mere part of civil liberty, because it involves considerations which belong to political liberty; and equally it is not a mere part of the latter, because it involves considerations which belong to the former. The close connexion between economic and political liberty may be traced from two different, and yet complementary, points of view. On the one hand, you may argue that the political status of the free citizen, with his share in controlling political government, demands the corresponding economic status of the free worker, with his share in controlling the government both of his general industry and of his particular factory. From this point of view you assume the existence of political liberty as a given and actual fact, and you argue from it to the existence (or rather the bringing into existence) of another and corresponding economic liberty to form its necessary corollary. On the other hand, and from another point of view, you may argue that political liberty is not a fact, and does not exist, until there is economic liberty, because the economically unfree worker is not, and cannot be, a politically free citizen. From this point of view you refuse to assume the existence of political liberty as a given and actual fact; and on the basis of that refusal you argue that economic liberty is a prior condition of political liberty, and not a corollary which follows upon it. But from either point of view—whether you adopt the liberal doctrine that political liberty precedes and entails economic liberty, or the more Marxian doctrine that economic liberty must always precede and can alone secure political liberty—you reach the conclusion that economic liberty is closely connected with political, and cannot be treated as merely a matter of civil liberty.

There are thus three forms of liberty in the State—the civil liberty of the individual person, 'in mind, body and estate'; the political liberty of the citizen; and the economic liberty of the worker, whether with hand or brain. These three forms of liberty, as has already been incidentally noted, may quarrel with one another. The liberty of the citizen in the political sphere may quarrel with that of the individual person in the civil sphere: for example, the enjoyment of intellectual freedom for the expression of thought and belief, which is one of the great articles of civil liberty, may come into conflict with a parliamentary majority, acting in the name of political liberty, if such a majority seeks to lay down conditions adverse to the free expression of some line of thought and belief, on the ground that it is seditious and calculated to excite disaffection against the government or to promote hostility between classes. Similarly the liberty of individual persons in the civil sphere may quarrel with that of the worker in the economic sphere; and the worker's enjoyment of some share in determining his wages and the conditions of his work may be challenged, as in the past it was, by a claim on the other side to the enjoyment of a freedom of contractual action which warrants the employer in practically dictating the terms of wages and conditions of work. Here political liberty can, and has, come to the rescue of economic liberty; but it is also possible that a parliamentary majority, acting in the name of political liberty, may seek to impose conditions adverse to the enjoyment of economic liberty as that liberty is conceived and claimed by the workers and their organizations. Liberty is indeed a complex notion, which at once unites men in its allegiance and divides them by its divisions; and if, in theory, we all claim to serve under the banner of liberty, in actual life we are faced by the question, 'Under *which* banner, and in the name of *which* liberty?' That is one[1] reason why we have different parties, all claiming to be parties of liberty. For the theorist it is sufficient to say (1) that liberty is one of the principles of justice, and one of the procedural rules on which the State and its law must act; (2) that in the actual application of that principle and rule, justice and law have both the difficult task not only of reconciling the liberty of one man with that of others, but also of reconciling the different liberties, or forms of liberty, with one another. But then the whole task and problem of justice, as we shall have reason to notice later, is the task and problem of conciliation; and indeed, as we shall also have reason to notice, justice and conciliation are fundamentally one. Justice, on a general view, has not only the task of conciliating the different liberties, or forms of liberty, with one another; it has also the task of conciliating liberty in general, in all its forms, with equality, and also, and in addition, the task of conciliating both liberty and equality with fraternity. Justice is the synthesis and the balance, holding together all the three and holding them all in an equilibrium.

§ 3. THE PRINCIPLE OF EQUALITY

JUST as each person, because he is a person, is a free legal agent in the scheme of the State, so also each person, because he is a person and as much a person as all other persons, has an equal standing, and counts equally as a legal factor, under that scheme. This is not to say that each moral personality is equal to every

---

[1] Only *one*. The principle of Equality is also a maker of parties, or at any rate of a party; and the principle of Fraternity, differently conceived by different groups, is another maker of parties, inspiring on one side the syndicalist and the communist, but also inspiring, on the other side, the nationalist who pins his faith to the cause of national fraternity.

other, in terms of total capacity and the power of developing such capacity; it is only to say that each legal personality is equal to every other in terms of *legal* capacity. The State which vests us with legal personalities, *personae*, or 'masks', vests us all with equal masks, partly because it simply cannot distinguish our differences even if it would (we are all plain indistinguishable integers in the millions of its members), but ultimately for the far deeper reason that we all matter equally before the law, whatever our differences may be, in virtue of the simple fact of being all equally persons, and as such possessing *some* measure of capacity and *some* power of developing capacity. We are thus arranged, as it were, in a level line at the starting-point of the race that lies ahead; and we start from that level line, so far as the State is concerned, with equal conditions guaranteed to each for making the best of himself—however much we may eventually differ in what we actually make of ourselves. (Equality is thus the beginning, not the end; the end depends on ourselves and on the use which we make of the equal conditions guaranteed to us, *as a beginning*, by the State.) The principle of Equality accordingly means that whatever conditions are guaranteed to me, in the form of rights, shall also, and in the same measure, be guaranteed to others, and that whatever rights are given to others shall also be given to me. Acting on that principle of distribution the law gives to all—of whatever class and whichever sex, as soon as the age of discretion is reached and the legal person has fully emerged—an equal right of owning property. This is not to say that it gives an equal right to owning an equal amount, which is an entirely different proposition; it is simply to say that it recognizes an equal capacity for owning. Burke's dictum, 'All men have equal rights, but not to equal things', is a truism, and not a sophism. Law is a giver of legal capacities, and of legal capacities only. If it gives such capacities evenhanded, it has obeyed to the full the principle of equality, and done all that in it lies to observe and follow that principle.

But this notion of equality as being essentially an equality of legal capacity, and consisting essentially in the equal standing of legal persons before the law, has been in the past, and is still today, a notion difficult to grasp and hold in its own true shape and form. Equality is a Protean notion: it changes its shape and assumes new forms with a ready facility. On the one hand, there has been in the past, among wealthy or cultured or otherwise powerful sections of the community, a feeling and an assumption, 'We are different in *general* capacity: our wealth means a larger stake in the country, and our culture a greater grasp of affairs: it is only fair that our superiority in general capacity should be accompanied by superiority in *legal* capacity, and that we should have something more than an equal standing before the law'. On the other hand, there is rising today, when the principle of legal equality has been generally asserted and vindicated, a feeling and an assumption among the less wealthy, or less cultured, or otherwise less powerful sections, 'We are now equal to you in legal capacity: it is therefore fair that we should also be equal in general capacity—in wealth and the opportunities it brings; in culture and the grasp it gives; in the general equipment and endowment of our faculties— and that legal equality should thus be crowned by social equality'.

The past has gone; but we cannot understand the thought of the present, or do proper justice to the feelings and assumptions which are widely current today, unless we take into our reckoning the legacy of the past. We have to remember that for century upon century legal capacity was either denied altogether, or given only in an inferior degree, to many classes of persons. There was a long reign of legal inequality. Down to 1772 the slave was denied any legal capacity on English soil; he was not a person in the eye of the law, and he had no share in the enjoyment of rights. Under the laws of settlement, as they were still interpreted in the eighteenth century, the potential pauper was condemned to an inferior degree of legal capacity by being denied the freedom of movement enjoyed by others; a man could not move to, or settle in, a new parish unless he could give security that he would never need poor relief from that parish. Under the laws regulating the suffrage down to the year 1918 a person in receipt of poor relief was similarly condemned to an inferior degree of legal capacity by being denied the right of voting along with and on the same terms as others. If the pauper was long assigned an inferior legal status, so too were women; and so, too, were all who dissented from the established Church. Under the common law relating to property, married women down to 1870 were destitute of legal capacity for ownership;[1] under the laws regulating the suffrage all women, down to 1918, were without any legal capacity for exercising a vote. The disabilities imposed on dissenters by a variety of Acts of Parliament, which made them unequal and inferior to members of the established Church, were only removed in the course of the nineteenth century: indeed, it was not until 1871 that the Universities Tests Act secured a general equality of admission to the benefits and privileges of the two old English universities. Generally, however, the principle of legal equality may now be said to have triumphed. Legal capacity has ceased to be a matter of degrees, some higher and some lower; all alike, irrespective of class, or sex, or confession, are now equal persons under the law of the land, and all now enjoy, at any rate in form, an equal degree of legal personality. Even so, there is still some measure of legal inequality. All may possess equal rights; but all have not an equal *power* of vindicating rights, so long as the vindication demands expenditure, and so long as some are more able than others to meet the expenditure demanded. In the actual operation of the courts, as distinct from the rules of the law of the land, inequality still remains, though it is steadily being diminished by reforms in their operation.

So far of the past, and so far of the slow and gradual victory of the principle of legal equality. We may now turn to the present, and to the problem of what is called 'social equality'. A cardinal question which confronts us today is how far the State and its law should go in promoting equality of culture and economic equality; how far, in a word, the State should add social to legal equality, or, more exactly (since the State is a legal association, and since any equality which it promotes must also be in its nature legal), how far it should extend its principle of legal equality into the field of culture and the field of economics. Is it possible to stop short at a bare conception of legal equality, or must that conception be extended and enriched by the inclusion in it of the idea of an increasingly equal distribution both of educational opportunities and of economic faculties?

In the matter of educational opportunities, the State has

[1] In regard to property, 'the very being or legal existence of the woman is suspended during the marriage, or at least is incorporated and consolidated into that of the husband'. (Blackstone, *Commentaries*, vol. i, p. 441.)

already secured an educational minimum open equally to all, and equally obligatory on all: it has also secured, by a method of selecting and endowing promise, a tolerably equal ladder of access to higher education for all who give some proof of the possession of higher capacity. But whatever the State has done, there still remains a considerable amount of educational inequality, and, with it, a gulf of culture between the few and the many. Culture is not everything; indeed it is far from being everything; and men can meet men as equals, in spite of differences of culture, on the broad common ground of good sense and mutual consideration. But a gulf of culture is still a sad gulf: it produces an awkwardness of social relations: it is an obstacle which hinders us all from attaining that general best society, richly and generally developed on the basis of the worth of all its members, in which alone each of us can be at his best.[1] The obstacle can only be removed by a steady raising of the educational minimum and a steady strengthening and lengthening of the ladder of access which leads to the educational maximum. On the other hand, we can hardly dream of absolute equality for all in education and general culture. We have to face two obstinate and irreducible facts. One of them is the natural existence of individual differences in mental interest and mental capacity. The other is the social necessity of different social functions, ranging from ploughmen and smiths to scholars and Ministers of State, and requiring for their performance a difference of mental equipment. Whether there is any correspondence between these two orders of fact: whether the natural existence of individual differences answers the social necessity of different social functions—that is an unsolved problem. We can only guess that nature has given us differentiated human material to use as best we can, and as justly as we can, to meet our different social needs. There is a difference in the material provided just as, and perhaps because, there is a difference in the needs to be met. It is our business to 'match' the differences. But whatever 'matching' we may achieve, the differences themselves remain. Man is infinitely varied in interests and varied in his capacities; that is the riches of his kind. The variety of men is consistent with equality of worth; but it is not consistent with identity of mental capacity and interest. Nor does equality

[1] *Supra*, Book III, § 7.

necessarily involve uniformity of education or identity of culture. Equality, after all, is a derivative value.[1] It is derived from the supreme value of the development of personality—in each alike and equally, but in each along its own different line and of its own separate motion. It has to be adjusted to that supreme value. What is derived must not divert, or defeat, the source from which it comes. But any equality which spelled uniformity would necessarily divert and defeat the spontaneous development of all the varieties of human personality.

In the matter of economic faculties, and the application of the principle of equality to their distribution, the State has a more difficult road to tread, and it is only at the beginning of the road. It has done something, since the beginning of the nineteenth century (the first Factory Act was as early as 1802), in the cause of economic liberty; but it did not face the problem of economic equality till the beginning of the present century. That problem may be said to be twofold. It is partly a matter of status; it is partly a matter of property and income. The matter of status raises the issue whether the State should seek to turn industrial production into something like a partnership of equals, and should introduce by persuasion, backed ultimately by legislation, a system under which the directing and managing element stands on a more equal footing, and accepts a more equal status, with the manual and operative elements. (Whether the State should itself take over branches of industrial production, and itself become the directing and managing element, is another issue, not indeed unrelated to the issue of industrial partnership, but largely independent of it, and turning mainly on considerations of national interest and national efficiency.)[2] In the matter of property and income the issue raised is whether, and, if so, to what extent and by what methods, the State should seek to correct inequality in their distribution. The policy of the State has been setting towards some measure of correction

[1] *Supra*, § 1 of this Book.

[2] It is true that the nationalization of branches of industrial production has been advocated on grounds of economic equality, and has been linked with the idea that each nationalized branch of production should be administered jointly by representatives of managerial and manual workers. But it is not clear that in actual practice a nationalized branch of production shows more equality of status between the elements concerned than do a number of private enterprises. When the State becomes the partner of the manual and operative elements, it may become a predominant partner.

during the last fifty years. On the one hand, limits have been imposed on the accumulation of wealth by differential taxation of the incomes of the rich; on the other hand, the incomes of the poor have been improved by the regulation and raising of wages and by various methods of social expenditure on public social services which are in effect equivalent to an increase of income. The combination of these two methods has introduced a greater equality into the distribution of wealth. But if the incomes of the poor have thus been increased, and the incomes of the rich diminished, there is still a large disparity of incomes; and when we turn from incomes to property, or the permanent ownership of capital resources, the disparity is still greater. There has indeed been an increase in the volume of popular savings, fostered by the State, which has meant some further diffusion of property; but this only touches the fringe of the problem of finding a general system for its more equal distribution. The State has still to grapple with that problem; it has still to consider, for instance, the method of profit-sharing, particularly in the form known as co-partnership, by which each worker in an undertaking shares in its profits by way of receiving an allotment of shares, and thus becomes a permanent owner of capital resources. Whatever arguments may be advanced against the method, whether by those who prefer the method of the general nationalization of undertakings, or by those who desire to keep labour free from 'entanglements' with capital, it would have the result of producing a greater equality in the distribution of property; and it may thus be fairly said that it is a question for consideration whether the State should not seek to introduce— once more by persuasion, backed ultimately by legislation— some policy of this order.

In both of these matters—the matter of status, and the matter of income and property—it is clear that there is much to be done before legal equality itself can become a fact and not merely a principle. The original and basic equality of the simple legal person—the member of the legal association simply considered as such, or, in a word, the citizen—is itself imperfect, and will remain imperfect, until some further equalization both of economic status and of economic possessions has made equal citizenship a fact: a fact in the law courts and in access to a career: a fact in the chance of entering Parliament and in the general opportunity of entering the service of the State. But this statement has a reverse side, which is also in the nature of a corollary. From the point of view of equal citizenship, the economic equality required is not a total or absolute equality: it is that amount of equality—no less, but also no more—which is relative to and necessary for the status of full legal equality in the system of State. Economic equality, after all, is relative to legal equality. But it is also relative to something higher and more original than legal equality. It is relative to, and must square with, that supreme value, consisting in the development of the capacities of personality, from which the whole principle of equality, in all its forms, is derived. That is the ultimate test and standard, alike of the idea of educational equality and of that of economic equality. Equality, in all its forms, must always be subject and instrumental to the free development of capacity; but if it be pressed to the length of uniformity, and if uniformity be made to thwart the free development of capacity, the subject becomes the master, and the world is turned topsy-turvy.

But the issue of economic equality, particularly in its aspect of equality of income and property, is too grave and pressing an issue to be dismissed with vague generalities. It confronts us with an immediate and urgent question, the question of the relation of economic endowment to moral growth and development. It has been argued above that such growth and development demand a system of equal legal rights and equality of legal personality. Do they also, and in addition, demand a system of equal economic possessions and equality of economic ownership? Or, if they do not, do they demand an approach, and if so, what degree of approach, to such a system? We must 'condescend upon particulars', and seek to give a definite answer, in particular terms, to these searching and definite questions.

In seeking to give such a definite answer we need not pause to inquire whether some persons may not be better qualified than others to *use* possessions as the tools and instruments of personal development, and whether, accordingly, on that ground of *use*, there may not be an argument for some measure of inequality in the distribution of possessions. There is a deeper and firmer ground of argument than that of use. This is the ground of *acquisition*. Our *nisus* towards the development of the capacities of our personality is closely and inextricably connected with the effort of acquiring possessions. That is one of the essential ways in which we try ourselves out: in which we become conscious of capacities, begin to see them externally expressed in results, and even find some sort of measure of what is in us and what we can extract from ourselves. The consciousness may be crude: the results may be merely material: the measure may be very far removed from a measure of genuine worth. But in the economy of our nature the *nisus* of personal development is mixed with this effort of acquisition and with its consciousness, results, and measure. The issue—granted our human variety—is a variety and inequality in the amount of possessions acquired by the different efforts employed. Can this variety and inequality (we may now proceed to ask) be modified or corrected without damage to the effort of acquisition and (what matters far more) to the *nisus* of personal development with which the effort is mixed? We may answer that it can be corrected without any peril or risk if, and in so far as, the amount of possessions actually enjoyed is not the result of individual effort, but of factors other than such effort. There are a number of such other factors. There is the factor of inheritance, not indeed wholly separate from effort (many men are spurred to effort by the thought of their children after them and the hope of handing on opportunity), but still, in the main, a substitute for effort. Above all there is the general factor of chance, in all its forms: the chance of fortunate investment; the chance of the local environment of effort; the chance of meeting the caprice of demand; a whole world of chance. So far as such factors other than effort are the cause of variety and inequality in the amount of men's possessions, there can be no moral argument—no argument based on the moral claim of the *nisus* of personal development—against the correction of inequality. But the correction of inequality on that ground, and within those limits, is one thing: the general abolition of inequality of possessions, and a general policy of economic equality, is something entirely different.

We may therefore dismiss, on moral grounds, any general policy of economic equality. Individually we should all be spiritually poorer (though many of us might be materially richer) through the blocking of a way of effort in which we try out our powers. Socially, we should lose the diversity and the dynamic process of movement which are necessary conditions of the best society in which each of us can be at his best. A static and immobile society of economic equality is not the environment in which the greatest number of persons can achieve the greatest possible development of the capacities of personality. Such achievement is a dynamic process which involves a dynamic society, with a rich variety of stations and functions and an easy movement of coming and going among those stations and functions. But to dismiss a general policy of economic equality is not for a moment to dismiss a policy of the progressive correction of economic inequality. On the contrary such a policy, as we have already seen, is a necessary corollary of legal equality, itself imperfect and unachieved as long as difference of economic means is such that it produces differences of civic standing and capacity. It is also a policy, as we have just seen, which is morally justified, and even morally demanded, in so far as the distribution of economic means is determined by factors and causes other than individual effort, and, more especially, by the factor of chance. The true policy of equality in the economic field is thus the correction of inequality, so far as such correction is demanded by the cause of legal equality, and so far as it is justified, and even demanded, by the action of factors other than effort in producing inequality in the distribution of means.

It remains to add that equality is not an isolated principle. It stands by the side of the principle of liberty and the principle of fraternity. It has to be reconciled with both, and, in particular, with the principle of liberty. Both liberty and equality matter; but there are reasons for thinking that liberty matters even more than equality. In its application and general extension it is, in our history, the older principle, asserted and vindicated in the course of struggles which now seem ancient history. But it is not by any means the stronger—on the contrary, it is rather the weaker—for being the older. It has not the vogue of fashion: it seems to be outmoded and outshone by the more recent star of equality. Yet the principle of liberty may still be argued to be the greater of the two. It is the greater because it is more closely connected with the supreme value of personality and the spontaneous development of its capacities. It is the greater because it entails the other: because we may say of it,

'Seek ye liberty, and equality shall be added unto you'; because, in a word, free men, by the mere fact of being free, are also peers and equals in the essential and cardinal attribute of liberty. It is the greater, finally, because the cause of liberty unites men together in something which each and all can possess; while the cause of equality, exclusively pressed, may make them sink into jealousy of supposed forms of invidious difference, and produce division rather than unity. The educational ideal is rather, and even more, the liberation of capacity than the equalization of opportunity. There must indeed be equality of opportunity before all capacity can be free to develop; but the major and ultimate aim is liberation of capacity. In the same way the economic ideal is essentially an ideal of liberation; and though here too there has to be achieved some greater measure of equality, both in status and in possessions, before the battle of liberty can be won, the major and ultimate aim is the liberation of all into the service of a free partnership, where all have a voice in determining the rules of work and remuneration, and all enjoy the common liberty of helping to frame the common law under which all work and serve.

§ 4. THE PRINCIPLE OF FRATERNITY (OR CO-OPERATION)

HERE we must begin by making a distinction, already suggested in a previous passage,[1] between the psychological fact of common emotion and the political principle of fraternity or (as it is better called) co-operation. (Fraternity is a dubious word, which may be used to denote both emotion and principle, but is perhaps generally used to denote emotion rather than principle.) Common emotion takes various forms, or at any rate appears under various names, at various stages of its manifestation. One of these names, current among the members of professions, is *esprit de corps*, a French term which, in English usage, serves to denote a feeling of attachment to some professional group and a particular regard for its honour and interests. Thus Bentham writes that 'a particular community . . . such as that of divines, lawyers, merchants, &c., has its *esprit de corps*, its corporate affections'. Another term, which is also of French origin, but which has a wider and larger significance, is soli-

---

[1] § 1 of this Book, *ad finem*.

darity: a term that has come, since its introduction into our language about a century ago, to denote especially the sense of unity and the feeling of a common cause pervading the members of occupations. When we move from professions and occupations to the area of the State, we come upon terms of a still wider significance, such as 'fraternity' and 'nationalism' or 'patriotism'. These terms, too, are all of French origin; but if they agree in their origin, they differ in their connotation and their associations. Fraternity, with its general suggestion of brotherhood, has the widest sweep, and may even serve (as it did at the time of the Edict of Fraternity of 1792)[1] to denote international or cosmopolitan emotion; but nationalism and patriotism are also terms of width. Nationalism, in its proper sense, is a term which belongs to the area of Society rather than that of the State: it is a feeling of attachment to the tradition and achievement of the whole national society, in all the varied range of its life, just as patriotism (if we distinguish it from nationalism) is a feeling of attachment to the very soil and the physical features of the whole 'land of our birth' or *patria*, in all its sweep and variety. But both of these terms, though they are terms of width, may also be terms of exclusion: they may ring and confine us within the circle of our particular national society, or our particular *patria*. It is a more serious matter that both of these feelings of attachment may easily be diverted from their original object, the whole of national Society and the whole land of birth, and transferred instead to the State, which is something different from both, even if it is based upon both. It is a still more serious matter that these feelings, when so diverted and so transferred, may readily be transformed into *étatisme* and *chauvinisme*: an internal idolatry of the organizing State and a missionary zeal for the spread of its external power. The penetrating genius of French thought, which has distinguished and named so many forms of common emotion, has not shrunk from the analysis and description of its final extremes.

These psychological facts are not principles, as equality and liberty are principles. They are in no sense rules of procedure, regulating and determining the action of the State in its dealings

[1] 'La Convention Nationale déclare au nom de la Nation Française qu'elle accordera fraternité et secours à tous les peuples qui voudront recouvrer leur liberté.'

with its members. They are simply, in themselves, mere facts of common emotion. In so far as the term fraternity is used to denote such a fact, it is not *in pari materia* with liberty and equality: it is not, as they are, a principle, but only a fact of feeling; and if it is yoked with them, in that sense and with that denotation, it is yoked illogically and improperly. But the term fraternity may be used, and has long been used, in another sense and with another denotation. It may be used, as it has already been provisionally used in the course of the argument,[1] to denote a principle or rule of procedure on which the State is bound to act in the course of its general function of providing for its members the conditions of their personal development. That principle, which, as we have seen, may also be called the principle of co-operation (a term less ambiguous because more free from emotional associations), is a principle dictating common provision for common needs. It commands, we may say, the provision of that common 'equipment' which is the necessary background and basis of all individual lives. As Aristotle taught in the *Ethics* and *Politics*, and as all experience testifies, personal development requires a *choregia* or equipment: a supply of 'external goods', or material means, which makes development possible, and without which we should live an animal life of struggle for mere existence. It is the business of each of us to provide, so far as we can, our own individual equipment. Such individual provision is a part, as well as a basis, of the whole process of our development; and the effort of acquiring possessions, as we have already seen reason for thinking,[2] is closely and inextricably connected with the general *nisus* of personal growth and the general unfolding of personal capacity. But whatever we may do in the way of providing an individual equipment, we need in addition, and over and above it, a common equipment on which all can draw, and which all must therefore provide by common and co-operative effort. It is here that the principle of co-operation, or fraternity, asserts itself, demanding this common equipment and dictating this common provision. The thoroughgoing and doctrinaire Socialist will press this principle to the length of contending that common equipment is the major need, or even that all equipment should be common. If we believe that there is value in the individual provision

---

[1] *Supra*, § 1 of this Book, *ad finem*.   [2] *Supra*, § 3 of this Book.

of equipment, and value, too, in the provision of equipment by the voluntary action of social groups (acting side by side with the State, but yet acting of their own motion), we shall limit the provision of common equipment by the State to the area of what cannot be provided, or at any rate cannot be provided adequately, by the joint action of individual effort and the effort of voluntary groups. The State will thus stand in reserve. It will provide the whole residuary equipment; it will complete that common basis, both of services and resources, which is the common need of all.

This common basis of services and resources is partly material and partly mental. On the material side it covers a large and constantly increasing range. It includes the provision of means of communication, and the general easing of free personal movement; it includes works of sanitation and housing, and the provision of medical service, to ensure the conditions of health; it includes schemes of provision for invalidity and old age, in order to secure a decent livelihood at the times and seasons in which individual effort is impotent or inadequate; it includes schemes for the development of general economic resources (such as forests, or mines, or electric power) by methods which go beyond the reach of private enterprise, and are intended solely for the common benefit; it includes the promotion of research into the general conditions of health and wealth for all (by bodies such as the Medical Research Council and the Department of Scientific and Industrial Research); it includes measures for the preservation of rural and urban amenities by the protection of natural beauty in the country and by promotion of the planning of towns with a view to decency and order. Measures such as the last just mentioned are, however, more than material, both in their intention and in their effects; and they form a natural bridge of transition from the material side of the common equipment to the mental or spiritual side. The common basis of services and resources necessary to a properly organized community is a matter of the mind as well as the body: it means a mental or spiritual as well as a material equipment. On this side the common basis is largely, as yet, a matter of educational equipment; but it is also, and it may become even more, a matter of general cultural equipment. The one involves the provision by the State of schools and colleges and universities—in collaboration with voluntary effort. The other involves the provision of galleries, museums, and libraries; the provision of social (or community) centres, public concert halls, and national theatres; in a word, the provision of all the common facilities needed for the common enjoyment of all the treasures of culture—but with the proviso, once more, that such provision should be made by the State in collaboration with voluntary effort. The proviso is important: indeed one may say that it is almost as important as the provision itself. If the common equipment of education and culture were all provided by the State, there would be a grave danger of uniformity and even of mechanism. The life of the mind is varied, and rooted in spontaneity. The State has a duty of serving that life, by helping to provide the equipment which it needs; but the wisest service will often consist in the helping of agencies other than itself. Our own State has shown that wisdom in its dealings with universities. In the interest of variety and spontaneity, so essential in the sphere of the mind, the same wisdom of caution and self-restraint may well be adopted as a general policy. Many may feel that the State should be generous and open-handed in its provision of the common equipment of education and culture. But perhaps it is most truly generous when it is generous in its help to voluntary agencies, and generous in the respect which it pays to the cause of variety and spontaneity.

A general reflection occurs to the mind in regard to this principle of fraternity when so conceived and defined. It is a reflection which also embraces the two sister principles of liberty and equality; but it springs immediately from the principle of fraternity or co-operation. It is natural enough that some fund of emotion should gather round the whole system of the State: round the law it maintains, the rights which it guarantees and distributes, and the principles on which it distributes those rights. Such emotion is something different from fraternity in the sense in which that term has just been defined, a sense which makes it not a state of mind but a principle of action; and yet it may be particularly and immediately inspired by a sense of the value and the beneficent effects of that particular principle. But however it may be initially inspired, this fund of emotion, as it gathers volume, attaches itself to the *whole* operation of the *whole* of the legal association; to its law, to its body of distributed rights, and to all the principles of their distribution. We may give the name of 'loyalty' to this fund and bank of feeling. It is the capital, or rather the credit, of the State; it is an accumulated confidence in the operation of law, issuing in a feeling of fidelity to law (*loialté, loyauté,* faith in the law). This loyalty is not a value, but a recognition of values: a common recognition of the values expressed and upheld in the law of the State: a common recognition which rises to the height of a common emotion attaching itself to those values. But it is not the only common emotion which moves the minds of the members of a nation. Because there is something beyond the State and its system of law, there is also something beyond the emotion of loyalty for the State and its system. This is the common emotion which the members of a nation feel for national Society itself, in the range of its operation which lies beyond (or rather around) the area of the State. It is national feeling, or nationalism, in the best and highest sense of that word. It is the sentiment of the long co-operative effort made by a national Society in the exploration and cultivation of a national way of life and type of civilization: the sentiment of the debt of each to the past and present of his Society, and of the obligation of all to its future.

Another reflection occurs to the mind which is at once a corollary and a corrective. Emotions are good servants; but they are also bad masters. Both the emotion of loyalty to the State and the emotion of nationalism for national Society are, or should be, controlled emotions. My loyalty to the State is controlled by the values for which it stands; and if the State should be unfaithful to them I may be bound by these controlling values to turn my loyalty into disloyalty, and to change a happy obedience into reluctant resistance. Similarly my emotion of nationalism for my national Society is controlled by the values of the way of life and type of civilization for which my Society stands. So far, therefore, as those values are shared by and present in other national societies, I shall feel an emotion for them not only as they exist in my own society, but also as they exist in those other societies; I shall therefore cherish a feeling for those other societies, as well as for my own; and thus my nationalism, being controlled, will not be exclusive. It is only uncontrolled nationalism which becomes exclusive nationalism; and such an exclusive nationalism is a negation of its own basis, because it refuses to recognize in others the very values on which it depends for its own existence. We may therefore conclude that while common emotions cluster immediately round institutions—the legal and political institutions of the State, or the social institutions of national Society in all its range—they are ultimately directed to, and controlled by, the values expressed (it may be imperfectly) in the matter and stuff of those institutions. But it is easy to fall into what may be called uncriticized institutionalism. This is a direct and immediate cult of the matter and stuff of the institution: the school or college; the State or nation; the class (if a class can be an institution), or the occupation or profession. All institutions need the motive power of a true, or balanced, institutionalism: a common belief in the values expressed and the purpose served by the institution: a common belief issuing in a common emotion, and resulting ultimately in a common will. But institutions may also run into an uncriticized institutionalism, which stops short at the matter and stuff; which is a cult of some group, with its institutions, in and for itself, and which therefore is an exclusive cult, repelling the members of other groups in the act of attracting to itself the members of its own.

The common emotion of a group for itself and its institutions may be compared to a head of steam in a boiler. It is in its place and measure a necessary motive power. But just as there may be too great a head of steam in a boiler for the ultimate end of motion, so there may be too great a head of common emotion in a group for the ultimate end of individual growth and personal development. Common emotion has its benefits in elevating men above the level of self-interest. It may also have its disadvantages, in depressing them below the level of self-knowledge and self-development. In these days of crowded populations and gregarious habits, common emotions are easily generated: the problem is not to create them, but to bring them under control. The problem is all the more urgent because a new technique of 'mass-communications' has made it easier than ever to move and fire great aggregations with a common ardour. The result is a sort of secular mysticism: a readiness to lose personal identity and individual responsibility, and to be merged in the movement of a common life. There is a world of difference between such secular mysticism and that of the religious mystic. The religious mystic may be a loyal member of a religious group, but he has a core of individual solitude; and if he is ready, and even eager, to lose himself, it is in union with a personal God, achieved through the ecstasy of active and personal contemplation, that he longs to be lost. The secular mystic has no such core: he begins and ends in surrender; and his surrender is not the surrender of a person to a person, but of a unit to an aggregation.

§ 5. THE FINAL PRINCIPLE OF JUSTICE

THE notion of Justice has already been discussed in the argument of the previous Book.[1] We have now to bring the results of that discussion into connexion with the argument here advanced on the nature of rights and the principles of their distribution. Justice, as we are now in a position to see, is a term of synthesis. It is the final principle which controls the general distribution of rights and the various principles of their distribution. It is, in a word, the general right ordering of human relations in, and by, the association of the State. As such, it gives to each person rights, as his share in the whole system, and it thus 'adjusts' person to person.[2] As such, again, it gives to each principle of distribution (liberty, equality, and co-operation) its share and weight in determining the distribution actually made, and it thus 'adjusts' principle to principle. This idea of justice as the general 'right ordering of human relations', or the final adjustment of persons and principles, may appear to be an abstract conception if we compare it with actual concrete law, which is its visible expression and actual embodiment. But it is not abstract; nor does it reside merely in the speculative mind of the thinker, seeking, by an effort of his own reason, to separate and distil some sort of quintessence from the matter and practice of ordinary life. The idea of justice resides in *all* minds, and it has been created and developed through the ages by a process of historical social thought, which has made it a common inheritance. In that sense, and from that point of view, it is not an abstract conception but a social reality: an actual content of actual minds: a content progressively greater and clearer as those minds think out more fully and consciously the problems of a general right ordering of human relations. This justice is not morality, and its code is not that of ethics; it is not a rule

---

[1] Book III, § 2 and the following Sections. [2] § 1 of this Book.

of the inward life, but a rule of the outward life—the life of the relations between the members of an organized Society acting as such. On the other hand, this rule of the outward life of relations is vitally and intimately connected with the inward moral life: it is a condition, or set of conditions, needed and designed for the free movement of that life: it is a removal of the obstacles, or a hindrance of the hindrances, which may impede that movement. If justice is not morality it is based upon it. If its code is not that of ethics, it is a code which, as we have seen,[1] is ultimately derived from ethics.

To elucidate the meaning of a term such as justice, built and vested with associations by an historical process of social thought, we shall do well to go back to its origin and the root from which it has grown. That root, which appears in many branches and has been prolific of many growths, would seem to be the notion of 'joining' (as in the Latin *jungere* or the Greek *zeugnunai*): of 'binding', or 'fitting', or 'tying together'.[2] Justice is thus, in its original notion, the quality or aptitude of joining: it ties together whatever it touches. Primarily, it ties *men* together, by the common bond of a right and 'fitting' order of relations, under which each has his position in the order and receives his due place (*suum cuique*); each has rights as his share of the general Right pervading and constituting the order; and each owns *jura* as the exemplification and concrete expression in his own case of the general *jus*. Accordingly the *Institutes* of Justinian define justice, considered as a subjective feeling and a consequent will for the general right and fitting order, as *constans et perpetua voluntas suum cuique tribuendi*. Similarly the *Institutes* define the three precepts of *jus*, considered as the objective expression of the right order in a recognized and enforced body of rules, as consisting in *honeste vivere* ('living', as we say, 'up to one's position'), *alterum non laedere* (not injuring the position of another), and *suum cuique tribuere* (actually and positively respecting another's position and rights). Aristotle, almost a thousand years earlier, had distinguished three different species of justice, as the *Institutes* afterwards distinguished and

---

[1] *Supra*, Book III, § 6.

[2] The original Indo-Euopean root was *yug*, which may be traced in the English 'yoke'. The Romans, as has already been noted, still used the word *jus* in the general sense of a bond or tie, as when they spoke of *jus amicitiae* (the bond of friendship), or *jura necessitudinis* (the ties of kinship).

defined three precepts of *jus*. The first is 'distributive' justice, which gives each person his proper position and due share in the political community: this is analogous to Justinian's *suum cuique tribuere*, but it also differs, as it is concerned only with the distribution by the city-state among its members of *public* or official position, and not with the giving of *general* position in the shape of a share in general rights. The second is 'corrective' justice, which corrects a loss of position and rights involuntarily sustained in the course of transactions between individual members of the community:[1] this is analogous to Justinian's *alterum non laedere*. The third is 'commutative' justice, or justice in exchange, which determines the proportion of one sort of goods or services to be rendered in return for another sort in voluntary transactions of buying and selling or letting and hiring: this has no analogy with any of Justinian's three precepts—unless it be taken as another form of Justinian's *suum cuique tribuere*.

Such is the primary way in which justice performs its function of 'joining' and 'fitting together'. But there is also a second and further way. Justice is a joining or fitting together not only of persons, but also of principles. It joins and knits together the claims of the principle of liberty with those of the principle of equality, and both with those of the principle of fraternity or co-operation: it adjusts them to one another in a right order of *their* relations. Equality may quarrel with liberty; for if its application be pushed to the length of what is called a 'classless' society, with absolute equality of possessions, it is at once brought into conflict with the liberty of each to try himself out in the effort of acquiring for himself some individual 'equipment'. Similarly the principle of liberty may quarrel with that of co-operation: on the one hand, men may stand on the claims of their liberty (whether the civil liberty of the ordinary individual, or the economic liberty of the worker) to the detriment of the claims of the community for the co-operation of all its

[1] Aristotle cites, as examples of loss thus involuntarily sustained, clandestine injuries such as theft or perjury (leading to the loss of a man's goods or good name), and open and violent injuries such as assault or murder. In Aristotle's own terminology the one term 'rectificatory' (or 'diorthotic') is used to cover the two sorts of justice distinguished in the text as 'corrective' and 'commutative'. Using that one term, he then proceeds to distinguish (1) the form of rectificatory justice which deals with losses involuntarily sustained, and (2) the form of rectificatory justice which is concerned with the voluntary transactions of exchange. But the meaning is made clearer if separate names are given to these two separate forms.

members; on the other hand, a party may press the claims of co-operation to the length of demanding the common provision and common possession of the whole equipment of life, and it may press them thereby to the detriment of the claims of the individual for civil liberty and personal freedom of effort. But not only may there be conflicts between one principle and another; there may also be internal conflicts inside the area of a single principle. In the area of liberty, for example, as the argument has previously suggested,[1] civil liberty may be pleaded in support of claims which run contrary to those of economic liberty; and similarly political liberty may be on occasion the enemy, even if it is generally the friend, of either civil or economic liberty. There must therefore be some final principle transcending that of liberty, as it also transcends the principles of equality and co-operation: a principle which can balance each of these principles against the others, as it can also balance against one another the different and possibly divergent modes of interpretation that may be present within the area even of a single principle: a final principle which, in a word, *suum cuique tribuit*. That final principle is justice, which balances, and thus reconciles (and thus, in the issue, 'joins'), the different claims. This balancing and reconciling, in its turn, implies some final and ultimate value in the light of which, and by reference to which, it is possible to strike a balance and achieve a reconciliation; for you can only balance different and possibly conflicting claims if you have something behind them all in terms of which you can measure the weight to be assigned to each. That final and ultimate value, on the basis of the argument previously advanced,[2] is the highest possible development of the capacities of personality in the greatest possible number of persons. Justice is therefore an order of persons, and an order of the principles regulating the distribution of rights to persons, which is measured and determined by this final and ultimate value.

It is an ancient commonplace that justice is the holder of a balance; and the visual representations of the personified figure of Justice accordingly show her with a balance in her hand and with eyes blindfolded as a sign of her impartiality. On the argument here suggested justice holds in the balance both the claims of persons to rights and the claims of different principles to

[1] *Supra*, § 2 of this Book.   [2] *Supra*, Book III, § 6.

determine the distribution of rights, and she measures them both by the standard of the maximum development of the capacities of personality in the maximum number of persons. A different view has been propounded by an American jurist, Dr. Roscoe Pound, in his *Introduction to the Philosophy of Law*. It is a view which invites discussion because in one form or another, under the general influence of socialist thought, it is widely current. According to this view the balancing of claims by reference to the standard of the development of personality is an outmoded fashion of the past. It belongs to a mode of thought which was current for the four centuries from 1500 to 1900; from the age of Renaissance and Discovery to the age of capitalism and imperialism. It was natural, and even valuable, in that age of individual expansion, to conceive justice as 'a making possible of the maximum of individual free self-asser-tion'.[1] The times, however, have changed, or so the argument runs. We live today in a crowded age of social groupings, in which a free field for the assertion of individual *wills* is a policy producing more friction than it relieves; and an open door for the satisfaction of social *wants* is now the urgent need. The problem is to harmonize the satisfaction of these wants; or rather (for Dr. Roscoe Pound despairs, in the issue, of finding any standard by which a true harmony can be achieved) it is simply to satisfy as many of these wants as can be simultaneously satisfied.

The difficulty of the philosophy of Dr. Roscoe Pound does not lie so much in his substitution of 'social wants' for 'indivi-dual wills', as in his failure to find any standard by which such 'social wants' can be brought into any balance or harmony. We may, indeed, deprecate his assumption that 'wants', 'desires', 'interests' (the terms are used convertibly) are the essential factors to be considered; and we may urge that beyond these factors, which seem to be conceived as mass or group fac-tors (the adjective 'social' is recurrently added to each of the nouns), there are individual persons, and capacities of individual personal development (which are something different from

[1] The reader will notice that 'the maximum of individual free self-assertion' is something very different from 'the maximum development of the capacities of personality in the maximum number of persons'. But the critic of what may be called a theory of 'personalism' readily turns it into a theory of 'individualism', and no less readily, on that basis, turns 'self-development' into 'self-assertion'.

'individual wills'), that matter, and matter profoundly. But the really grave difficulty in Dr. Pound's view is his surrender of the notion of any criterion or standard of value by which different wants, desires, and interests can be measured and adjusted. All wants would appear, in the issue, to be equal: equally final; equally absolute. He does, indeed, speak of the problem of grading and valuing wants. But he seems to confess that it is insoluble, and that all wants must thus be regarded as on the same footing of value. This seems to reduce justice to a mere *de facto* balance of different social wants, controlled by no criterion, but attained by the registration of any actual equilibrium which the clash of equally valuable wants has attained for itself at any given time. It would justify a balance in which the wants of one particular type, if it were the most powerful or the most numerous or both, had tilted the scale. It leaves us accordingly with a pragmatic justice of the *fait accompli*, destitute of foundation or reference. This pragmatic justice necessarily has for its fellow an equally pragmatic system of law. Law, which is the visible expression of justice, becomes accordingly a simple activity of 'social engineering', which drives the best-graded road that it can through the intricate hills of social wants with a view to surmounting as many as possible with the greatest possible ease.[1]

§ 6. THE TRANSLATION OF JUSTICE INTO LAW

Justitia must become *jus*: the idea of a right ordering of human relations, a due 'joining' of the positions of persons and of the principles on which such positions are assigned, must be translated into the fact of recognized and enforced law. Logically—but not chronologically—we may distinguish three

---

[1] 'I am content to think of law as a social institution to satisfy social wants . . . by giving effect to as much as we may with the least sacrifice, so far as such wants may be satisfied by an ordering of human conduct through politically organized society . . . in short, [as] a continually more efficacious social engineering' (Pound, *An Introduction to the Philosophy of Law*, p. 99). But it would be a drab world in which there were only 'social wants' and 'social engineers' for their satisfaction. The actual world is a world of persons; and because it is, it is also a world of values, which persons are capable of apprehending, and in the light of which they are capable of acting. Such a world is not a fact of the past, or of the centuries from 1500 to 1900: it is a fact of all time. It is also a world which needs something more than efficacious social engineering—though there is room for some 'engineering' in the way of removal of obstacles, if only there is a vision of what is to be attained when the obstacles are removed.

stages in that translation. First, there is the idea and ideal of a system of justice for the right ordering of the relations of persons who are brought into contact with one another by the facts of neighbourhood and social intercourse. Next, there is the creation, by a constituent act, of a legal association, within which the ideal can be realized, and which is the prior condition of its realization. Finally, there is the formulation, in and by that association, of concrete rules of law intended to make the ideal, so far as is possible, a fact.

In connexion with the last of these stages we naturally speak of an act of law-making. We easily go even farther. We begin to think and to speak as if law-making created, and brought into existence, something which never existed before; and we continue what we have thus begun by thinking and speaking as if law-making were the same as commanding, and as if law proceeded, in the form of an act of commanding, from the will of a person or body of persons entitled to issue commands which are simply and solely commands.[1] But these prima facie notions are open to a double challenge. The first challenge is that law does not emerge from a vacuum by an act of sudden creation. The second challenge is that, when it emerges from its previous background, it does not emerge as a command or indeterminate act of legislative will which can be this or that at pleasure. In support of the first challenge it may be argued that the idea and ideal of a proper order of human relations were already present in social thought, as the inevitable result of men's thinking about the problems of social intercourse, and that what we call law-making is therefore only the declaration or manifestation of the result of that thought. We may thus say that law emerges from social thought about justice, and not from a vacuum, and that when it emerges it does so as a manifestation, and not as a creation. In support of the second challenge it may be argued that a conviction of the imperative character of the idea and ideal of justice, and of their implications, is an attribute and property of the whole association and all its members (otherwise the association would not exist), and is not confined to any particular person or body of persons; and therefore law-making, even if it is immediately the act of a particular person or body of

[1] On the notion of law as command see also the previous argument in Book III, § 1, p. 92.

persons, is ultimately, and in the last resort, the general expression of a general conviction made *through* that person or body.

If these arguments—and especially the latter—are accepted, it follows that law-making is not a matter of commands, addressed by a superior having power to inferiors who are under power, and ordering that this or that rule *shall be henceforth* obligatory upon them: it is a matter of declarations, issued by some agent or organ acting on behalf of a legal association of free and equal members, and stating that, in the general opinion of that association, this or that rule *is now* regarded as obligatory on all and will continue to be so regarded. We may even add that there is a form of law—the form termed 'customary'—which need not be declared at all by an agent or organ, because it is already apparent in common usage and is thus declared, immediately and directly, by the association itself.[1] In this way we reach the definition of law suggested by Gierke: 'Law is the conviction of a human community—either manifested directly by usage or declared by a common organ appointed for that purpose—that there exist in that community external standards of will: in other words, limitations of liberty which are externally obligatory, and therefore, by their very nature, enforceable.'[2]

When, on this basis, we turn to consider the agents and organs of the declaration of common conviction, we have only to repeat and expand a passage in our previous argument.[3] Both in the past, and still today, the judges first spring to the

---

[1] A well-known passage of the jurist Julianus, quoted in the *Digest*, explains how *consuetudo* may be regarded as a form of law made immediately and directly by a *populus*: see above, Book III, § 1, p. 95.

[2] Gierke, *Johannes Althusius*, p. 319 (translated in Gierke's *National Law and the Theory of Society*, vol. i, p. 225). But in the act of citing this passage of Gierke the writer cannot but remember two passages in a letter written to him by Lord Atkin in 1932. The first relates to the process involved in the declaration of written law. 'Have we ever sufficiently considered how much actual law is due to the particular intellectual (or other) processes of individual men? I am not thinking only of the traditional law-givers: Moses, or Solon, or Napoleon. In these days a good deal of law is the result of the impulses of a government clerk who gets his department to adopt a bill, and gets it put through mechanically by the Government majority. How are you to get a principle which correlates this process with those in other countries, or find the "tendency" which has led him to his results?' The second passage relates to the origin of customary law. 'I have a strong feeling that in many cases of custom the origin is the will of some chief or wise man who laid down the rule so, though he might just as well have laid it down differently, and then enforced the rule with all his power.'

[3] *Supra*, Book III, § 1, *ad finem*.

mind as the agents declaring, from day to day, the rules of law which ultimately proceed from common conviction. They not only declare them in the sense that they re-enunciate old rules in deciding upon new cases: they also declare them in the sense that from time to time they enunciate new rules, to meet new cases of peculiar novelty, by giving decisions upon such cases which afterwards come to be accepted as not merely decisions for the case in question, but as general rules for all similar cases. It is such enunciation which is judicial declaration *par excellence*. Here there is obviously no question of will: the action of the judge is rather that of collecting and distilling opinion—immediately, we may allow, that of the legal profession, but ultimately that of the public at large, whose sense of justice is always there, if it is only there in the background. But if the judges first spring to the mind as the agents declaring the rules of law, there is also the great and massive organ which is called the legislature. This, by its very name, may seem to be not only a declarer, but also a maker, of law, and indeed of the great bulk of law. What, then, is to be said of the function and power of the legislature in regard to the issue of law?

There is one thing to be said of its history, or at any rate of its history in England. The English legislature, or Parliament, would seem to have been in its origins, as the style of 'High Court of Parliament' still indicates, a judicial body which declared the law, in the last resort, in particular cases. In a word it was a part, if a very high part, of the judiciary, rather than a legislature separate from it. But at an early date it added to this original function, by a natural and easy development, the further function of declaring the law not by a particular decision in a particular case before it, but by a general decision applicable to all cases that might afterwards come before any tribunal. For a long time, however, such general decisions, couched in the form of statutes, were comparatively infrequent; and indeed the conception and practice of a specifically legislative organ, regularly and annually producing a crop of statutes, is little more than a century old, and may be dated from the era of reform after the passage of the 'Reform Bill' in 1832. Today we are familiar with the action of a sovereign legislature, exercising its power of sovereignty (or final decision in the last resort)[1]

---

[1] *Supra*, Book II, § 5.

by a continual process of legislation which seems, prima facie, to proceed from its own original will. But even the modern legislature is a common organ appointed for the purpose of declaring common conviction: and it confesses its nature when, as is generally the case with a new declaration on a matter of more than ordinary importance, it uses the argument that the matter has been considered by the community, in and during a general election, and that the declaration now made is based on the conviction then expressed by the community.[1] If, therefore, the legislature is sovereign, it is sovereign only in the sense that it possesses the final power of declaring common conviction, and that, possessing such power, it can amend or abrogate such declarations as are issued by the judges (otherwise its colleagues) when they too use their declaratory power in the enunciation of 'case law'. The action of the legislature is not creation, but declaration; and its essential function is to declare the implications of the idea and ideal of justice, or the right ordering of human relations in an organized society, and to declare them as they are generally felt by the members of that society and as they are expressed in the form of its common conviction.

It has been said that the State is both the child and the parent of law; at once its creature and its creator. It is the child and creature of law in so far as it is begotten by an idea of justice; is brought to birth by the primary law which constitutes it as a legal association and gives it a constitution; and is henceforth bound by its nature to act in accordance with that primary law. It is the parent and creator of law in the sense that, acting through the agents and organs commissioned for that purpose under the primary law of the constitution, it declares the rules of ordinary or secondary law which ultimately spring from the

[1] It should be noted that some acts of the legislature are 'declaratory' in a special sense: they declare and explain, for the purpose of removing doubt, what the existing law *already* is, and has previously been, even before the declaratory act is passed. This is, of course, something different from the declaratory function of the legislature exercised by it when it declares what the common conviction of the community has just become, and what, accordingly, the law *now* is and will henceforth continue to be. But these two things, though different, may occasionally blend with one another; and one and the same act may be both declaratory in the special sense and declaratory in the larger and more general sense. The Trade Union and Trade Disputes Act of 1927 is entitled 'An Act to *declare* and *amend* the law'; and accordingly it not only declares what the existing law already is, for the purpose of removing doubt, but also declares new rules of law now brought into force as new expressions of common conviction.

common conviction of all its members, and stamps and seals them, by such declaration, with a validity which they would not otherwise possess. This secondary law is not valid law unless and until it is declared by the State through its legislative and judicial organs; but when once it is so declared it is valid, and continues to be valid, even if it conflicts with the ideal of justice and the common conviction about the implications of that ideal. On the other hand, a rule of law which is in such a state of conflict, though still retaining validity, loses the value which depends on conformity with the ideal of justice and the consequent support of common conviction; and a valid law which has lost that value gradually loses also validity, because citizens cease to obey it, juries cease to give verdicts in accordance with it, and the courts are thus unable to enforce it. This was the case with many of the provisions of English criminal law at the turn of the eighteenth century.

§ 7. THE ENFORCEMENT OF LAW AND THE PURPOSE OF PUNISHMENT

THE figure of personified Justice not only holds a balance: it also bears a sword. Law, as the concrete expression of Justice, must also wield the sword: the words *gladius custos legis* are written on the gate of the Palace of Justice in Paris. How shall we explain the sword of the law; the employment of force by the State which is formed for the negation of force and the substitution of law; the conjunction of the violent and the legal? We have seen that law is essentially and ultimately a conviction of of the existence of rules or external standards of action, a conviction common to all, including the potential breakers of rules. But a rule about human actions, unlike a rule about the action of natural bodies, does not exist of itself, or continue to exist of itself. In order to exist at all, it must be thought into existence, and become a common conviction. In order to continue to exist, it must be willed into continued existence: in other words, the common conviction that a rule exists must be backed by a common will that it shall continue to exist. Bare conviction is not enough: there must also be volition of the object of conviction. Nor is this all. Besides conviction and volition, there is also a third thing needed. If you will that a rule shall go on existing, you must also will that infractions and obstructions shall *not* go on existing, and you must back that will by an effort for their negation and removal. That effort is force, which enforces the law and fortifies justice.[1] In the realm of human relations, as distinct from the realm of nature and the relations of natural bodies, a rule will not be a rule, and law will not be law, unless it is backed by effort as well as conviction and will.

It has been said that behind the fairest show of right dealing there stands the armed force of the community. The saying is true enough, if we remember that force does stand behind, and is not placed in the forefront. Force is not the origin, but the ultimate consequence of law: the consequence which follows on will, which in turn follows on conviction, which in turn, and in the last issue, is the origin of law, and indeed *is* law. Generally, and on the whole, conviction, standing in the first rank, wins the victory of law by itself: we obey the law, 99 times out of 100 (but that is an under-estimate), in the simple strength of a conviction, wrought into our very fibre, that it expresses for us and others a right order of human relations. Force operates as a rearguard; it acts only in the hundredth case, when, as the Romans said, you fall back on the *triarii*, or the soldiers of the last rank. Force and punishment enter when conviction has fallen as it were asleep, as with a careless driver or a negligent trustee, or when men consciously break a rule, though still convinced of its general advantage, because they think they can gain in that way their own particular advantage and are therefore somehow exempt from the rule. Then, and then only, comes force: the memento to careless forgetting, and the corrector of vicious reasoning; the unsleeping 'knocker up' of the sleeping and the unerring critic of the erring. Force, in a word, is a servant of the conviction called law, a servant who keeps his master from either sleeping or straying.

If that is the relation of force to law we may now proceed to consider, in the light of this conception, the relation of force to

---

[1] Pascal says somewhere, when he is thinking in sadness of what men may actually do, 'Ne pouvant pas fortifier la justice, ils ont justifié la force'. There is a dilemma presented to men's choice by the nature of their minds: they must either fortify justice or, if they fail to do that, proceed to justify force. It is curious, by the way, to notice in how many forms the same root recurs—'force', 'fortitude', 'effort', 'enforce', 'fortify'. The fundamental notion is not that of violence, but of strength: the strength of a good courage (*fortitudo*) and of effort shown in upholding a cause against any enemy attack.

the individual, or the nature and purpose of punishment. The problem is really the same: there is only a difference of approach. The basis of punishment of the individual is the assumption of a society of rational agents, sharing a common conviction about a right order of their relations, and therefore responsible to one another and to the whole society for negligence or infraction of the declared rules of that order. The assumption thus made, in the act of punishment, that each agent is individually responsible, and that all alike are responsible, is a tribute to the principles of liberty and equality, and thereby to the ultimate and intrinsic value of human personality from which those principles are derived. Punishment is the black shadow of those principles and that value; but we respect them most if we recognize that they do, and must, cast a shadow. The danger of psychological and sociological theories of punishment, or at any rate of some of those theories, is that they attenuate the offender and make him, like the man in the fairy-tale, a person without a shadow. If we respect personality, we must respect responsibility. If we respect responsibility, we must respect the right of offenders to be punished for their offences.

There are, indeed, psychological aberrations and abnormalities, where the assumption made in the act of punishment ceases to be possible, and where all that can be done is to apply, if it be possible, some method of psychical therapeutics. Samuel Butler, in *Erewhon*, went to the length of thinking that all offenders alike were abnormalities. In his Utopia crime is held to be the result of some prenatal or postnatal misfortune which has produced a mental lesion; and therefore, without being judicially punishable, it is remitted to 'a class of men trained in soul-craft', called by the name of 'straighteners', for the application of treatment and cure. This is an extreme view, which abolishes altogether both responsibility and punishment. We must indeed admit that there is a sort of borderland in which the rational responsible agent shades off by various degrees into the irrational and irresponsible: we must allow that some wrongdoing belongs to this borderland; and we must confess that wrongdoing of this order is, or may be, a matter for 'straightening'. But the normal presumption is sanity, and therefore responsibility, and therefore the right of offenders to be treated as responsible agents and punished as such for their offences; nor can the normal presumption be waived except in the face of cogent proof of its invalidity. Normal wrongdoing— if that phrase may be used (for in one sense wrongdoing is always abnormal)—is the action of normal responsible persons; and the law will normally treat it as such. There is, however, a qualification, or rather addition, which has to be made. Responsibility is not the same as intentionality. A man may be a responsible person, and yet his act, in a given case, may be wholly or mainly unintentional. But *some* amount of intentionality, *some* degree of will and conscious volition, is necessary to constitute a living act, or, in other words, an act that rises above the level of mere automatism; and it is only for a living act, based on some amount and degree of intentionality, that a man is legally liable. The difficult question is the simple question, '*How* much?' This raises the problems of duress, 'extenuating circumstances', and the like. It would be irrelevant here to enter upon this question, or to discuss these problems. It is sufficient for the present argument to note that the question of the degree of intentionality to be attached to some particular action of a responsible person is a different question from that of the degree of responsibility to be attached to the mind of a person alleged to be more or less irresponsible.

Just as there are psychological theories which attenuate the offender and extenuate the offence, so there are sociological doctrines which lead to a similar result. The gist of these doctrines is that a great amount of wrongdoing is not the conscious and deliberate action of persons responsible for themselves, but the automatic and inevitable action of persons for whom Society is responsible, in the sense that it has created the set of social conditions in which they have been born and bred, which have made them what they are, and which have produced their acts. It is impossible to deny, and indeed it is a duty to admit, the evil results of overcrowded tenements, of the lack of facilities for healthy recreation, and of the abundance of the facilities for drink and dissipation. But the difficulty of a doctrine which transfers responsibility for wrongdoing from the wrongdoer to Society, and to the conditions created or tolerated by Society, is that persons living in the same set of social conditions differ greatly from one another in their behaviour and action. If some are impelled to wrongdoing, a great many more are law-abiding;

and it cannot therefore be said that a given set of social conditions inevitably and uniformly produces a corresponding type
of action. The most we can say is that one set of social conditions,
such as that of the slum, is accompanied by a greater amount of
wrongdoing than another set, such as that of a new housing
estate; though in either set of conditions by far the greater number will be law-abiding citizens. It follows that the wrongdoer
living in a set of bad social conditions may be regarded as less
responsible for his action, though still (let us say) nine-tenths
responsible; and it also follows that Society ought to alter those
conditions, because it is (say) one-tenth responsible for the
wrongdoer's action by creating or tolerating the conditions by
which his action is partly produced. What does not follow is that
persons born and bred in bad social conditions can be treated on
a different basis from other persons; though in determining the
particular degree or character of punishment the judge may
well take into account the milieu of such persons.

In the light of the previous argument we can now discern and
define the purpose of punishment. The purpose of punishment
is to affirm, against all negligence and infraction, a universal
mental rule, which because it is mental must live in the mind,
and because it is universal must live in all minds. Because *all*
minds are in question, the essential purpose of punishment is a
purpose of *general* prevention. It exists to prevent all minds,
including that of the offender (but not, for a moment, his only),
from neglecting or rejecting the content of common conviction.
From this point of view it may even be said that each single act
of punishment is a universal act. All are concerned and intended
in each particular act of punishment, and all may therefore
say, 'There, but for the grace of remembering and obeying the
law, go I, and with this reminder before me I must continue to
remember and obey'.

If we cling to this conception of the universal aspect of every
particular act of punishment, we shall readily acknowledge that
its primary and essential purpose is the purpose of prevention.
When, however, we turn from the universal aspect of punishment to the particular, and when we consider it as *immediately*
concerning and intending the one person punished, though
ultimately it concerns and intends all alike, we may say that
there is a sense in which the purpose of punishment is also

reformatory. But punishment is reformatory in the sense that it is intended to *revive*, in the mind of the person punished, the mental rule which he has neglected or rejected, and, along with it, the whole of the system of such rules. In other words, punishment is a reformation of the wrongdoer only in the sense of being intended to *prevent* him (as well as others, and along with others) from neglecting or rejecting the particular mental rule he has broken and, with it, the whole system of such rules. It follows that the reformation intended is simply a consequence, or by-product, of prevention, and that it therefore affects, as such, others besides the wrongdoer, and others along with the wrongdoer. So far, therefore, as punishment is reformatory, it is reformatory of all, and not of the criminal only, though it may, and should, be particularly and especially reformatory in his case. But the fact remains that punishment is never reformatory in the sense of being intended to re-form or re-shape the character of the particular wrongdoer. That is his own business, which he has to do for himself, as all men have to do their moral business for themselves. We should not only insult the moral autonomy of the wrongdoer, but we should also break against it, if we attempted to do his own business for him.

Finally, there is a sense in which punishment is retributive. But here we have to ask who it is who retributes, and what it is that 'pays back'. It is not the injured person who retributes or pays back; it is not even the whole community of persons, considered simply as persons. It is the mental rule of law which pays back a violation of itself by a violent return, much as the natural rules of health pay back a violation of themselves by a violent return. The *lex talionis* does not mean that the person or body of persons you hurt shall hurt you in return: it means that the order you disturb will disturb you in order to restore itself.[1] It is true that if you regard this order as existing in the thought of the community, and as issuing from that thought, you may say that the thought of the community returns, as it were, in retribution on any disturbance of itself; and in that sense you may even say that the community retaliates. But that is different from what is meant by the ordinary man when he uses the phrase, 'vengeance belongs to society'. In the sense in

---

[1] St. Augustine, in Book XIX, c. xiii, of the *De Civitate Dei*, expresses subtly, and with a deep insight, this notion of the 'return' of order upon the offender.

which he uses the phrase, vengeance does not belong to society, or to any person or body of persons. The only sense in which retribution, or retaliation, or vengeance, can be said to belong to society is that it belongs to, and proceeds from, the order or system of mental rules which lives in the thought of society. Punishment is terribly personal, so far as concerns the person punished: it touches him to the quick. But it is also absolutely impersonal, so far as concerns the persons punishing: they are only the agents of the return of the order violated. It was this impersonality of punishment which Kant had in mind when he said that 'even though a society were about to be dissolved by agreement, the last murderer in prison must be executed before it breaks up'.[1]

[1] It is possible to exaggerate the impersonality of punishment. On the other hand, it is dangerous to let personal considerations obtrude. It may be argued that a strong popular opinion against punishment in a given case, or against a given mode of punishment, or, conversely, a strong popular demand for severity against a particular wrongdoer or a particular class of wrongdoers, is a matter of importance, because it is an expression of the thought of the community. But we have to ask ourselves whether such an expression or demand is really an expression of social thought, or only of an uncriticized sum of personal emotions.

BOOK V

THE DUTY OF THE CITIZEN TO THE GOVERNMENT

or the Grounds and Limits of Political Obligation

§ 1. THEORIES OF THE GROUND OF POLITICAL OBLIGATION

THE term 'obligation' is a term derived from Roman Law. Obligation is defined in the *Institutes* of Justinian as 'a legal bond (*juris vinculum*) in virtue of which we are tied by necessity to some performance'. Such an obligation may be either civil or political. When it is civil, and takes the form of a bond between private persons, I am tied as a private person to perform some act for another such person, and the necessity by which I am tied is that of enforced law. When the obligation is political, and takes the form of a bond between me as a citizen and the governing authority as such, I am tied as a citizen to perform an act, or rather a number of acts, for the governing authority; but what is here the necessity by which I am tied to performance? Above me as a private person and any other private person there stands the necessity of enforced law, as something apart from us both. What is the nature of the necessity which stands above me as a citizen and the governing authority as such, and which is something apart from us both? It cannot be enforced law; that is simply a mode or aspect of governing authority, and not something above it and separate from it. Some other answer has to be found. We may begin by considering three different theories which have been propounded by way of answer.

(a) *The Theory of Divine Right*. Upon this theory the necessity which stands above and apart from the citizen and the governing authority is that of the Divine Will and ordinance. I am obliged to obey the governing authority because I am obliged to obey God, and because any governing authority is essentially an emanation and delegation of divine authority. This theory goes back to the East and the ancient Eastern monarchies; but in its European form it is based on the teaching of St. Paul. 'Omnis anima potestatibus sublimioribus subdita sit: non est enim potestas nisi a Deo: quae autem sunt a Deo, ordinatae sunt.'[1] St. Thomas Aquinas, as has already been noted,[2] followed the teaching of St. Paul, and accordingly ascribed to God the *principium* of all authority. But knowing also the doctrine of the Roman lawyers, that the *princeps* derives his authority and power from an act of the people in delegating and transferring to him *omne suum imperium et potestatem*, and knowing too the doctrine of Aristotle that the assembled people should have the right of electing its magistrates initially and calling them afterwards to account, St. Thomas adds a rider to the teaching of St. Paul.[3] If God Himself gives the *principium* of authority, the people determines its *modus*, or permanent constitutional form, and it also confers the *exercitium*, or actual enjoyment and employment of power by the person or body of persons possessing it for the time being. (St. Thomas also suggests that the people may criticize, and in the event of misuse withdraw, the *exercitium* which they have conferred: indeed in one passage of the *De Regimine Principum*[4] he even says that 'a ruler who fails to act faithfully, as the office of kingship demands, in the government of a community, deserves to suffer the consequence that his subjects should refuse to keep their *pact* with him', thus appearing to combine a theory of social contract with the theory of divine right.)

The theory of St. Thomas, which was the generally accepted theory of the Middle Ages, was thus a theory that the king, as the head of a body politic, had a claim to the necessary obedience of each member of that body in virtue of an authority coming *from* God, but coming, in its course, *through* the body politic of which he was head. The thought of the sixteenth century, departing from that of the Middle Ages, amputated as it were the body from the head: it rejected the notion that authority came to the head through the body: it left the head

---

[1] Romans, c. xiii, v. 1.   [2] *Supra*, Book III, § 3.

[3] The doctrine of the Roman lawyers is expressed in the dictum of Ulpian, repeated in the *Institutes* of Justinian (L. i, tit. 2, § 6), that 'the will of the *princeps* has the force of law because the people confers upon him and into his hands all its authority and power'. The doctrine of Aristotle is stated in c. xi of Book III of the *Politics*, and especially in §§ 8–9 of that chapter.

[4] Book I, c. vi.

with a solitary authority unqualified by any act of the people. It is in that century, but not before, that we find a new theory of divine right as the right of a bodiless head.[1] This bodiless head may either be regarded as receiving authority directly from God, or he may be held, as he is by Sir Robert Filmer, to have received it indirectly through a patriarchal succession from Adam who received it originally and directly from the hands of his Maker. The result of the latter view is a theory of divine hereditary right, with the emphasis on the word 'hereditary'; but both views alike involve a theory of divine right which leaves no room or place for the body of the people. The medieval theory had been monarchico-democratic: the theory which emerges in the sixteenth century is purely a monarchical theory, and it is especially so in the seventeenth-century version which makes the line of heredity the line of the transmission of right.

It is not necessary here to accept or reject the theory of divine right. There is a sense in which, at any rate to the theist, it is eternally true that all power is of God, and that every holder of power is responsible to God; and if it is also eternally true that the holders of power are responsible to the community, we have seen that the medieval version of the theory, if not in the later versions of the sixteenth and seventeenth centuries, recognized and proclaimed this truth. But the form and vesture of the theory belong to a vanished age, in which kings governed as well as reigned; and while we may recognize a permanent core of truth in its essential doctrine, we must also recognize that the setting of the core is now an antiquity. Indeed in the sixteenth century thought was already moving away from the idea that kings derived authority from God, and was seeking to give them a different title.

(*b*) *The theory of prescriptive possession.* Upon this theory, which began to be advanced in France, and which may be termed the theory of legitimism, the monarch rules by customary right: not *jure divino* (though that right might also be alleged as an additional support), but *jure consuetudinario*. Long possession, ripening

---

[1] F. W. Maitland, in an essay on 'The Corporation Sole' (*Collected Papers*, vol. iii), notes that in 1522 a judge could still declare that 'a corporation is an aggregation of head and body, not a head by itself or a body by itself', but that later, by 1550, the conception of the King as a corporation sole, in himself, is establishing itself and 'the personality of the corporate body is concentrated in and absorbed by the personality of its monarchical head'.

into property, is the title of kings to governing authority; and from this title, upon the assumption that men are tied by necessity to respect all property-rights, the conclusion is drawn (though, as we shall see, it is not a logical conclusion) that subjects are tied by necessity to respect the property-right of kings to the exercise of governing authority. Bodin, in his *De Republica* of 1576, connected a theory of this order with a theory of patriarchy, though he did so without bringing into his argument, as Filmer afterwards did in his *Patriarcha* of 1680,[1] the idea of a divine commission of authority to the original patriarch Adam. The theory of Bodin may be resumed in three propositions. The first is that the family is a given natural fact, which you must simply accept, and that it naturally involves for its head a right both of property in possessions and of authority over persons, which you must also simply accept. The second is that the family is the source and origin of the State. The third, which follows logically on the second, is that the authority of the head of the State is the same authority, with the same natural title, as that of the head of a family, inasmuch as the State is only a derivative and extension of the family. The theory of Bodin is in one way superior to the theory of divine right current in his day. He makes the king not a bodiless head, but the head of a family; and by thus introducing the idea of the family he gives to governing authority not only the title of prescriptive possession, but also a natural title grounded in human feeling. The objection to his theory is that the State has long ceased to be, if indeed it ever was, an extension of the family, and that the position of the head of a State is therefore not the position of the head of a family—still less (as he seems to assume) the position of the head of a family vested with that peculiar degree of *patria potestas* which was practised among the early Romans.

Another French jurist, Loyseau, in his *Traité des Offices* of 1614, is more thoroughgoing than Bodin, and puts his trust in the simple theory of prescriptive possession, which is the essence of legitimist ideas. He does not seek to justify the claims of governing authority to impose obligation on subjects by basing such authority upon something exterior to itself, as even Bodin does when he invokes the name and sanction of the family: he is content to base it upon itself, if only it includes within itself

The book was posthumously published: Filmer died in 1653.

the element of duration. Kings, he holds, have *arisen* in different
ways, some by popular concession, others by simple force and
'ancient usurpation'; but as they now exist, after the process and
passage of time, 'they have all acquired by prescription the
property in sovereign power'. In other words, continuous use
has given them something more than the exercise of authority:
it has given them *ownership* of authority; and their subjects are
thus tied to them, and to the authority which they own, by the
necessity of respecting ownership and all the rights which it
carries. This mere legitimism could, and did, ally itself with
ideas of the divine right of kings, on the plea that a long-time
warrant was also the warrant of God. It might carry weight in
that conjunction; but in itself, and taken by itself, it fails to explain why the subject is tied and obliged to governing authority.
It degrades authority over persons to the level of property in
things; and it brings the problem of political obligation down
into the area of civil obligation, to which it does not belong
and in which it cannot be solved. Moreover it is a theory which
has a sole application to monarchy, and to monarchy which is
a governing as well as a reigning monarchy.

(c) *The Theory of Contract.* Upon this theory[1] in its simpler
form the citizen is tied to the governing authority, first, because
he, in common with all other citizens, has made a contract with
a person or body of persons, under which that person or body
receives authority in return for the protection and service of
declaring and enforcing a system of legal rules, and, secondly,
because he and his fellows are bound by natural law to respect
and perform the terms of that contract. But reflection soon suggests to the mind that this simpler form, taken by itself and in
itself, is inadequate and incomplete. How could men bargain
collectively with the person or body of persons to be vested with
governing authority, unless they were already of the nature of
a collective body, and how are we to explain their being already
of that nature? In order to answer that question thinkers of the
school of contract were ultimately forced to the conclusion that
there was a double contract, or more exactly, two stages of
contract: first the contract of society, the *pacte d'association*, as it
is termed by Rousseau, or the *Gesellschaftsvertrag*, as it is termed

---

[1] The theory is discussed in more detail by the writer in Essay IV of the second
edition of his *Essays on Government*.

by Gierke, or 'the social contract proper', as it may also be termed; and secondly, the contract of government, or the *pacte de gouvernement*, or the *Herrschaftsvertrag*, or the social contract loosely (and even improperly) so called. Under the 'contract of society' all persons in a given area, an area supposed somehow to be definite, agree with one another to form and to be a collective body of the nature of a *societas* or partnership. Under the 'contract of government', or the social contract loosely so called, this *societas* or partnership, once it is formed, agrees with a person or body of persons, supposed somehow to be separate from it, to institute a *potestas* and to confer it upon that person or body on certain conditions. The first contract thus creates *societas*, and the second *potestas*; or, as we also say, in the specific terms of Roman law, the first contract is the result of an act of simple consent expressing itself in the form of partnership or *societas*, and the second the result of a similar act expressing itself in the form of agency, or, as it was called by the Roman lawyers, *mandatum*.

Is there any element of truth in the first of the two contracts thus distinguished: the contract of society? If the notion of a social contract is meant to explain the nature and the existence of a national Society, as the use of the word 'social' implies, it fails to achieve its object, not only because a national Society is never actually the product of contract, but also because it is totally unlike anything that could possibly be produced by contract. A national Society, as we have seen,[1] knows no limits to its purposes, as contractual partnerships always do: it cannot be dissolved by agreement, as partnerships can be: it has, as a national Society, no organization or administration, as partnerships always have. If, however, the idea of a social contract is meant to explain the nature and existence not of national Society, but of the national State—the State as distinguished from national Society, the State as a legal association superimposed on such a Society—then it may be said to achieve its object. Though we cannot apply the idea of contract to national Society, and though the adjective 'social' is a misnomer, we can apply the idea of contract to the national State, and we may not improperly speak of a political contract. But the 'political contract' of which we may thus speak is something entirely

[1] *Supra*, Book IV, § 4.

different, as the course of the argument will show, from the 'contract of government' assumed by the old thinkers of the school of contract. If it has to be distinguished from the contract of Society, it has equally to be distinguished from the contract of government as that contract used to be conceived.

How, then, are we to conceive the nature of this political contract? We must begin by admitting, or rather contending, that it does not serve to explain, and is not for a moment meant to explain, the chronological antecedents of the State in general, the State at all times and places in all its manifestations. It serves only to explain, and is meant only to explain, the logical presuppositions of the State in particular: the State as it exists at the present time, and as it exists at the present time in the Western world—the world of Western Europe, the British Commonwealth, and the Americas. If we look at the State in general, as it arose and grew in the course of past time, we are bound to recognize that it did not arise and has not grown in the climate of contract. It was formed and developed by a variety of factors: the bond of kinship uniting, or supposed to unite, a people or group of peoples; military force and diplomatic policy welding different peoples into some sort of union; the bond of neighbourhood joining the residents of some definite area in a common system of economic and social relations, apart from, or over and above, any bond of kinship or any employment of force and policy. But if we look at the State in particular, as it exists in our own time and in the area of the Western world, we are equally bound to recognize that it lives and has its being in a climate of contract, and of all the concomitants of contract: mutual concession, mutual toleration, mutual discussion, and general give and take. The modern State of the Western world is a legal association. As such it depends upon, and is constituted by, a memorandum of association, or a set of articles of association, or in other words a 'constitution', which states the contractual terms on which the association is made and under which it henceforth acts. The constitution of a State may thus be regarded as the contract on which its action, and the action of its members in their capacity of members, is ultimately dependent; and from this point of view political obligation may be regarded as contractual obligation. This is especially plain where there is a written constitution, as there is in the great majority of the States of the Western world, but it does not cease to be plain where the constitution is partly or even largely unwritten: there is, after all, no difference of kind between the 'written' and 'unwritten' constitution, and indeed the sense of obligation may be felt as much to the 'unwritten' as to the 'written' constitution.[1] The contractual nature of the constitution, and the contractual nature of the obligation incumbent under it on each citizen, becomes even more plain when the constitution contains not only a 'frame of government', or a statement of means and methods, but also a 'declaration of rights', or a statement of ends and purposes; for such a statement of ends and purposes is even more obviously a formulation of contractual terms than is a statement of means and methods.

We may now turn from our examination of the truth of the first form of contract, the contract of Society, to an examination of the truth of the second, the contract of government. Here we may say at once that the logic of the previous argument necessarily involves us in the rejection of any idea of a separate contract of government. If we accepted that idea, we should be committed to the view that the citizen is tied or obliged to the governing authority by the necessity of a contract separately and specifically made with that authority: a contract other than, and additional to, the political contract expressed in the constitution. There is no need for any such view; and if it were adopted, it would unduly exalt the governing authority by making its members a body separate from the general civic body, and independent enough to negotiate on equal terms with that body. The one political contract expressed in the constitution is sufficient for every purpose, and adequate in itself to explain the basis of governing authority. That one contract, so expressed, determines all positions in and under the constitution: it determines governing position as well as, and along with, the general civic position of the ordinary citizen. A person who is a member of the governing authority simply adds to his general civic position, in which he is already placed and obliged by the terms of the political contract, a further and particular governing position, in which he is also placed and obliged by the terms of the very same contract. If he differs from the

[1] *Supra*, Book II, § 4.

ordinary citizen in having two positions, and not one only, he owes both of the positions which he holds to the same origin in the same contract, the one and only contract expressed in the constitution. When once we grasp the idea that the constitution of the State is the one and only contract, we can see that, fundamentally, the citizen and the holder of governing authority stand on the same footing by virtue of an identical title. The idea of a separate contract of government, giving a separate title to the holder of governing authority, could only arise in the absence of a constitution: it was a rudimentary attempt to provide the rudiments of a constitution, in the form of a bilateral contract regarded as simply determining the position of governing authority in its relation to the general body of citizens, and determining nothing more. Actually the constitution, as men saw in the light of further experience (beginning with the American Revolution of 1776, and continued in the French Revolution of 1789), determines much more than that: it determines *all* positions: it regulates equally, and in the same way, the position of governing authority and the position of ordinary citizens. When once men grasped the breadth of the contract of the constitution, the rudimentary idea of a contract of government had served its turn, and faded away.

§ 2. POLITICAL OBLIGATION AND THE IDEA OF JUSTICE

Is it a final solution of the problem of political obligation to argue that we are bound by our own contractual act in forming and continuing to accept the constitution of our State? That argument certainly provides us with a legal bond in virtue of which we are tied to performance by a necessity: not the necessity of enforced law, which is what holds us to our civil obligation, but the necessity of the constitution, which is what holds us to our political obligation. But the question may be raised, Why is the constitution itself necessary, or in what sense is it a necessity which we are bound to accept? We may reply to that question by saying, or repeating, that the constitution, after all, is our act (though the communist or the revolutionary might rejoin that it was not *his*), and that our acts, when they are once established as objective facts in the external environment of our lives—when once they have gone out of us as promises made to others, on which others rely and on the performance of which they count—oblige us necessarily as things now beyond recall. *Fides est servanda.* But our minds crave something more even than the sanctity of promise and pledge. We want to know not only that we *are* now bound and tied, but also that we *ought* to be: we want to know not only that there has been an act of our own, but also that the act has value, or is directed towards a value, so that we are bound not only by the act as an act, but also by something valuable in it or above it. We are thus led to ask ourselves where, and in what, we can find the final and ultimate ground of political obligation. The answer to that question is suggested by the argument of the previous Book. The ultimate reason why we are obliged is not that the State is our act and deed: it is because the State represents and realizes, and in so far as it represents and realizes, that system of political values, and that general idea of justice controlling and co-ordinating the system, which finally claim our obedience. If the State does *this*, and to the extent that it does *this*, our obligation is perfect.

It is not, therefore, the fact that the State has a basis of contract which finally commands our allegiance. It is the fact that the State is the expression and organ of justice. We are obliged to the governing authority of the State, and we obey and perform its commands, because the State as a whole is, on the whole, such an expression and organ. If the State fails to be that, or in so far as it fails to be that, we are left with an obligation which hangs, as it were, in the air, and has no final support. Then there arises the problem, 'Which is the true obligation: our obligation to the State, or our obligation to justice?' It is the problem which confronts the communist in a non-communist State: it is equally the problem which confronts the liberal and the democrat in a State which is neither liberal nor democratic: it is, in a word, the problem whether the major obligation is simply to the State-expression of justice, or to a demand of justice which the State either fails to express or falls short of expressing fully.

To that problem we shall return at the end of the argument of this Book. Meanwhile we are left with the proposition that the State as a whole is, on the whole, the expression and organ of justice, and that this is the final source of political obligation.

The proposition involves both a positive and a negative implication. Neither of these implications will justify any and every act of the governing authority of the State: both of them justify only the action of the State *in general* (or in other words the State as a whole), and that only in respect of the *general trend* of such action. The positive implication is that when the State is declaratory—when it declares, in the form of law, the body of deductions which flow from the idea of a right order of human relations, as that idea now stands at this given stage of common conviction—we are actively obliged to accept and to carry into effect the law so declared, because it is ultimately a declaration of the dictates of an order which we ourselves acknowledge to be obligatory. In fulfilling the law which the State declares, we obey, and we are obliged to obey, our own idea of what a right order of human relations should be. The negative implication is that when the State is compulsory—when it compels us by the use of force to recognize in a particular case, and that our own case, the general rule which we recognize as binding for all cases—we are passively obliged to accept and suffer the compulsion so applied, because, once more, it is ultimately the compulsion of an order which we ourselves acknowledge and acknowledge to be obligatory. In undergoing compulsion we are being made to obey, not the State as a will or a power impinging on our own will or power, but the something behind the State which is not a will or a power, but a system of right order which we believe to be right as a system, even though we may have infringed it at a particular point.

§ 3. POLITICAL OBLIGATION AND THE 'GENERAL WILL'

Two lines of thought have been followed in the argument hitherto advanced. Along the first line an attempt has been made to explain political obligation in terms of contract, and as the result of the political contract embodied in the constitution. Along the second the attempt has been made to explain it in terms of justice, and as being a logical consequence of the idea of a right order of relations which is at once demanded and supplied by our own reason and thought. We have now to draw the two lines together and to combine the two explanations. If they are left unconnected, difficulties ensue: explanation ceases to be valid, and obligation does not oblige. If obligation be regarded as simply a matter of contract, we are faced by the possibility of two opposite consequences, both of them disastrous, if diametrically different. On the one hand some of the parties to the contract may stickle and cavil about the State's action, and arguing, 'This was not in the bond', they may refuse accordingly to be obliged. On the other hand, the contractual association, acting as a whole, or at any rate by a majority decision, may hold that its own will and deed is final, whatever that will and deed may be, provided only that the form of the constitution is duly observed: indeed, since an act of the association, or that of a defined and prescribed majority within it, can alter the form of the constitution, the will and deed of the association may even be held to be unconditionally final, without proviso or qualification. In that case the members of the association will be obliged by the necessity of obeying mere will, as such and apart from its content. These are the difficulties which ensue from a simple reliance on the notion of contract. But there are also difficulties which ensue from a simple reliance on the notion of justice. If obligation be regarded as simply a matter of justice and of obedience to the dictates of justice, then it will follow that a governing authority which wills and enforces those dictates will necessarily oblige us, even if it is a pure autocracy, in no way based on consent, and therefore destitute of any contractual element. This may seem an abstraction, or even a fantasy. In effect it *is* a fantasy; for if justice is a *common* conviction, then it and autocracy can never be yoke-fellows. But it is a fantasy which haunted the benevolent despots of the eighteenth century, and has haunted in our time the leaders and dictators of the twentieth century. Nor has it haunted them only. It has also been accepted by many thinkers, who have believed that the cause of impartial justice is best served by the mind of the 'one best man' who is lifted above all passion.[1]

The problem before us is that of reconciling the principle of a common will, expressed in the notion of contract, with the principle of a common rule, expressed in the notion of justice.

[1] The idea of the 'philosophic' or 'scientific' autocrat is an idea both of Platonists and Comtists. It was also an idea cherished by Hegelians, in the days of Prussian monarchy, when they preached that the unity of the State must be incorporated 'in an actual individual' lifted above sectional interests and conflicts and holding an impartial balance.

In other words we have to combine democratic might with sovereign right: to unite the volume and dynamic power of a common will with the stability and control of a common rule of reason. It is an easy escape from this problem, illustrated in the writings of Rousseau,[1] to proclaim the sovereign right of democratic might. But it is an escape, and not a solution: not a reconciliation of both of the terms, but an elimination of one at the expense of the other; not the joint dominion of a common will and a common rule, but the single dominion of a will which, because it is merely will, is ultimately nothing but might.[2] Is it also an escape, or is it a solution, if we start at the other end: if instead of attaching sovereign right to democratic might, we seek to attach democratic might to sovereign right? Does that too eliminate one of the terms at the expense of the other, or does it succeed in reconciling both? At any rate there is a case for inquiry. We may therefore inquire where the argument leads if instead of beginning—and ending—in will, we begin with the 'rule of right' or common rule of reason. On this basis we take our start from the idea of a right order of relations postulated and given by reason and therefore prior to will; and we seek to discover how this sovereign right proceeding from reason can acquire democratic might, by becoming the common conviction of the whole of a community, and by inspiring and enlisting in support of itself the common will of the members of that community.

The inquiry involves three stages. In the first of these stages we are confronted by the idea of a sovereign right, as the ultimate source of obligation—the idea of justice the orderer, 'joining' and 'fitting together' both the positions of persons and the principles on which those positions are assigned,[3] and thus pro-

---

[1] It is true that on Rousseau's own theory the common will, or *volonté générale*, is not the quantitative will of the community, but a qualitative will for the common good, which may be the will of one man in the office of 'legislator'. But it is also true that in practice he identifies the *volonté générale* with the will of a primary assembly voting freely and at discretion in the absence of party organization or any other similar system of order.

[2] 'Wo der Wille den Willen normirt, ergibt sich mit logischer Notwendigkeit immer nur der Begriff der Macht': 'where will is conceived as controlling will, the result, by a logical necessity, is always nothing but the conception of might'. In other words, a clash of wills can only be solved by the victory of the more powerful will, and in that way a doctrine of will ends in a doctrine of power. (Gierke, *Johannes Althusius*, p. 318.)

[3] *Supra*, Book IV, § 5.

ducing what we have called a right order of human relations. This was the fundamental meaning of the theory of Natural Law, as that idea was expressed by the Stoics and the Roman lawyers in antiquity, by the Fathers and the schoolmen of early and medieval Christianity, and by thinkers of the secular school of Natural Law in the seventeenth and eighteenth centuries. But there was an imperfection and an abstraction in the theory of Natural Law, particularly in the last of its phases. We cannot assume, as the thinkers of the seventeenth and eighteenth centuries did, that there are truths of a 'natural', or ideally rational, justice to be discovered and deduced by the reason of the solitary jurist, as there are truths of geometry to be discovered and deduced by the reason of the solitary geometrician. Still less can we assume that, even if they could be discovered and deduced by such a process, they would remain thenceforth unchangeably true. There are differences between geometry and justice. For one thing, geometry is concerned with impersonal space, which does not think; justice is a matter of a personal system of human relations, and therefore of living persons who themselves think about those relations, whose thought constitutes that system, and who, in a word, think justice into existence. It is not the solitary jurist who discovers the truths of justice: it is the whole body of persons who stand in relation with one another and think out together the problems of the right order of their relations. For another thing, geometry is concerned with a space which is constant and invariable, and it remains accordingly constant itself; justice is a matter of human relations which change and grow in the process of time with changes of social thought, and it adjusts itself and changes accordingly. There is, indeed, a constancy of justice; but justice has also life and growth, and therefore mutability. It is an 'ever-fixed mark'; but it is also an ever-flowing stream.

This brings us to the next and second stage of our inquiry. If justice, as a matter of human relations, involves a society of persons thinking about their relations and thinking into existence a right order of those relations; if again, as such a matter, it also involves the possibility of a change of relations, and therefore of thought about relations, and therefore of the scheme of right order created for them by thought; it follows that we can add to the idea of sovereign right, which confronted us in the first stage, the idea of creative general thought, busy in a constant process of disengaging this sovereign right from the multitude of relations and the constant flux of their change. Justice is made by the general thought of all the members of a community engaged in relations with one another; or, more exactly, it is always in process of being made by that general thought, and it is therefore always in a state of 'becoming' or development. The general thought of the community is the maker of sovereign right, and it is always making it afresh. We can see an example of its making and remaking if we take the instance of marriage, or the relation of husband and wife. Thought has created and sustains the idea that permanent monogamy is the justice or right order of that relation. It has been a long work: it is a work which is still being changed and modified. Greater equality has been introduced into the relation by the reduction of the power of the husband: greater liberty is being sought (sometimes with too little regard to the principle of co-operation, in the rearing and training of children, which is also a principle of marriage) by the extension of facilities for divorce in the event of grave disagreement. At point after point, and in stage after stage, the general thought of the community, which originally applied the idea of justice to the relation of the sexes, is constantly applying it afresh, and therefore constantly changing the general opinion about the right order of that relation and, with it, the law which reflects and declares that opinion.

The third and last stage of our inquiry confronts us with the question, 'What is the product that issues from this general thought of the community, and what is the form and shape in which it is distilled and expressed?' Gierke, as we have noticed,[1] seeks to express the product in the term 'common conviction' (*Gesammtüberzeugung*). Rousseau sought to express it in the term 'general will' (*volonté générale*). Both of these terms are shorthand, and either of them is the half rather than the whole of the matter. Perhaps we shall answer our question best if we put the two terms together, and if, in the course of doing so, we also seek to indicate, more precisely than has yet been done, both the area in which the general thought of the community acts and the time-span of its action. On that basis we may say that, as the result of a *long-time* process of thought, moving in the

[1] *Supra*, Book IV, § 6.

area of Society and being therefore a process of *social* thought, there emerges a *common conviction which is also a general will* about a right order of human relations and the obligatory nature of that order.

The *long-time* character of the process of thought is a fact of primary importance. Burke stated this fact in memorable words, 'Man is a most unwise, and a most wise being. The individual is foolish. The multitude, for the moment, is foolish, when they act without deliberation. But the species is wise, and when time is given to it, as a species, it almost always acts right.'[1] If we substitute 'Society' for 'species' the statement of Burke is the expression of an indubitable truth. The benefit of time is needed for the production of the common conviction which is also a general will. It was the error of Rousseau to ascribe to the meeting of the multitude for the moment a *volonté générale* which can only be the fruit of slow time and of something more than the multitude.

That something more (and here we come to another fact of primary importance) is Society, national Society, as defined and explained in the beginning of the whole argument;[2] and it is accordingly *social thought*, in the strict sense of the word, which produces, by its working in time, a common conviction and will. The area in which the general thought of the community acts is essentially and primarily the area of Society, and not the area of the State. This is not to say that such thought is not operative in the area of the State: it is only to say that it operates there, as it were, at a remove, and by a translation or transference from its original area. The State, as such, is the area of electoral votes, parliamentary statutes, executive orders and regulations, judicial decisions, and all the formal declarations which constitute, in one way or another, the scheme of positive law. All these declarations register social thought. But that thought is prior to the registration; and it acts, in its original motion, elsewhere than in the area of registration. It acts in and through the social organs which precipitate social thought and conduct with one another the discussion of what they precipitate: it acts in and through the churches, the clubs and societies and parties (not in

---

[1] Burke's speech of 7 May 1782 on Representation (in the Rivington edition of his works, vol. x, p. 97).

[2] *Supra*, Book I, § 2; see also Book II, § 4.

themselves a part of the State but rather a part of Society, however much they impinge on the State),[1] the professional and occupational groupings, the newspaper and pamphlet and book, and all the other organs for the ventilation and the comparison of different social ideas. We can thus see social thought in all its forms and with all its organs, which correspond to the multiplicity of Society,[2] proceeding by the way of discussion, which is its great and sovereign way; and we may even begin to see in advance the emergence of the idea of democracy, which is a system of 'government by discussion', and therefore a transference of the method of social thought into the area of the State and government.

Proceeding thus by way of discussion, social thought produces a mental output (and here we come to still another fact of primary importance) which is partly a conviction of the value, and partly a will for the establishment, of a general order of social relations and the general rules of that order. It would be an error to concentrate attention exclusively on the element of will in this output: it would also be an error, and a still greater error, if, having so concentrated our attention and isolated the element of will, we ascribed that element exclusively to the State. The will is conviction as well as will, and conviction before it is will; and the primary area of its residence is Society, even if its effects are transferred and translated into the State and the State's legal system.

But the term 'general will' has come to be used in political theory as a shorthand term for that common conviction-and-will which, arising in the area of Society, transmits its action and operation into the area of the State. There is some reason for the use of the term; but there are also reasons for using the term with caution, and with reservations and qualifications. In favour of its use we may argue that a national Society, as such, and as distinct from the State, develops in the course of its common life a growing general conviction about the just and proper order of the relations between its members, and a growing general will for the establishment and maintenance of that order as its own way of life and type of civilization. This has been the line of development of French national society; it has equally been the line of development of British national society.

[1] *Infra*, § 4 of this Book. [2] *Supra*, Book II, § 1.

Upon this basis we may go on to argue that the national State, as the legal incorporation of a national Society, should acknowledge this general will at each stage, in the form and expression which it has attained at that stage, as the ultimate standard of its action. Thus conceived, the general will, as a contemporary thinker has said, is 'the standard by which political willing should be guided': in other words it is the ultimate and permanent will (if we can rightly use the word 'will') by which the immediate and day-to-day will of the governing authority ought to be determined, as it also is the ultimate will (if again we can rightly use that word) by which the will of the citizen ought to be obliged.

But though we may thus speak of the general will as the standard by which political willing should be guided, alike in the governing authority and in the citizen, we must also remember the qualifications to which any use of that term is subject. The first qualification is a matter of the *mental character* of this will. The will is a conviction as well as a will, and a conviction before it becomes a will. The essential and primary thing about it, as Gierke has said,[1] is a conviction that something already is, and that a standard exists and is there, rather than a will that something shall be. From this point of view we may also say, as Rousseau strove to say, that the essence of the general will is not the persons or 'subjects' willing, but the things or 'objects' of their will: the things or 'objects' which are primarily a content of common conviction, and which only become a content of common or general will because they are already a content of common or general conviction. The second qualification, which ensues upon the first, is a matter of the factor of *time*. So far as the general will is will, it is not an act of willing at a given moment of time: it is a permanent trend of will, which is growing as well as permanent, and which, we may even say in a paradox, shows its permanence most clearly in its capacity of growth. The third and last qualification, which ensues in turn on the second, is a matter of the *area* or residence of this general will, thus operative through time as a permanent and yet growing trend of the mind in the members of a community. The area or place of residence is not the legally organized State. The 'general will' is not political willing, and its home is not the political sphere. It belongs to the social area: it is a function of Society.

[1] *Supra*, Book IV, § 6.

The qualifications are so numerous that we may well come to the conclusion that the general will is almost of the nature of a will-o'-the-wisp. The truth which that term is designed to express may be stated more simply in other terms. Instead of committing ourselves to the notion of the primary or supreme sovereignty of the general will, we may prefer to speak of the primacy of a socially created and socially developed conception of justice—that last and most majestic sovereign which stands behind and above the 'sovereign' constitution, as that, in its turn, stands behind and above the 'sovereignty' of the parliament of the State. Upon this basis we may proceed to enumerate a series of propositions.

1. The supreme sovereign which stands in the background of any politically organized community is justice: justice in the sense of that right order of human relations which gives to the greatest possible number of persons the greatest possible opportunity for the highest possible development of all the capacities of their personality.

2. Justice is mediated by, or comes through the medium of, a process of social thought, which in the course of its operation produces a body of common conviction about the dictates of justice, backed by a common will or purpose of acting in the strength and under the guidance of that conviction.

3. This product of social thought is mediated in turn by the State, in the sense that it undergoes a process of being declared and enforced by a legal association contractually formed for that object by the creation of a constitution, and acting henceforth in virtue and under the rules of that constitution.

4. The citizen is obliged, at the end of the whole process, to obey the law so declared and enforced by the State, for the immediate reason that the State is based on his own contractual act, but for the ultimate reason that the State expresses the product of social thought which itself is the expression of justice.

A number of problems are raised by, or involved in, these propositions. (*a*) The third of them raises the problem of the proper method of the mediation of social thought by the State;

it leads us to inquire whether the democratic form of constitution and the democratic method of government are the most correspondent, in their own nature, to the form and method of social thought, and the most likely, in their results, to translate the product of such thought into a clear and effective expression. (*b*) The first proposition, and especially its first clause, confronts us once more with the problem of sovereignty: it leads us beyond what has already been said about that problem at an earlier stage,[1] and involves us in an inquiry into the ultimate nature and final residence of sovereign authority. (*c*) The fourth proposition, in its final clause, suggests, or implies, one of the gravest (if not the gravest) of all political problems. Granted that the citizen is obliged to obey the law of the State because the State expresses in its law the product of social thought, which itself is the expression of justice, does it follow that he is obliged to obey when that reason is not present? If and so far as the State does *not* express in its law the product of social thought, but expresses something different from, or even contrary to, that product, does obligation then to that extent cease; is disobedience then justified; and, if it is, may it even be carried to the length of resistance? This is the problem of the limits of political obligation: it is also, at its furthest reach, the problem of the right, or duty, of resistance. It is a problem as old as the *Antigone* of Sophocles, and indeed as old as the State itself; but it is always assuming new shapes, and if in the past a Creon or a Caesar was challenged in the name of religious conviction, today democracy itself is challenged in the name of the economic creed of communism.[2]

§ 4. POLITICAL OBLIGATION AND THE DEMOCRATIC SYSTEM

If the State can be regarded as mediating social thought about justice to its members, and as expressing in its law the product of such thought, we may draw from that premiss the conclusion that the State should itself correspond, in its own

[1] *Supra*, Book II, § 5.

[2] The three problems here suggested—that of the relation between political obligation and democracy, that of the relation between political obligation and sovereignty, and that of the limits of political obligation and the right or duty of resistance—are discussed in the three following sections in the order in which they have just been stated.

nature and operation, to the process of social thought which it
mediates, and should thus be a broad open channel for the
flow of the product which it expresses. The process of social
thought is a process in which all the members of Society can
freely share, and to which they can all contribute freely. It follows that, if there is to be correspondence and a broad open
flow, the process of the activity of the State should also be a process in which all its members can freely share and to which they
can all freely contribute. We may argue that this demand is
satisfied, and satisfied only, by the democratic State. Indeed we
may argue that it is satisfied doubly by the democratic State;
first in the form of its constitution and the way of its coming into
being, and next in its method of government and the way of its
operation.

In their actual coming into being, as has already been noted,[1]
States are historical products of very various patterns, due to a
variety of historical causes. But the question before us here is not
a question of the far-off origins, back in the mists of time, of the
States we know today in their changed and developed form as
the modern States of our Western world. It is a question of the
basis and *raison d'être* of the modern State *as we know it now*,
in the form which it has now assumed in the world in which
we now live. What set of ideas, and what motions of the mind,
have formed and brought into being the State we now know in
the form it now has? Some answer to that question has already
been given; and it is only necessary to summarize briefly the
heads of the answer. A national Society, in the course of a process of social thought, creates and sustains an idea and ideal of a
right of order relations between its members: an idea and ideal of
justice. But it cannot attain its ends, or turn the idea into fact
and the ideal into reality, without an organized system for the
declaration and enforcement of the dictates of justice. We must
therefore conceive the society as making itself, or 'constituting'
itself, an organized system *for this purpose*, or, in other words, as
forming itself into a *legal* association or State, while still continuing to exist and act as a Society, and still continuing, as
such, to maintain and develop that process of social thought
which is continually fertilizing the idea and ideal of justice.
This act of the 'constitution' of a State by the members of a

[1] *Supra,* § 1 of this Book.

national Society results, and expresses itself, in a 'constitution' in another and further sense of the word: the Constitution with a capital C; the articles of association (both written and unwritten) which warrant, authorize, and control the actions and the organs of the legal association. We may say that this Constitution, or set of articles of association, is of the nature of a contract, which we may call the political contract; and in that sense, as has already been noted,[1] we may say that the State has a contractual basis. We may also say that the constitution of a State by a national Society and by all the members of that Society, or in other words by the people, is the first stage and the foundation of the democratic method of government. In it, and by it, the people have given themselves the basis of political action by a first democratic act of creation. Will they not then go on, still following the same path, and give themselves a method of government and a way of permanent operation in which they are equally active?[2]

To find a firm basis for a theory of the democratic method of government in the modern State, we must go back to the process of social thought from which the State issues and to which it always remains attached. The process of social thought is naturally and necessarily a process of discussion. Ideas emerge here and there: each emergent idea becomes a magnet which attracts a clustering group of adherents: the various ideas, and the various groups they attract, must either engage in a war of competition with one another to achieve a victory, or attempt a method of composition which fuses and blends them together in peace. The military idea of a war of competition between ideas is prominent in the philosophy of Hegel. His dialectical idealism (which Marx turned upside down, or as he preferred

---

[1] *Supra*, § 1 of·this Book.

[2] To avoid misunderstanding, and to make the argument clear, it should be noted that the argument here advanced is simply, and only, an argument that the modern State is the product of a shift of ideas, which may be traced in England from the beginning of the Civil War to the Revolution of 1688 and the Hanoverian settlement; which showed itself in North America and France in the last quarter of the eighteenth century; and which spread over Western Europe, South America, and the countries of the British Commonwealth, during the nineteenth century. Whatever the State may hitherto have been, it became, with this shifting of ideas, a specifically legal association, created by the sentiment and action of the national Society, and based on a constitution which is of the nature of a contract. It would be a folly to argue that the State (in the sense of all States, at all times) is based upon contract. It is not a folly to argue that the modern State, in all the parts of the world which have been stirred by this shift of ideas, is so based.

to say 'right side up again', in his dialectical materialism) assumes a war of ideas, in which 'one shrewd thought devours another': a battle of thesis and antithesis, in which each side fights for itself. But even Hegel's military conception of the war of ideas ends in a sort of composition between thesis and antithesis; or, more exactly, it ends by producing the synthesis of a higher truth in which the partial truths of the thesis and the anti-thesis are abolished and transcended. It has thus, after all, some approach to the principle of discussion; but Hegel's theory of discussion is rather that of a logical process inside a solitary mind (even if that mind be conceived as the 'objective' mind of a whole Society) than that of a social process among and between a number of minds. The theory which is implied in Aristotle's *Politics*[1] is much nearer to the idea of such a social process. Instead of assuming a war of two conflicting ideas, to be ended by a transcendent and triumphant synthesis, he assumes a plurality of social ideas, to be fused and blended to-gether in a 'scheme of composition'. Just as it takes all sorts of men to make a world, so it takes all sorts of ideas to produce a 'catholic' and all-round view. Aristotle applies this conception to the field of culture and the province of artistic judgement: here, he says, 'some appreciate one aspect, and some another, but all together appreciate all'. But he also applies it generally to the whole field of social thought; and he applies it, in particular, to matters of political judgement. The Many, he holds, 'when they meet together', and put their minds fairly to one another, can achieve a composition of ideas which gives their judgement a general validity.

If we follow the guidance of Aristotle, we shall say that social thought proceeds by the way of a plurality of ideas, by the way of debate and discussion between the different ideas, 'when they meet together' and come into contact with one another, and by the way of a composition of ideas attained through such debate and discussion. We shall also say that this social way must also be, and also is, the political way: in other words it must also be, and also is, the method of the State's government and the way of the State's operation. This is not only because the State should be true to the Society from which it comes,

[1] Book III, c. xi. The reader is referred to the writer's translation of the *Politics*, and to the notes appended to that translation.

and on which it continues to rest: it is also because the way of Society (the way of plurality of ideas, debate among them, and composition of them) is right in itself and universally right— right for Society, right for the State, and right wherever men are gathered together and have to act together. The one way to get at practical truth, the right thing to do, the straight line of action, is, in any form of group, the way of thinking things over together and talking them over together, with a view to finding some composition of the different threads of thought. It is the way of the Friends, when they seek what they call 'the sense of the meeting'. It is the way of democracy, which is not a solution, but a way of seeking solutions—not a form of State devoted to this or that particular end (whether private enterprise or public management), but a form of State devoted, whatever its end may be, to a single means and method of determining that end. The core of democracy is choice, and not something chosen; choice among a number of ideas, and choice, too, of the scheme on which those ideas are eventually composed. Democracy is incompatible with any form of one-idea State, because its essence is hospitality to a plurality of ideas, and because its method (which is also its essence) consists in holding together a number of different ideas with a view to comparison and composition of their difference. The democratic criticism of the one-idea State is not a criticism of its object (which may also be the object of the democratic State, or at any rate part of its object): it is a criticism of its whole process of life.

This last phrase, 'process of life', suggests a further consideration which is of vital importance in the theory of democracy. One of the archbishops of Canterbury, Frederic Temple, once said that there were two schools of political thought: one which held that politics existed for the production of a result, or the *ergon* school; and another which held that politics was valuable in itself as a process of activity, or the *energeia* school. The school of production judged politics by the results which it produced: the school of process preferred to judge on a different basis, and it was content, and more than content, if the process of the political life of a community elicited and enlisted for its operation the minds and wills of its members, thus aiding, and indeed in its measure constituting, the development of their capacities as persons. The distinction here suggested, which goes back to Aristotle,[1] is a just and pregnant distinction. We are naturally apt to think of politics in terms of making, rather than of doing, as if our political activity were directed wholly to achieving an object outside itself (and not immanent in itself), such as a scheme of legal order, or an adjustment of economic relations, or some other similar structure. But this is not the whole of the matter, or even the greater part. It is certainly true, and indeed it has already been urged in the course of our argument, that the State as a legal association must necessarily produce a result: it must produce a scheme of declared and enforced law which gives expression to the idea of justice. But there are two other things which must also be borne in mind. First, the ultimate purpose behind justice, and therefore behind law, is the development of the capacities of human personality in as many persons as possible to the greatest possible extent. That is the final result which the State must produce—or rather help to produce; for the result produces itself in each person through his own internal activity, even if it needs help, in the way of removal of hindrances and the offering of opportunities, in order to produce itself fully. This first reflection naturally leads to the second. If we hold that behind and beyond the *production* of law by the State there is a *process* of personal activity and personal development in its members, we may go on to say that the production should itself be drawn into the process. In other words we may argue that the productive effort of the State, the effort of declaring and enforcing a system of law, should also be a process in which, and through which, each member of the State is spurred into personal development, because he is drawn into free participation in one of the greatest of all our secular human activities.

These reflections suggest a second main justification of the democratic system. Not only is it justified, as we saw at the beginning of this section, by the fact that it makes the State true to the method of general discussion and composition of ideas which is the method of Society; it is also justified, as we now see, by the fact that it makes the State, in the very process of its own

---

[1] The distinction between production (*poiesis*) and action (*praxis*) is discussed in the *Ethics*, Book VI, cc. iii–v. The gist of the argument is that 'Production has an end other than itself: action cannot have; for good action is itself its own end.'

operation, true to the fundamental purpose which lies behind its operation, the purpose of the development in action of the capacities of personality. This is the justification urged by John Stuart Mill in his *Considerations on Representative Government*. Arguing, in his second chapter, that 'government is at once a great influence acting on the human mind [according as it elicits, or fails to elicit, its energy] and a set of organized arrangements for public business' [that is to say, for producing the result of a scheme of legal order], he lays stress on the sovereign importance of the first of these two aspects. He has a strong sense of the 'practical discipline which the character obtains' from the demand made upon the citizen to exercise some function; he has an equally strong sense of the intellectual discipline which is also obtained by the mind, when the citizen is required to rise above private partialities, and to apply principles and maxims which are based on the idea of the common good.[1]

If we accept the democratic system as justified, we must also accept the party-system. Party is a great and necessary factor in any method of general discussion; and that is its permanent justification. A party begins as a set of connected and coherent ideas (an 'ism', as when we talk of socialism or liberalism or conservatism), emerging and acting in the area of social discussion. It becomes, in the process of its development, a body of persons united in entertaining such a set of connected and coherent ideas: a body of persons, forming a social group in the area of Society, who discuss their common ideas among themselves, formulate them in a policy or programme, and vindicate that programme in discussion against other similar groups in the same social area. Finally, and in the culmination of its development, a party becomes an organization, with its own accredited leaders, for the purpose of carrying a programme into effect by securing for it a majority of the votes of the political electorate, and by then proceeding to turn its leaders into the political government. In all these stages, but particularly in the last, party serves as a mediator between social thought and political action; and this is a reason why it is a great and necessary factor in the democratic system. We may accordingly say

---

[1] In the same sense General Smuts, in a Sidgwick Memorial Lecture on Democracy delivered at Cambridge in 1929, urged that 'the end of government is not merely good government, but the education of the people in good government'.

that a party may be defined as a social formation which (1) serves as a social reservoir for the collection of a set of connected ideas from the area of voluntary society, and also (2) serves as a political conduit or channel by which the ideas collected from that area flow from their social reservoir into the system of the State and turn the wheels of political machinery in that system. So conceived, party performs the service of enabling society to run into the State, and thus of keeping the action of the State constantly and wholesomely responsive to the play of social thought. This is a reason why we may deprecate any legal regulation of party, unless such regulation is made imperative by serious flaws and defects in the working of the party system. The effect of legal regulation is a transmutation of party, which ceases, when such regulation is applied, to be an informal organ of society freely expressing a trend of social thought, and freely seeking to transmit that trend into the area of political action, and tends to become instead a formal and legal organ of the legal association. To regulate by law the meetings of party organizations, and to prescribe their methods of nominating candidates, may be, on occasion, a 'cruel necessity'; but it is, in itself, a grave alteration of the proper relation between the State and party. Regulation should only enter, as a desperate remedy, when the general system of parties, in the act of carrying over a current of social thought into the area of the State, becomes clogged by the manipulation of party managers, and when the State, as a liberating agency, is thus called on to clear the channel of transmission by providing that the meetings and actions of parties shall be free from any such clog.

But there are other and larger conditions which party must also satisfy if it is to perform its proper function in a system of democracy. In the first place, there must necessarily be a plurality of parties. A one-party State is a one-idea State: it is a falsification, and not a mediation, of social thought and of that general process of social discussion which must in its nature include a number of different ideas. On the ground of principle, and looking at party as a set of ideas held by a body of persons within the process and for the purpose of social discussion, we must demand at least two parties as the necessary condition of any discussion; and we may demand even more than two, or in other words a multiple system of parties, if that is the proper expression of the varieties actually present in the process of social thought and discussion. On the ground of practice, and looking at party, in its other aspect, as an organization for the purpose of creating and supporting a government—and also an opposition which will criticize the government and keep it effective—we may welcome a two-party system; but equally we may deprecate a multiple-party system, on the ground that it turns the creation of a government into a matter of temporary and interested coalitions, as it also makes the support of a government uncertain and incoherent. Considerations of principle and considerations of practice are thus agreed in postulating more than *one* party; but they are not agreed when the issue is one of more than *two*, for then considerations of principle may be in favour of more than two, and considerations of practice will be in favour of two and two only. We can only say that, in such a case, considerations of principle may have to overbear considerations of practice, and that when social thought develops more than two trends of opinion it will be necessary to have more than two parties, even though the presence of more than two parties may involve coalitions and shortlived governments. It would be a pity if *raison de gouvernement* were allowed to have the last word, and if the whole rational process of social thought and social discussion were subordinated to that *raison*.

A second condition which party must satisfy if it is to perform its proper function in a system of democracy is that each party should be a set of *general* ideas, backed by a *general* body of persons. A party must not be a set of particular ideas about a single interest, backed by a particular body of persons connected with that interest. This is what Burke had in mind when he defined a party as a body of men united for promoting the *national* interest upon some particular principle: he meant that all parties alike should be concerned with the same general object, and that each should be partial or partisan only in its particular angle of approach. It is true, indeed, that a one-interest party may sometimes express a trend of social thought which is broad enough, and unselfish enough, to warrant such a form of expression; an abolitionist party, or even a prohibitionist party, may be held to be of this order. On the other hand, a one-interest party, composed of a one-interested body of persons, cannot be in its nature an organization for the purpose of creating and supporting a government, or even for the purpose of helping to create and support a government; and a party cannot perform its full function, as a channel of mediation between Society and the State, unless it is able, at the very least, to *help* in the creation and the support of a government.

§ 5. POLITICAL OBLIGATION AND ITS RELATION TO SOVEREIGNTY

WHEN we survey the whole process which begins with the formation of social thought and ends in its translation into terms of political action, we find ourselves confronted by a problem which has already arisen in other connexions, but which arises more particularly here, in connexion with the theme of political obligation. This is the problem of sovereignty. Where, and at what point of the process, is the last word said to the citizen— the word of words which carries a final and conclusive authority —about what he is bound and obliged to do as a member of the State? And who, or what, says that last word? We may begin our answer by seeking to recapitulate the preliminary conclusions already attained in previous stages of the argument.

At the first of these stages,[1] when our view was still confined within the limits and the four walls of the legal association, and did not, as yet, embrace the wide area of Society and social thought beyond those limits and outside those walls, we attempted a preliminary view of sovereignty in purely political terms. On that view sovereignty was regarded as being, in its nature, the power of final adjustment within the association; the authority of last resort in the State, which said the last word within the State. Sovereignty upon this view, is not public power, or State-authority, as a whole, in the whole of its range: it is the summit, and not the mountain; it is the topmost rung of public power or State-authority, where the final word is pronounced on legal issues which get so far as to rise to that rung. If that is the nature of sovereignty, conceived in purely political terms and viewed purely as an attribute of the State, the place of its residence must be regarded as being the summit of the structure of public power and State-authority. That summit, at its highest peak, is the constitution itself, and the constitution is

[1] *Supra*, Book II, § 5.

thus the ultimate or normative sovereign; but under the constitution, and subject to the constitution, we may ascribe the possession of immediate or active sovereignty to the legislature, and we may accordingly say that the legislature is the immediate sovereign when, and in so far as, it acts by the norm of the constitution.

At a second stage of the argument,[1] though our view was still confined within the limits of the State, we made a fresh step, and added a new consideration, which affected further our view of the nature of the immediate sovereignty of the law-making body. The gist of this new consideration was that 'law-making', as it is called, is not the creating of law in the sense of issuing a command to the community, in the imperative mood, about what *shall* or *shall not* henceforth be done, but is rather the declaring of law in the sense of issuing a statement to the community, in the indicative mood, about what already *is* the standard of will and action accepted by common conviction. It follows from this view that the immediate sovereignty of the legislature, acting within the limits and the four walls of the State, is not only subject to the ultimate normative sovereignty of the constitution: it is also subject, in itself and by its own very nature, to the limit imposed by the fact that it is an organ for the expression and declaration of common conviction. This common conviction, resident in the members of the legal association, is a conviction about the idea of justice: a conviction about the dictates or deductions which issue from that idea: a conviction that justice is the value of values, and that standards of will and action flow from this supreme value. We may accordingly say that the immediate sovereignty of the law-making body is inherently and by its own nature subject to common conviction, and thereby to the content of common conviction, and thereby to the idea of justice, and thereby to the standards of common life that issue from that idea.

Finally, at a third stage of the argument,[2] we went still farther, and going beyond the limits and the four walls of the State we took into our view the area of Society and social thought which lies outside those limits. Here we arrived at the conclusion that the idea of justice had its ultimate origin in Society, and originally sprang from a process of social thought

[1] *Supra*, Book IV, § 6.   [2] *Supra*, § 3 of this Book.

proceeding by way of social discussion. We thus advanced beyond the conclusion of the previous argument. We moved from the view that a common conviction about the dictates of justice, resident in and entertained by the members of the legal association of the State, was the basis of law and the inspiration of the law-making body; and we rose to the higher and broader view that social thought about the nature of a just order of human relations, moving in the area of Society and developed by social discussion, was the basis of the existence and the inspiration of the activity of the whole legal association. We thus gave justice, as it were, a new bodily habitation, by arguing that it resided not only in the common conviction of the legal association as such, but also, over and above that, in the social thought of national Society as such, standing behind and rising above the walls of the legal association. We also gave this justice, with its new bodily habitation, a new and final authority as the ultimate sovereign of sovereigns: we made it the extra-legal or supra-legal sovereign, sovereign even over the constitution, which is an instrument it has created, and sovereign therefore over the legislature, which is an instrument of that instrument.

We may now seek to draw together the conclusions attained at these different stages. When they are thus drawn together, they may be enunciated in two propositions, which have already been implied in the previous course of the argument.

(*a*) Prior in order of thought to the State and to the form (or forms) of its sovereignty, though the State in its early condition of a power-organization may itself have been prior in order of time, there is the idea of justice and of the sovereignty of justice, resident in the social thought of the members of a national society about the right order of their relations. There are those who would seek to separate the idea thus resident in thought from the thought in which it resides; who would argue that the idea of justice is one matter, and the seat of its residence another; and who, having made that distinction, would proceed to contend that it is social thought, under the name and style of 'the general will', which ought to be deemed to be sovereign, rather than the idea of justice. But we cannot make a distinction between the sovereignty of the idea of justice and the sovereignty of social thought. The two are inseparable. There is no justice but social thinking makes it so; and conversely there is no social thinking about the order of human relations but issues in the idea of justice. We may therefore speak of the supreme sovereignty[1] of a socially created idea of justice, which is brought into being by social thought and the process of social discussion. Upon that basis we may make an admission, which is also, at the same time, a contention. There was, after all, a great measure of truth in the ideas of the votaries of natural law. When they urged the cause of the supreme sovereignty of natural law, and even went to the length of making null and void all laws and acts of government which were contrary to such law, they were groping after the idea of the sovereignty of the idea of justice. The one thing they failed to grasp was the fact of the social creation of the sovereign they sought to enthrone.

(*b*) When the State has emerged into action as a legal association, for the purpose of realizing the idea of justice by translating it into a system of declared and enforced law, it is, in the last resort, subject to the supreme sovereignty of the idea of justice by which it was created and by which it is sustained. But considered in itself and by itself it develops within its own limits two other sovereigns or forms of sovereignty. They are both of them legal sovereigns or forms of sovereignty; and as such they are both distinct, and different in kind, from the social sovereignty, as it may be called, of the idea of justice. The first of these legal forms of sovereignty is the ultimate sovereignty of the constitution which is the creative act, as the idea of justice is the creative spirit, that brings the State into being and controls its subsequent action. The second legal form of sovereignty is the immediate sovereignty of the law-making body; the body of persons, legally subject to the constitution, and inherently limited by its own nature as an organ appointed for the purpose of declaring common conviction, which is concerned with the issue, and has a general control of the enforcement, of the rules of positive law. Within the State, and looking only at the State, we see only these two sovereigns. If we go beyond the State, and take into account the play of Society and social thought out-

---

[1] There is some want of logic, and of consistency, in using the term 'sovereignty' in any other sphere than the legal. It is properly, as has already been noted (at the end of Book II, § 5), a term of legal art, belonging only to the legal sphere. But there is a point in insisting that the last word in the legal sphere is not the last word in life, and that there is something above legal sovereignty.

side the State, we see a third sovereign beyond these two; a sovereign idea of justice, moving and finding expression in the play of social thought, which is not a sovereign in any legal sense, and yet is the standard and final control of all legal action and legal sovereignty.

It is tempting to reduce the three sovereigns to one, and instead of being content with a hierarchy to seek a single and simple unity. It is particularly tempting to seek such unity in a personal source of will, whether the source be a single person or some one body of persons. We are naturally apt to think in terms of a Sovereign Will or a Sovereign Sanhedrim of Wills. But we cannot thus deify will, whosesoever the will may be; whether the will of a decreeing person or a body of such persons, on the ground that they are creators of the rules by which we live, or the will of the People itself, on the ground that it is the super-creator which limits, and may even control, the decreeing person or body. If we make will final, we really make force final, for a will which prevails just because it is will, without regard to the object it wills or the standard by which it wills, is a force.[1] We may allow, indeed, as we have already done,[2] that a law which has issued from the will and action of a law-making body, acting as the organ of common conviction, is legally valid and finally conclusive within the area of the State, provided that it is duly enacted according to the rules of the constitution which are the final arbiter of legal validity; and in that sense, and to that extent, we may admit the sovereignty of legislative will and action. But we must also allow that a law which has issued from that source, even if it possesses legal validity and imposes legal obligation, will not possess moral value or impose moral obligation unless it squares with the idea of justice, as formed in and expressed by the movement of social thought. That still leaves us with a hierarchy rather than the simple unity of a single personal factor. In the sphere of social and political theory, which is bound to embrace both Society and the State, there is no one and only sovereignty of which we can say 'Its will is our peace'. The peace of acquiescence in such a will is denied us by our own nature.

---

[1] *Supra*, § 3 of this Book.
[2] *Supra*, Book IV, § 6, *ad finem*.

§ 6. THE LIMITS OF POLITICAL OBLIGATION AND THE PROBLEM OF RESISTANCE

THE very fact that this problem is presented to us is itself a proof that we cannot enjoy the peace of acquiescence in a final will. It is, in effect, a double problem. The first of the problems is whether there is a sphere of life and conduct in which there is no political obligation. The second is whether political obligation, in the sphere in which it exists (whatever that sphere may be) is absolute, or conditional.

Mill, in his *Essay on Liberty*, assumed the existence of two different spheres of conduct. One sphere or part of the conduct of anyone, he argued, is that which concerns others; and for that he is 'amenable to society'. The other part is that which merely concerns himself; and here 'his independence is, of right, absolute ... and the individual is sovereign'. The assumption made by Mill is open to a double criticism. In the first place, as his critics have urged, he separates the inseparable. The conduct of any man is a single whole: there can be nothing in it that concerns himself only, and does not concern other men: whatever he is, and whatever he does, affects others and therefore concerns them. In the second place, it would also appear that Mill fails to separate the separable. He lumps together, as the phrase 'amenable to society' suggests, both the social and the political: he vindicates the liberty of the individual, in one breath, both against the Mrs. Grundy of social convention and the St. Stephen's of political enactment. We cannot separate two different compartments of individual conduct; but we *can* separate the sphere of Society from that of the State. Because we cannot separate our individual conduct into two different compartments, and because we are bound to regard the whole of our conduct as concerning others no less than ourselves, we have to admit that the whole of our conduct is controllable— *so far as the criterion of its concerning others is the criterion of judgement.* But because we *can* separate the sphere of Society from that of the State; because we are able, and even bound, to regard the one as the sphere of voluntary action, proceeding by the method of free co-operation, and the other as the sphere of uniform and regulated action, based, in the last resort, on the method of compulsory enforcement; we are free to contend that there are some things which are best left to the first of these methods, and others which are best left, and indeed must be left, to the second.

How are we to decide which things belong to the sphere of Society, and which to that of the State? That question has already confronted us, and an answer to it has already been attempted, at an earlier stage of the argument.[1] In general terms, the answer is that since the State acts by the method of compulsory enforcement, the things that belong to it are the things which had better be done under compulsion than not be done at all; and since Society acts by the method of free co-operation, the things that belong to it are the things which, in their nature, must be done freely if they are to be done well and to have any value. If we seek to translate these general terms into detail, we may say that the things (if they may be called things) which are best left to the sphere of Society are the expression of thought and opinion, in matters of the mind; the exercise of the moral virtues, such as, for example, the virtue of temperance; the practice of religion, not only in private profession, but also in public worship and the public propagation of belief; the development of culture, in the sense of a general way of life or type of civilization, and (along with that, and as part of it) the making and changing of social customs, habits, and fashions. But it cannot be said that any of these things belong to Society so wholly and so absolutely that no factor or element in them can ever belong to the State. On the contrary, there may well be factors or elements in each (for instance, even in the expression of thought) which had better belong to the State, and be brought under State-regulation, because they involve the method of compulsory enforcement. There is no fixed category of things which must always and in all cases be left to Society; there is only a fixed principle about the sort of things which it is better *generally* to leave to Society—*exceptis excipiendis*.

This notion of 'exceptions' may appear to be dangerous, and particularly dangerous when it is applied to the expression of thought. We all assume it as an axiom that the expression of thought, opinion, and belief is a matter for free social action, limited only by the decencies of courtesy and consideration for

[1] *Supra*, Book II, § 2.

others. So it is, in the main: but it cannot always be left there. There are elements or factors in the expression of thought which enter the area of the State and are amenable to State-regulation. If an author's expression and publication of his thought and opinion is adjudged by the common conviction of the members of the political community to be a nuisance—that is to say an injury to the health of their minds, as being unclean and obscene, in the same way as an open sewer is an injury to the health of the body—it will be the duty of the State, in the course of declaring and enforcing common conviction, to deal with the nuisance by its own method of compulsory enforcement, and to vindicate the community's claim that it should not be made to suffer injury against the writer's claim that he should be free to express his thought. The issue, if we probe the matter, is not in the last resort an issue between the writer and the State. It is an issue between two parts or sections of the community; between two trends of opinion; between the claim of one part or section to a right of expressing its opinion, and the claim of the other to a right of keeping its own opinion uninjured and undamaged. There is a danger of shock or collision between the two opposite sides; and the State has to act, as it were, in the office of a buffer for the purpose of absorbing the shock. It must diminish the collision by adjusting the conflicting claims; but in doing so it will act as an arbiter, and not as a party in the case.

The issue, however, is far from simple. How can we be sure of the fact that there is a common conviction? And even if we are sure of the fact, a further question arises. Why should the writer be required to obey a conviction which in his view, and possibly also in the view of his profession generally, is mistaken; and why should the claim of others, however numerous, to be free from suffering the supposed nuisance of the expression of his thought overbear his claim to express his thought for what he believes to be the benefit of the public? An answer may be made to these questions which is cogent enough so far as it goes. Within the political community a claim of the members, endorsed by a common conviction formally expressed in law and thereby registered as a fact, has the validity of a right, and a writer is thereby *politically obliged* to respect that right in his expression of his thought. But there is an answer to this answer.

The writer whose works are challenged on this ground may plead that there is something higher than political obligation: that his final obedience is due to the demand of that something higher, the cause of beauty or the cause of truth; and that political obligation accordingly ceases when it is contrary to that demand. This plea, in effect, is a plea that political obligation is conditional, and not absolute; due under certain conditions, when it does not clash with a higher demand, but not due under all.

We are thus confronted with the second of the problems raised at the beginning of this inquiry. Is political obligation, within its sphere, an absolute obligation, which is due under all conditions, or are there occasions and conjunctures in which a member of the community, or a group of members, are justified in refusing obedience, or in offering resistance? Various grounds have been taken, in the course of the history of political thought, by those who have sought to find an answer. First (and this is the oldest ground) there is the ground of natural law. Here the contention advanced is that all positive enactments and administrative acts contrary to natural law are null and void. They may therefore be disobeyed; they may even be resisted, if an attempt is made to apply them by force. The paradox of this contention, if the term 'natural law' be interpreted strictly, is that it results in the proposition that law may be legally disobeyed. But the real gist of the contention is something less, or more, than that. It is that law may be disobeyed *justly*, and that it is possible, in the name of justice, to disobey a law which does not express, as all law should, the idea of justice. This was the ground adopted in the American Declaration of Independence of 1776, with its appeal to the laws of nature and of nature's God; and with some modifications it is a ground which, as we shall see, may still be defended. There is less to be said for a second ground, which is that adopted by the Utilitarians at the end of the eighteenth century. On this ground the issue between the acceptance and the rejection of political obligation was reduced to a calculus of material utility. According to Bentham it was 'allowable to, if not incumbent on, every man . . . to enter into measures of resistance . . . when . . . *the probable mischiefs of resistance* (speaking with respect to the community in general) *appear less to him than the probable mischiefs of obedience'.*[1] By virtue of this calculus, as Paley frankly admitted,[2] 'the justice of every particular case of resistance is reduced to a computation', with danger and grievance on one side and the probability and expense of redress on the other. There is little satisfaction to the mind in a computation of this order, which weighs the consequences but omits the cause. More may be said in favour of the ground which is taken by the French jurist Duguit, when he argues for the limited and conditional nature of all political obligation.[3] His contention is that all laws or other acts of the persons styled 'governors' may be resisted passively, defensively, and even aggressively, if they conflict with the Rule of Right (*règle de droit*) deduced from the basic fact of economic solidarity. The ground thus taken enthrones Right above law, and makes the obligation of obedience to law conditional on the conformity of law to Right; but the Right thus enthroned by Duguit is only a derivative or expression of economic fact and process, or rather of a part of such fact and process.

Is there anything to add to these answers, or any way of drawing them together in a comprehensive view which does justice to the elements of truth they contain? We may begin by drawing a distinction which has already been implied in the previous course of the argument. (1) Within the State, and so far as concerns the State and its operation, there is an absolute and unconditional obligation, incumbent upon its members as such, to obey a law duly passed by the legislature in conformity with the constitution, or an act of government duly done under a law so passed. Even here, however, and even within the limits of the State, obligation to a law is conditional upon its being in conformity with the constitution; and it may thus be contended that, in a strict sense, the only unconditional obligation is the obligation due to the constitution. The proviso is just; but it need not prevent us from laying it down that just as a law is unconditionally and absolutely valid when once it is duly passed in conformity with the constitution, so obligation to a law so passed is unconditional and absolute, *within the State and in terms of the State*. (2) If we transcend the terms of the State, and

---

[1] *Fragment on Government*, c. iv, § xxi.
[2] *Moral and Political Philosophy*, Book VI, c. iii.
[3] *Supra*, Book III, § 5.

take into view the play of Society and the activity of social thought in creating and developing the idea of a just order of relations, we have to amplify, or rather to qualify, our view of the nature of political obligation. Upon the assumption, previously made, that the socially created and socially developed idea of justice is the supreme sovereign, we are bound to admit that obligation, even to a law duly passed in conformity with the constitution, is after all in *some sense* conditional upon its squaring with the idea of justice. The distinction which has just been drawn would appear, prima facie, to involve a contradiction. We seem to be saying in a breath that political obligation is unconditional and that it is, 'in some sense', conditional. What exactly is meant by the latter of these sayings? It is not meant for a moment that political obligation ceases, for a man or a group of men, when once they conceive that a law, or a set of laws, fails to square with the idea of justice entertained in their minds. The view suggested is entirely different. Political obligation, *as such*, remains: indeed we may even say that, *as such, and within the State*, it remains an unconditional obligation. But a new and super-political obligation enters as soon as we take into our view the socially created and socially developed idea of justice: an obligation which we may call 'social', in the sense that it springs from Society and from the product of social thought. This super-political or social obligation may conflict with, and be pitted against, the political obligation which exists in the area of the State. A dilemma then arises. What is to be done in this dilemma? What is the weight of political obligation, and what is the weight of the super-political, when the two are opposed to one another? How is the State to act to the 'protestant' who pleads against it the cause of justice, and how is the 'protestant' pleading that cause to act to the State?

Because political obligation, as such, remains, and because it remains, as such, absolute and unconditional, we may lay it down that in any case of disobedience or resistance to law, based on the idea of social justice and social obligation, it is the clear duty of the judge, in his capacity of judge, and of all the organs of government, in their capacity of organs, to enforce the established law (it is not their business to recognize, far less to enforce, any idea of justice other than that expressed in such law); and it is equally the clear duty of the disobeying or resisting citizen to obey, as a citizen, the established law, by accepting the legal consequences involved in his disobedience or resistance. But because social obligation is also a fact, and because, to the 'protestant' penetrated by a conviction of its sovereign nature, it is the highest fact, it is also his duty to accept its demands and to offer his testimony to its sovereignty.

Here, however, a problem arises, which must always vex the mind of every serious and reflective 'protestant'. If the higher obligation is *social*, how can a mere individual, relying on his own idea of justice, or even a group, relying on an idea entertained only by its members, defy the general run of opinion? Must not any challenge to established law be based upon, and be backed by, some measure of general *social* support? This difficulty disappears if we reflect on the nature of social thought and the process of its formation.[1] The process is one of the initial production, the subsequent discussion, and the eventual composition, of a number of different ideas. Each individual, and each group, has something to throw into the pool of discussion in order to stir the waters. Sometimes the contribution must be made in pain if it is to achieve that stirring. A group which feels its idea to be a vital element in any just order of relations will then feel bound to stake itself upon that idea: it will disobey, or even resist, any law to the contrary: it will seek, by the visible testimony of its disobedience and its acceptance of the legal consequences, to impress the value of its idea on others, to get it incorporated in social thought, to make it part of common conviction, and ultimately to secure its adoption as part of the law of the State. Many causes have followed this way in the course of the centuries: the cause of the abolition of slavery, for instance, in the United States, and the cause of the enfranchisement of women in the United Kingdom. It is not, in itself, a way of revolution, though it may sometimes seem to approach the verge. It is at once a rejection and an acceptance of political obligation: a rejection, so far as it denies that obligation on a particular issue: an acceptance, so far as it affirms it in general and on the whole, and so far as it attests its affirmation by facing and accepting the legal consequences of the partial denial. Indeed we may almost say that resistance of this order is still in

[1] *Supra*, § 4 of this Book.

the area of debate, and is a method of persuasion rather than a recourse to force. The resister puts his plea into the arena of debate, and stakes himself upon it: and if he invites the application of force to his own person, he does not seek to apply it to the persons of others.

But the resister who thus courts martyrdom (which in the original Greek from which it is derived meant the simple giving of witness, but with us has come to mean the giving of witness in and by the suffering of pain) can never escape the dilemma in which he is necessarily involved. In following to the uttermost some idea which is part of himself he is also breaking, at some point, the scheme of political obligation which is also part of himself. Nor is that all. There is more in question than the breach of political obligation at a *particular* point. The resister who defies a law is also disturbing (and incidentally encouraging others—less scrupulous than himself and more intent on private ends—to disturb) the *general* scheme of law and order, and the *general* validity of obligation. He has therefore to ask himself whether the contribution which he may make to social thought about justice, by staking himself on the particular idea he wishes to add, is worth the possible cost of disturbance of the whole scheme of existing law and order, itself based upon and itself expressing the idea of justice. This is to make a calculation, and as such it is something like—and yet also very unlike—the calculation of which Bentham and Paley wrote. It is like, in so far as in either case mischief has to be measured against mischief: it is very unlike, in so far as the mischiefs to be measured differ greatly in the two cases—the mischiefs weighed in the one case being mischiefs to the cause of utility, and those weighed in the other being mischiefs to the cause of justice.

There is no simple rule for the weighing of the mischiefs of obedience against the mischiefs of resistance. There is only the general rule that weighing is needed in every case in which a conflict arises between political obligation and the obligation which is super-political. The weighing itself will differ according to time and place; and the decision will depend on the degree of stability of law and order existing in a given country at a given period. The common love of use and wont, the strength of convention, the habit of tradition, are sometimes a sufficient guarantee of the stability of law and order; and where and when that guarantee is present, the electric disturbance of a new idea, pressed to the point of resistance, may serve to correct men's tendency to settle down on the lees of custom. On the other hand, it may well be said that the age in which we live is already sufficiently electric; and it may also be said that new ideas which are ready to appeal to force always introduce an incongruous and explosive element into the peaceful process of social thought and persuasion. This is only a 'dusty answer'. But it is also the only answer which the mind can ever get, however hot for certainties it may be.

BOOK VI

THE DUTY OF THE GOVERNMENT TO THE CITIZEN

or the Relation of the Functions of Government to the Rights of Individuals

§ 1. FUNCTIONS OF GOVERNMENT AND RIGHTS OF PERSONS

IT is easy, and perhaps even natural, to oppose the functions and powers of government to the rights and liberties of persons, as if they were mutually exclusive and each of them began at the point where the other ended. They may, indeed, be distinguished in thought, but they are inseparable in operation. Functions of government cannot be separated from rights of persons, except in the sense in which the reverse of a coin can be distinguished from the obverse. On the one hand, the functions of government are a condition of the rights of persons, because they are necessary to the enjoyment of those rights and because they exist in order to secure them. On the other hand, the rights of persons are a condition of the functions of government, because they are the source and the cause of the existence and action of government. To claim, for example, a right to the enjoyment of personal security is also to claim a right to protection against any invasion of that security; to claim that right to protection is also to claim the exercise of a function of giving protection; and to claim the exercise of that function is also to claim an organ, possessing power or authority, by means of which it is exercised. We may accordingly say that government is a service on behalf of rights, and not a power outside their range: 'servitium propter jura, non potestas praeter jura'. We may add that the service rendered by government to rights is both a consequence and a part of the general rights of persons. I have a right to the service, and the service is thus a part of my rights, because, and as a consequence, of the other and general rights belonging to me as a person.

The same view of the relation between functions of government and rights of persons may equally be attained if we follow another line of reflection. The State is, in its essence, a legal association. The mode of its action is law. The function of its organs of government is the declaration and enforcement of law. What, then, is the nature of the relation of law to rights? Does it abridge them, or does it contain them? The answer, as we have already seen,[1] is that law contains rights, and indeed *is* rights. Law and rights are simply two aspects of something which is essentially one: law is its 'objective' aspect, or the thing as regarded from outside, and rights are its 'subjective' aspect, or the thing as regarded from inside, that is to say from the point of view of the 'subject' or person concerned. If we look at a sum or system of rights objectively, and regard it accordingly as an object projected outside ourselves or a fact confronting us, we think of it primarily as law; but we also think of it as apportioning both the rights which we ourselves own as persons and the consequent duties which we owe to others, as similar persons, in order that they may own similar rights. Conversely, if we look at the same sum or system subjectively, and regard it accordingly as existing in us and ourselves as participating in it, we shall think of it primarily as rights; but we shall also think of these rights, with their consequent and correlative duties, as parts and portions of a sum or system which in the gross is law. If law is thus rights, and rights are thus law, a conclusion necessarily follows in regard to the functions of government. The function of the organs of government, in declaring and enforcing law, is also and equally a function of recognizing and guaranteeing the rights of persons. To declare and enforce law is also, and indeed is the same as, to recognize and guarantee rights. We are thus led once more to the conclusion that the function of government is the service of rights.

There is a corollary to this conclusion. If we think in terms of ownership, we shall say (as indeed we have already done) that the members of a political community are the owners of rights. We may also say, in addition, that along with their rights, and as a consequence and a part of those rights, they own the services required by their rights, and are therefore the owners of the functions of government which serve and secure the actual enjoyment of the rights which they own. The question may then

[1] *Supra*, Book IV, § 1.

be asked, 'What do the governors own, in their capacity of governors?' Shall we say that they own authority—the authority of declaring, interpreting, and enforcing the law? It is impossible to use such language. The members of the governing organs (legislative, judicial, and executive) certainly exercise authority; but they do not own what they exercise. They exercise authority as the appointees, direct or indirect, of the community which owns it, and which owns it as a consequence and part of its general ownership of rights. Authority in the sense of a function of government (or rather the sum of its functions) is not something *owned* by governing persons, but something which they *owe*, in virtue of their appointment, as a mode of service of rights. We may therefore conclude that governing persons own nothing as such (though as members of the political community they own rights equally and in common with other members): they owe rather than own. They owe the exercise of the authority which is necessary for the secure enjoyment of the rights of persons: they owe the service, remunerated by pay or prestige or both, of declaring, interpreting, and enforcing the law which is the objective side of rights of persons: we may even say, if we look only at immediate sovereignty, that they owe the service of sovereignty, in the sense of declaring, in the last resort, what the law is and is henceforth to be. All authority, and all the functions of government, including the function of immediate sovereignty, are services *owed* to rights.

§ 2. THE CLASSIFICATION OF RIGHTS

IF rights are thus prior to functions of government, we shall do well to enumerate and classify rights before we examine the functions of government and the methods of their operation. It has already been noticed[1] that there are three principles, or procedural rules, which regulate the distribution of rights among the members of an organized community: the principle of Liberty, the principle of Equality, and the principle of Fraternity or Co-operation. They preside together, and in common, over the whole of the distribution of rights; but we may none the less regard each of the three as having a particular connexion with a particular set or cluster of rights, and as regulating particularly the distribution of rights in that set or cluster. We

[1] *Supra*, Book IV, § 1.

may accordingly seek to classify rights under the three heads of Liberty, Equality, and Co-operation. In doing so we shall not only be concerned with the full legal rights which are already recognized and guaranteed by law: we shall also extend our view to include the nascent rights which are being convassed in the process of social thought, and which, as they become a part of the common conviction of the political community, and come to be formally endorsed by the organs of that community, are ultimately turned into legal rights in the full sense of the term.[1] The reason for this extension of view is that it is necessary to an understanding of that growth of the functions of government which is a feature of our times. It is the growing-pains of rights which cause the growing labours of government.

We may begin our classification under the head of Fraternity or Co-operation, reserving to the end the rights which come under the head of Liberty.[2] It has already been noticed[3] that the French jurist Duguit, using the term 'solidarity' or 'mutuality' in lieu of the older term, enumerates three particular rights with which the principle of fraternity is particularly connected—the right of education, the right of public assistance, and the right of employment—and that on this basis he would impose corresponding duties on 'governing persons' to provide these rights. The view of Duguit is suggestive, but it is also extreme. It is too narrowly economic—and too closely connected, at that, with a particular brand of economics—to offer any safe guidance. We shall do better to interpret fraternity in the sense of a general co-operation, which is not merely economic, but as wide as the general life of society; and on this basis we may proceed to argue, as indeed has already been argued,[4] that there are two main rights which fall under this head, and two corresponding functions of government. The essence of both of the rights is that men need, and ought to enjoy, a common or public equipment of services and resources, which goes beyond the equipment that individual effort and the effort of voluntary groups are able to provide, and which can be provided only by

[1] *Supra*, Book IV, § 6.
[2] The reason for this order is the fact that the rights which come under the head of Liberty have a peculiar and intimate connexion with the structure of government and naturally form the immediate prelude to the study of that structure which follows in § 3.
[3] *Supra*, Book IV, § 5.   [4] *Supra*, Book IV, § 3.

the common co-operation of all. We may regard this equipment as twofold, or as being both material and mental; and this is why we may hold that it issues in two different rights. The one is the right of persons to enjoy collectively a common or public equipment of *material* necessities unattainable except by the co-operation of all, and ranging from means of public transport and methods of public sanitation to schemes of national insurance and plans for the national development of national economic resources.[1] The other right is a similar right of persons to enjoy collectively a common or public equipment of what may be called *mental* necessities, ranging from schools and places of learning to galleries, museums, libraries, and the like, and thus including not only the facilities needed for public education but also those that are needed for the general national enjoyment of the accumulated treasures of culture.[2]

Under the head of Equality the jurists and thinkers of France, basing themselves on the Declarations of 1789 and afterwards, have enumerated four rights—the right to be treated equally with others, and on the same footing as others, in the eye of the law and in all legislative acts; the right to be treated equally with others in matters of justice and in courts of law; the right to be treated equally with others in matters of taxation, so that each man pays the same proportion of his means as is paid by others; and, finally, the right to be treated as equally admissible with others to public honours and offices of employment. These four rights are all rights of the citizen in respect of the exercise of governing authority: they are claims, acknowledged and recognized by law or general custom, that governing authority should deal equally with all, alike in its legislation and its jurisdiction, its imposition of taxes and its distribution of honours and offices. But the progress of social thought has given

[1] In the Universal Declaration of Human Rights (1948) this right, or one main element of it, is expressed in the Articles (23 and 25) which declare 'the right to social security' and, in more detail, the right to an adequate standard of living, including medical care and necessary social services, and the right to security in the event of lack of livelihood due to causes beyond individual control, such as unemployment, sickness, and old age.

[2] In the Universal Declaration of Human Rights this right is expressed in the statement that 'everyone has the right to participate in the cultural life of the community, to enjoy the arts, and to share in scientific advancement and its benefits'. (Article 27, Section 1.)

a wider sweep to the notion of equality and to the nature of the rights which it involves. We have learned to think not only of what may be called political equality, in relation to the action of governing authority, but also of economic and cultural equality, in relation to the general life of the whole of the organized community; and we have accordingly come to believe that there are further rights which ought to be added to the rights of political equality. These further rights are still, as it were, in process of construction: they are emerging from social thought, and beginning to pass into the common conviction of the political community; but the proper nature of their form, and the exact extent of their dimension, have still to be determined by the continuing process of social thought and by the method of tentative experiment. They are rights which men are beginning to claim, not in relation to governing authority and the distribution of its incidence, but in relation to one another: they are rights to a greater measure of general equality between man and man, partly in economic status and the distribution of economic possessions, and partly in educational opportunity and enjoyment of the general treasures of culture. These new and nascent rights of equality are obviously linked with the similar rights which have already been suggested under the head of co-operation. The greater the provision of material and mental necessities in the form of a common or public equipment in which all alike can share, the greater will be the achievement of equality on both the material and the mental plane. But in addition to common and equal sharing in the stock of common or public equipment there is also needed a greater measure of equality in the enjoyment of individual status, in the possession of individual equipment (or 'private property'), and in the opportunity of individual access to the benefits of education and general cultural development.[1]

The rights which came under the head of Liberty are all the greater, and the more numerous, because Liberty is a multiple principle. Within the State, and apart from the area of Society

---

[1] A special problem of equality, and of the rights of equality, is raised by the position of women. It may be noted that the Universal Declaration of Human Rights states (1) that 'every one, without any discrimination, has the right to equal pay for equal work' (Article 23, § 2), and (2) that men and women 'are entitled to equal rights as to marriage, during marriage and at its dissolution' (Article 16, § 1).

(which has also a social liberty of its own), there are, it has been suggested,[1] three divisions or regions of liberty. These three divisions are the political, the civil, and the economic. We may accordingly classify the rights which come under the head of Liberty according to these three divisions.

The rights of political liberty generally include the right of the citizen to participate in the election of the legislature, and thereby, indirectly, to share in the choice of the government.[2] When the jury system exists, along with a system of unpaid magistrates drawn in large numbers from the general public, the rights of political liberty also include the right of the citizen to participate in the administration of justice and to form, in a sense, a part of the judicature. The right to form political parties, and the right of such parties, when formed, to play a part in the election of the legislature and thereby in the choice of the government, is a sort of border-land right, essentially connected with political liberty but formally a part of civil liberty and a product of the civil rights of freedom of the expression of opinion and freedom of association and meeting.

The rights of civil liberty have been divided by French thinkers into two different groups, distinguished from one another by the historical fact that the one group is earlier than the other. The first and earlier of these groups, already evident in the Declaration of 1789, includes the three rights of personal freedom, personal security, and personal or private property. The second group, gradually developed in the thought and expressed in the legislation of the century which followed the Revolution, includes some half-dozen rights; liberty in the choice and conditions of employment, and in the conduct of trade and industry; liberty of the press; liberty of assembly; liberty of association; liberty of teaching;[3] and liberty of conscience and worship. This historical division of the rights of civil

---

[1] *Supra*, Book IV, § 2.

[2] In countries, such as the United States, where the government is of the presidential type, the citizens share directly in the choice of the government, concurrently with their participation in the election of the legislature. It may be added that in States which adopt the institutions of the referendum and the initiative, the rights of political liberty also include the right of the citizen to participate actively, along with the legislature, in the work of legislation; see above, Book II, § 5.

[3] *Liberté de l'enseignement*: the right of individuals or groups to organize and to offer courses of instruction on a voluntary basis.

liberty into two different groups may square with the facts of French history, but it does not suit the history of England, where no such distinction can be traced, and it cannot be generally applied. Abandoning, therefore, any chronological scheme of division, we may suggest a logical classification of the rights of civil liberty into three different groups, based on the nature and character of the activity concerned.[1] The first group will consist of the rights which come under the head of freedom of physical activity; it will include rights such as personal security (whether from arbitrary arrest and detention, or from torture and inhuman punishment, or from arbitrary interference with the privacy of home and domicile), and such, again, as freedom of movement and residence inside a country, along with the right to seek and enjoy an asylum in other countries. The second group will consist of rights which come under the head of freedom of the activity of the mind: this will include rights such as the right to freedom of conscience and religion, the right to freedom of opinion and its expression, and the right to freedom of meeting and association. The third group will consist of rights which come under the head of freedom of practical activity, or, as we may also say, freedom for the exercise of will and choice in the general field of contractual action; this group will include the right to the acquisition and disposal of property, the right to marry and found a family on the basis of full and free consent, and similar rights of that order. It may also be made to include a number of rights connected with the choice and conditions of employment and the conduct of trade and industry; but rights of this order, as has already been noted in an earlier part of the argument,[2] are best treated as belonging to a separate class, and are most properly classified under the head of the rights of economic liberty.

The rights of economic liberty were already expressed in some detail in the part of the German Constitution of 1919 which dealt with 'Economic Life', and they have recently found their place in the Universal Declaration of Human Rights.[3] If we

[1] *Supra*, Book IV, § 2.   [2] *Supra*, Book IV, § 2.
[3] They are set out in Articles 23, 24, and 25 of the Declaration. Article 23 declares the right to work, with free choice of employment and under just conditions; the right to just remuneration; and the right to form and join trade unions. Article 24 declares the right to rest and leisure, with limitation of working hours and with regular holidays. Article 25, as already noted (p. 230, n. 1), declares the

seek to formulate them broadly, in terms of contemporary life and the growing demands of social thought, we may suggest that they fall into three main groups. We may regard them as extensions and expansions, into the economic sphere, of the old three rights of civil liberty already declared by Blackstone in England and by the revolutionary thinkers of France in the latter half of the eighteenth century—the right of personal freedom, the right of personal security, and the right of personal property. They are extensions and expansions entailed by the flood of economic development (often termed the 'industrial revolution', though the term is hardly adequate) which began to flow about 1750, and is still flowing swift and deep. The group of rights which is an extension of the old civil right of personal security includes the rights of workers under Factory Acts (the first of the rights of economic liberty to be formally acknowledged), their rights under Workmen's Compensation Acts, and their rights, under various acts, to insurance against the risks of sickness and unemployment and age. The group of rights which may be regarded as an extension of the old civil right of personal freedom includes already the right of workers freely to form trade unions and to bargain freely through such unions about the conditions and remuneration of their work: it may also come to include the further right, now beginning to be claimed, to the enjoyment of the status of free partners in the general control and conduct of industry. Finally, the group of rights which may be regarded as an extension of the old civil right of personal property may be held to include the right of workers to some share in the capital of the particular industry in which they are engaged. This means their right to acquire, by virtue of the rendering of permanent service, some permanent property in the undertaking for which they work, over and above their weekly remuneration: it means, again, the right to participate in a diffusion of ownership which makes personal property as general in its scope as personal freedom or personal security.

This attempt at a classification of rights may seem to be little more than an academic exercise. But it is, as has already been noted,[1] something more than that. It is the necessary prelimi-

right to an adequate standard of living, and the right to security in the event of a lack of livelihood due to causes beyond individual control.

[1] At the beginning of this section.

nary to any study of the functions of government, which are services owed to rights and can only be understood in the light of the rights they serve. On the other hand, classification is also the creation of compartments; and the creation of compartments, if it may be a help to clear thinking, can also be a danger to the breadth and sweep of thought which not only apprehends but can also comprehend. For one thing we have to remember that the movement of human life does not proceed in compartments. The same general problem recurs, if in different forms, under the different heads of our classification. The future of industry and the development of a fair system of economic rights is at one and the same time a matter of the rights which come under the head of liberty, of those which come under the head of equality, and of those which come under the head of fraternity or co-operation. We cannot think of the problem properly in the limits of one compartment; and we are driven back, in the issue, on that general and comprehensive idea of justice which seeks to reconcile the principle of liberty with that of equality, and both with the principle of co-operation, and which thus controls and co-ordinates the rights belonging to each. There is another thing also to be remembered; or rather there is another aspect of the same general truth. No right is absolute and inviolable, or entrenched by itself in its own inexpugnable iron compartment. The right of personal property is indeed a right; but it is a right which has to make terms, and to enter into combination, with a variety of other rights. Not only has my right to acquire property, as a condition of the development of the capacities of my personality,[1] to be reconciled with the right of others to acquire it, as a condition of the development of the capacities of their personality: the right of each person to such acquisition has also to be reconciled with other rights in other spheres, such as the right of workers to enjoy the status of free partners in the general conduct and control of industry, a right which cannot be simply defeated or abrogated by the right of the owner of property to the free use and disposal of his acquisitions.[2] Once more we are driven back on the general idea of justice by which one sort of right is 'mortised and adjoined' to another.

---

[1] *Supra*, Book IV, § 3.   [2] *Supra*, Book IV, § 2.

§ 3. THE RIGHTS OF POLITICAL LIBERTY AND THE STRUCTURE OF GOVERNMENT

'EVERYONE has the right to take part in the government of his country.'[1] The origin and basis of this right have already been suggested at a previous stage of the argument.[2] We saw, at that stage, that discussion is the necessary and vital process of the life of an organized community, and that each and every member is entitled to contribute to this process. To be entitled to contribute to discussion is the same thing as to have 'the right to take part in the government'; for the process of political discussion is the essential activity of government in a politically organized community. The process of political discussion has evolved, in the course of time, a number of organs for its operation. These organs, distinct and yet connected, form a successive series, in which, as in a relay race, each of them hands to another the task of 'carrying on' from the point which it has reached itself. We may distinguish four of these organs, and proceed to trace their connexion.

The first of the organs of political discussion is party. Party, as we have already seen,[3] is a social formation which also discharges a political function and has thus, as it were, one foot in Society and one in the State. Each party is a voluntary association; but each party also formulates a political programme for the consideration and choice of the political electorate, and each party submits to the vote of that electorate candidates for election to Parliament who offer themselves as symbols and exponents of its programme. At the first stage or lap in the process of discussion each party discusses in its own counsels the programme which it proposes to formulate; and each, when the programme is formulated, proceeds to discuss and debate it in public, before an attentive electorate, with the other party or parties.

The turn then comes for the second organ, the political electorate. That too is an organ of discussion, at any rate in periods of election (which is not to say that it is dead, or ceases to think and interrogate, in the intervals between such periods[4]);

---

[1] Universal Declaration of Human Rights, Article 20, § 1.

[2] Book V, § 4.   [3] Book V, § 4.

[4] The contact between members and their constituencies, during the life of a parliament, becomes increasingly intimate; and the results of such contact may on

it canvasses and considers the programmes, and examines and cross-examines the candidates, submitted to it for choice; and when it has made its choice, it hands over the further conduct of discussion to the representatives whom it has chosen, trusting them to carry it into far greater detail, and to carry it on with a far greater degree of continuity, than it can possibly do itself.

The third organ then succeeds in its turn to the same double task—the task of conducting discussion itself, and the task of preparing the way for further and later discussion. This organ is the representative body; the core and centre of the whole system of representative democracy; the Parliament which, as its very name indicates, is peculiarly engaged in the activity of 'parley' and constant discussion. But the function of Parliament, like that of the electorate, is a twofold function. It is not only an organ of discussion itself, engaged in a process of constant debate intended to translate a general programme into legislative enactments: it also helps to create,[1] and it continually serves to support, a government which it expects and trusts to carry discussion into even greater detail, and to conduct it even more continuously and intimately, than it is able to do itself.

We thus come to the fourth and last organ in the successive series; the responsible government or cabinet, which is the organ of government *par excellence* (though also, and at the same time, only *one* of a number of organs of government in the wider sense of the word), and which is therefore commonly called '*the* Government'. This government is 'responsible' in the sense that it must necessarily command the support of the representative body from which its members are drawn; but it may also be

occasion be decisive, as they were said to be at the time of the abdication of Edward VIII.

[1] The creation of a government, as has already been noted, is not a matter for the representative body in countries where the government is of the presidential type: it is a matter for the electorate, which chooses both the government and the representative body. But even in countries where the government is of the cabinet type, and therefore in the nature of a committee of the representative body (in the sense that it necessarily consists of persons who are members of that body), we cannot say more than that the representatives 'help to create' this government. The creation is generally a mixed sort of act, in which the Head of the State first invites a member of the representative body (designated by the fact that he is the leader of the majority party in that body) to become the head of a government, and the person so invited then proceeds, as we say, to 'form a government' which must of necessity be able to command the confidence and support of a majority of the representative body.

said to be responsible in another and even deeper sense. It is responsible for carrying the process of discussion to that crucial and final point at which it issues in decision. A responsible government, organized under its head, is at once the innermost core of discussion and the originating motor of action. Not that the decision at which it arrives, and the impulse which it accordingly gives, is necessarily final or absolutely conclusive. The decision, on any grave issue, will flow back, as it were, to the representative body for approval and confirmation; it may even flow back to the electorate, either for informal approval by what we call public opinion, or even for formal approval by an electoral vote in a general election at which a proposed decision is made the main or a dominant issue. The process of discussion may thus return on itself; and after flowing from the electorate to the representative body, and from that to the responsible government, it may in turn flow back from the government to the representatives, and then from them to the electors.

There is thus a general system of discussion which operates through a number of organs. The difficulty of this system is to reconcile two necessities: the necessity, on the one hand, that each organ should concentrate on its work with a free vigour and a fresh impetus, as if everything hung upon the conclusion at which it arrives; and the necessity, on the other, that each of the organs should also keep in touch and harmony with the rest, acknowledging that they too, as organs of the same general process, have the right and duty to do *their* work, in their place and at their time, and that their right and duty must always be respected. The peril of the system is that one or the other of the organs concerned should lay an exclusive emphasis on the first of these necessities, and arrogate to itself an exclusive and predominant importance. If that is done, the results will in any case be unhappy, because they will necessarily involve a disturbance of the whole system; but they will vary according to the nature of the organ on which an exclusive emphasis is laid as being the organ of discussion *par excellence* and therefore the dominant organ. If it is the organ of party which asserts its predominance, you may have the open tyranny of a single party (whether of the Right or the Left), or the secret tyranny of a cabal which unites the leaders of several parties in an interested coalition and controls behind the scenes both the representative body and the nominal government.[1] If, on the other hand, it is the representative organ which is particularly conscious of its own importance, you may have a parliamentary autocracy, with the enthroned deputies installing and evicting governments as and when they think fit. The system of political discussion is a delicate as well as a difficult system. To remember, and to seek to observe, the two necessities which it imposes is to face the problem of doing simultaneously two different things which seem almost contradictory: on the one hand, leaving each organ free to act with an original vigour to the full stretch of its capacity; on the other hand, keeping each organ within the limits of its capacity (so that, in the Platonic phrase, it 'does its own business' and no more than its business), and thus keeping all the organs in harmony and co-operation. This is the general problem of representative democracy; and there is no way of avoiding the problem—except by substituting the dictatorship of one organ for a system of discussion divided among several. To do that is to abolish discussion, at any rate as a general process in which all, at some stage, have the right to participate. (There may be left some fragment or simulacrum of discussion within the organ which holds the dictatorship; not that a fragment or simulacrum is anything more than a travesty.) But if discussion be the vital process of the life of any organized community, to abolish discussion is suicide and the end of the common life.

Representative democracy, considered as a system for giving effect to the rights of political liberty, is often defined as a system of government by all, or of government by the people. It *is* that; and yet it is something more than that. The right of everyone to take part in the government of his country is not a simple matter of all men saying, as a single aggregate, what is their will and what is the object of their volition. On the contrary it is a complex matter of all discussing, through a variety of organs which are necessary for the purpose of full and thorough discussion, what is their thought, what is the content of their

---

[1] The exaggeration of party may thus flourish in the multiple-party as well as in the single-party State; and in such a State it may be encouraged by the device of proportional representation, which tends to stimulate each party to secure its full pound of flesh and to push its claims *à l'outrance*.

common conviction, what is the idea which they consider right and ripe for realization. Ideas have quality in them, as well as quantity behind them; and while the quantity of wills assembled behind an idea matters, and matters greatly, the quality or value in an idea is also something that matters, and matters at least as much. That is a reason, a fundamental reason, for the time and the pains which we spend on the process of discussion, (It is not the only reason; for we also exercise and breathe our minds, and develop the capacities of our personality, in the course of the process.) We want to get at the quality and value of the ideas presented to us, and we cannot do that without taking discussion through stage after stage, sifting and sifting at each new stage. The courts of law and the methods of justice offer an analogy: there, too, 'the rights of the matter', which are the object of search, are sifted and clarified by a process of inquiry which rises from instance to instance by a progressive refinement. The short cut of an immediate decision is tempting; but the only sure way of arriving is the way of successive stages. The electorate is one stage; but it is only a stage, and a general election is neither the beginning nor the end of the matter. Government by all, in its true and full sense, takes time: it is not only a matter of the voting of all the electors: it is also, and even more, a matter of the deliberation of all the organs concerned and involved in the process of mature and considered decision.

§ 4. THE STRUCTURE OF GOVERNMENT IN ITS RELATION TO THE RIGHTS OF CIVIL AND ECONOMIC LIBERTY

WE have seen how the rights of political liberty affect the structure of government, and how they issue in 'government by all' in the sense which has just been defined. We have now to see how the structure of government, when it is true to the rights of political liberty, affects in its turn the rights of civil and economic liberty. We have, in a word, to see what manner of fruits it produces: we have to inquire whether 'government by all' will not in its nature be 'government for all'.

It has already been argued[1] that government by all has an intrinsic value, and is, of itself and in itself, something which is for the benefit of all and makes for the common good of all.

[1] *Supra*, Book V, § 4.

Considered simply as a process, and apart from any results or product outside the process, it is a way of the development of the capacities of personality. But it has also an extrinsic value; it is also valuable for the results which it produces, and for the new rights—other than those of political liberty, and over and above them—which are added by its operation to the common fund of enjoyment. If we look at the matter historically, we are led at once to the conclusion that during the days of struggle men pressed for the political right of government by the people not as an end in itself, or not only as an end in itself, but because they wished to secure for themselves and their fellows, by the exercise of this right, the enjoyment of other rights hitherto denied, or at any rate confined to the few. The Chartists, for example, were vehement in urging the justice of their six political points; but the ultimate aims of their endeavour were economic aims. If that was true in the days of struggle, it is also true, as experience shows, that the actual achievement of political rights raises at once in the days of attainment two questions of economic rights: the question, first, of the economic rights which ought to follow on political rights by the logic of consistency, in order to secure more liberty for the worker in the course of his work and thus make the economic system correspond better with the political;[1] and, secondly, the question of the economic rights which will inevitably and in any case follow on the acquisition of political rights by the simple logic of fact, or, in other words, as a result of the fact that the mass of the people now have the vote and will tend to use it in order to secure economic rights which they regard as the necessary conditions of economic liberty.

It follows then, alike by the logic of consistency and by the logic of fact, that an extension of the rights of political liberty must involve a similar extension of the rights of economic liberty. When the structure of government is altered, by the extension of political rights, the altered structure of government will alter in turn the economic structure, and it will do so by means of the extension of economic rights. This extension of rights will take two forms. One of these forms is the extension to all of old rights, already recognized as belonging to the members of a section of the community, but not hitherto recognized as

[1] *Supra*, Book IV, § 2.

belonging to the members of the community as a whole, irrespective of section or class. The other form is a still further extension by the recognition of new rights, not hitherto recognized at all, and their general distribution to all the members of the community. In brief, we have both an extension of the number of those among whom rights are distributed and an extension of the number of the rights distributed.

For the present we may confine ourselves to the extension of the number of those among whom rights are distributed. That rights are for all, and not merely for the members of a single section, is a simple proposition which now seems self-evident; but the actual extension to all even of old and long-recognized rights has been a slow historical process. The width of vision which sees that 'a man is a man for all that', whatever the rank and the guinea's stamp, is a slow historical acquisition. There was long a defect of vision, honest and genuine in its own day, which made men as it were near-sighted, and prevented them from seeing beyond a small and limited circle. Privileged classes, accepting the idea of the general social necessity of different social functions arranged in an ordered hierarchy of ascending degrees or stations, proceeded from that idea to a firm conviction that the masses were confined by the nature of their functions—as ploughmen and artificers—to the one office of manual work, and were not intended, and indeed were not fit, either for the political right of the suffrage or for the civil and economic rights (full personal security, full personal freedom of movement, and the full ownership of personal property) which they themselves enjoyed. We may almost say that they naturally thought in terms of 'two nations', or even of two grades of humanity and two classes of human beings. Three movements of thought, two of them belonging to the eighteenth century, and the third emerging in the course of the nineteenth, have radically altered these terms.

The first is the movement of humanitarianism, mainly based (at any rate in England)[1] on the foundations of the Christian Gospel, and inspired by a fervent conviction that the benefits of the Gospel belonged to all and must be extended to all—to

[1] On the Continent, in the age of Enlightenment, the humanitarianism of Voltaire and the Encyclopaedists, who were no less zealous in their reforming passion, found its basis in rationalism.

the slave, the prisoner, the factory-worker, and whoever else needed the comfort of a recognition of his common humanity and his common human rights. Whether this Christian humanitarianism were Evangelical or Catholic, whether it proceeded from the Low Church or the High, it changed and widened men's view of the distribution of rights, and altered the narrow terms in which they had hitherto thought. The other two movements which have worked in the same direction, however different they may be both from Christian humanitarianism and from one another, are the Benthamite utilitarianism which emerged at the end of the eighteenth century and the Marxian socialism which began to grow from the middle of the nineteenth. The Benthamites, going on the principle of the greatest happiness of the greatest number, and holding that all were capable of happiness and had therefore the right to enjoy it, attacked the limitation of this universal right by the sinister interests of a privileged few, and advocated a structure of government under which all alike had a voice and a vote and the majority could use their voice and their vote to counteract sinister interests and to enthrone general happiness. The Marxians, going on the assumption (not altogether unwarranted by the history of the past) that the existing structure of government was based on the domination of a small and interested social class, which made law to suit its own interest and thus limited rights to its own members, urged that the largest and the most numerous social class, the class of the workers, should acquire domination in its turn, and should then extend and generalize rights by instituting a workers' State in which all would be workers and all would enjoy the common rights belonging to workers. There is an obvious difference between the Benthamites and the Marxians. The Benthamites laid their primary emphasis on the rights of political liberty: they held that the extension of the suffrage was the key to a greater enjoyment of happiness by a greater number of individuals: they expected a peaceable extension of the rights of civil and economic liberty, following easily and naturally on a similar extension of the right of political liberty. The Marxians were primarily concerned with economic liberty: they held that its attainment demanded effort, and even violence: they respected less the rights of individuals than the rights and the status of a whole class. But great as is the difference between Benthamism and Marxianism, the effects of both have been so far similar, that both have tended towards the extension of rights to all, and both have helped to abolish the old assumption of a graded society marked by a graded enjoyment of rights.

§ 5. THE EXTENSION OF RIGHTS IN ITS RELATION TO THE EXTENSION OF THE FUNCTIONS OF GOVERNMENT

THE argument has hitherto turned on the extension of existing rights to a greater number of persons. We may now turn to consider the extension of the number of rights, or in other words the creation and the general allocation of new and added rights, particularly in the sphere of economic liberty. The distinction between the two modes of extension is perhaps verbal rather than real. Actually the extension of rights to a greater number of persons is, *for them*, the creation of new and added rights. Actually, again, the creation of new and added rights is not so much a matter of the creation of something new as of the broader and more liberal interpretation of something old. The new and added rights in the sphere of economic liberty are really new and extended versions of old and recognized rights in the sphere of civil liberty—the right to personal security, the right to personal freedom, and the right to personal property.

We may begin with the extension of the right to personal security. That right had been recognized, however imperfectly, since the end of the sixteenth century, under the old system of poor relief: and a new recognition was added, from the beginning of the nineteenth century, under the system of factory legislation. Still another recognition has been added, in the course of the present century, under the system of joint or social insurance. There are thus three stages of recognition (first the poor law, then factory legislation, and then social insurance); but they are all stages of a continuous process, and though we may cherish a vivid sense of the value of the third stage, and associate it particularly with a conception of the 'welfare' State, we have to remember that it is part of a process, and that the whole process has been inspired by the one fundamental idea of the right of personal security. It has become customary to apply the term 'social services' to the developments of this third stage.

But services are secondary and consequential things, entailed by the primary fact of rights, which are the cause and source of all services; and we shall do well to begin any study of the nature of these developments not from the services in which they end, but from the rights in which they begin. From this point of view we may say that our century has been marked by a new and more social interpretation of the right of personal security. This new and more social interpretation has led us to regard the right of personal security as including (1) the right of the worker to be protected against the risks of sickness, unemployment, and age; (2) his right to be so protected by a method of joint or social insurance (producing a joint or social security, and thus broadening and strengthening personal security), under which he is linked with his employer in a partnership of contribution to the cost, and both are linked again in a similar partnership with the State; (3) his right to enjoy the necessary services of government, loosely called 'social services',[1] which the method of social insurance demands. The general result is an extension of the rights of economic liberty under the head and rubric of the right to personal security. But it is also at the same time— necessarily, because an extension of rights is also an extension of services—an increase of the functions of government and an extension of governing authority.

The two results go together: they are indissolubly connected. It is here that we may possibly find a limit, or a principle of limit, to the extension of our rights to the enjoyment of personal security. There is always a cost involved; and it is wise to count the cost in advance. The cost is partly financial, or a simple matter of money: it is partly also spiritual, or a more serious matter of control. The financial cost is that involved in the payment of contributions by the worker, the employer, and the general taxpayer, to meet the expenses of a system of joint or social insurance. The spiritual cost is that involved in the extension of the area of compulsory uniformity and administrative control. The double cost may be well worth the while: what is certain is that it must always be paid. The extension of our

[1] In reality, the services of government are always *public* services, either military or civil. The so-called 'social services' are thus public civil services rendered by government to the operation of the method of joint or social insurance. They are 'social' in the sense that they serve that method, but not in the sense that they are services rendered by society or by any social organ.

rights to the enjoyment of personal security is thus subject to a double proviso: the proviso that the members of the community are ready and able to pay the cost of the benefits which they receive; and the proviso that they are willing to accept the extension of the functions of government, and the increase of administrative control, which are also the price of their receipt of benefits. In a word, new rights are new commodities which, like other commodities, have their price, and, like other commodities, must be bought. The commodity bought may be well worth the price; and the liberty gained by the greater enjoyment of personal security may be greater far than the liberty surrendered by the increased acceptance of administrative control. The fact remains that it is always wise to count the cost. Rights are not to be had for the asking, or as a matter of pure gift. There is always a sense in which they are bought; and they are only sure when they are fairly bought by an honest bargain.

We may now turn from considering the extension of the right to personal security, and proceed to consider the extension of the right to personal freedom and the right to personal property —two rights which in their nature are closely interconnected, and which come into question together as soon as we seek to examine the further and fuller extension of economic liberty. The extension of the right to personal security still leaves us with something which may be called *passive*; for though the new system of social security, attained by the method of social insurance, demands the contribution and co-operation of all, workers as well as others, it remains none the less, in its essential nature, a protective system of shelter in which the worker can find a refuge from the risks and chances of the economic process. The question then arises whether there is not also needed something which may be called *active*: some system of participation or partnership under which all workers can actively share in the conduct and management of the economic process; some extension of the right of personal freedom, and also of the right of personal property, which will give them a voice and a stake in the undertaking in which they serve. We have already seen[1] that there are two general reasons for answering that question in the affirmative. The first is that you cannot well have, in the same community and at the same time, two separate worlds, one of

[1] *Supra*, Book IV, § 2.

political democracy and the other of economic autocracy. The second is that, if we assume the general principle that the ultimate purpose of all institutions is the greatest development of the capacities of personality in the greatest number of persons, we are bound to conclude that there must be room for such development in the working of the system of economic institutions which occupies so many hours of the daily life of so many persons, even though the immediate purpose of that system is simply the purpose of producing the maximum of material necessities at the minimum of cost. We may therefore admit, on these two grounds, that there is a presumption in favour of active economic rights; and we are then confronted by the question, 'What is the method, or methods, by which such rights may be secured and guaranteed to all the workers engaged in the general business of production?'

One method which has long been advocated, and partly put into practice, is the method of nationalization. This means, in effect, that the capital resources of some particular branch of production are taken over by the State, and that the business of production, in that branch, is thenceforth handled, directly or indirectly, by the State which owns the resources. Such a method eliminates, in any range in which it is applied, the right of personal property in capital resources; and it eliminates, along with that right, such elements of value (initiative, variety, and personal responsibility) as are involved in its exercise. That is the price to be paid. On the other hand there may be argued to be corresponding gains which are even greater than the price. In the first place the nationalization of capital resources makes each worker, in his capacity of a member of the nation, an owner of capital resources, vested as such with a right of property which he did not hitherto enjoy. In the second place it makes each worker, again in his capacity of a member of the nation, an active agent in the conduct of the business of production: indeed, it may even do more, and if there is devolution of the conduct of the business of production on the workers and technicians of each particular nationalized branch, it may make each worker an active agent in his capacity of a member of that particular branch. But it may also be argued that these gains are not so great as they seem to be, and are illusory rather than real. In the matter of ownership, or, more exactly, in the matter of a new and larger enjoyment of the right of property, we have to notice that the ownership is collective, and the right of property enjoyed is not a personal right vested in an individual person. The extension of collective ownership is *not* an extension of the right of personal property: it makes each man not an owner, but (in a State of fifty million members) a fifty-millionth part of an owner. Again in the matter of status, or the new enjoyment of the right of personal freedom arising from the new position of being an active agent in the conduct of production, we have equally to notice that the status is collective, and that the activity of each agent in the conduct of production is merely a fractional activity. When the business of production in the whole of a particular branch is undertaken by the State, directly or indirectly, through the length and breadth of the country, the scale of the undertaking is so vast that the personal activity of the individual worker in the conduct of business is necessarily infinitesimal; and experience appears to suggest that the result is a central mechanism, ponderous and impersonal, in which there is less play for the personality of the worker than there is in a smaller undertaking, even under the system of private ownership of capital. It may thus be argued that the method of nationalization does not attain the end which alone can justify the means—the end of extending personal and individual enjoyment of rights, and thereby extending the area of the development of the capacities of individual personality.

We may therefore turn to inquire whether another and different method would not be better calculated to promote the attainment of this end. We may begin by assuming the existence, and the continuing right to exist, of personal property in capital resources vested in individual owners. That right, it is true, is not an absolute right of the *Noli me tangere* order. On the contrary, it is a relative right (as rights in general are) which has to be properly adjusted to the rights of other persons. The problem before us is accordingly a problem of the proper adjustment of the right of the capitalist to those other rights. The right of the owner of capital resources, if it is not an absolute right, is grounded on something more than the mere prescription of continuous possession in the previous course of history. In other words, it is something more than a mere historical right which can only plead the fact that it has been in favour of the claim that it should continue to be. The right of the owner of capital resources is grounded on permanent titles, which belong to the present and the future as well as to the past, and consist in the social and moral advantages which accrue from the possession and exercise of the right. These advantages are various; but they may be classified summarily under three heads. In the first place, the right of the individual owner of capital resources is favourable to the play of personal initiative. It encourages responsibility for taking a personal decision, immediately and directly, at the point where the problem arises; it prevents decision from being centralized in one focus, and therefore mechanized; it remits it to, or distributes it among, a number of separate and living centres, thus following a biological rather than a mechanical pattern. In the second place, the right of individual ownership of capital resources is favourable to variety of experiment and to the method of trial and error. It encourages competition between undertaking and undertaking, and serves, by encouraging such competition, to raise the level of all and to improve the service of each; so that here again it may be said in a metaphor, and in no ignoble sense, to follow a biological pattern. Finally, the right of individual ownership of capital resources, as we have already had reason to notice,[1] is connected with and favourable to that *nisus* towards the development of the capacities of personality which is an essential element of our nature: it provides a way in which we try ourselves out, and become conscious of our capacities by seeing them externally expressed in results. It is easy to exaggerate the importance of such external expression, and to forget that the development of capacity, even if it is encouraged by being expressed in external results, matters infinitely more than any result by which it may be encouraged. But results matter none the less; and men do more, and develop more, when they are moved to action by the incentive of visible results.

We may therefore hold, on the ground of these various advantages, that individual ownership of capital resources has a continuing social and moral title over and above the title of prescription and vested interest. But there is another side to the matter, and it is a side which is still more important. Uncriticized and unadjusted, the right of the owner of capital

[1] *Supra*, Book IV, § 3.

resources at once does harm to *him* and depresses the workers whom he employs. It does harm to him, in so far as it gives him a power over the lives of others which corrupts, or tends to corrupt, the possessor, as uncriticized power always does: it does harm to him again, in so far as it makes him, or tends to make him, a member of a privileged and almost parasitic class, enjoying results which may not be the results of personal capacity or of personal effort, but of mere inheritance or of pure chance.[1] Just as it does harm to the owner, so too an uncriticized and unadjusted right of private ownership of capital resources also depresses the worker. It depresses him to the almost servile status of a 'hand' (or, in Aristotle's phrase, 'a living tool') in the undertaking for which he works. It depresses him also to a 'propertyless being', with no share in the right of personal property, when by the same title of effort and output of personal capacity which the capitalist pleads he too should have his share in the capital of his undertaking. It follows that both in the interest of the capitalist and in that of the worker the State is forced to undertake the function of adjusting and reconciling the right of the owner of capital resources to the worker's rights of personal freedom of status and the enjoyment of personal property. This is a matter, once more, of the general task of the State: the task of achieving a right order of human relations, and thereby realizing the reign of justice, by adjusting the rights of one set of its members to the rights of another. Here the particular task is that of adjusting the old rights of the owners of capital resources, long recognized in positive law, to the worker's new rights, or more exactly his new claims to rights, which are now being recognized in social thought and are moving forwards to the further stage of legal recognition.

The method by which the State will seek to perform this task, if it remains true to its own proper nature and continues to follow the line of action which it has hitherto followed, will not be the method of 'nationalization,' but the method of 'supervision'. It will not assume the new form of the socialist State, annexing the means and administering the business of general production: it will keep its old form of the supervisory State, still watching and easing the play of rights, as it has always done, but extending the range of its vision and increasing its work of

[1] *Supra*, Book IV, § 3.

adjustment. Recognizing the right of individuals who are owners of capital resources as a necessary part of the process of production, it will at the same time supervise the whole of the process of production with a view to co-ordinating this right, belonging to these individuals, with the other rights of other individuals which are also a necessary part of the process. It will see with the eye of its vision individual persons and personal rights, and it will think in terms of such persons and rights; but at the same time it will 'over-see' them and think them over together (which is the true sense of 'supervision'), and it will seek to adjust them accordingly. If we can imagine the State engaged in reflection, and expressing its reflections in speech, it might address itself and its members in words such as these:

'I am by my nature, and I must remain if I am to be true to my nature, a legal association. As such, I am not an agent of production, except where the principle of co-operation compels me to produce some system of public or common equipment[1] (a postal system, or a system of fuel and power, or a transport system) which is needed by all and must be provided by the co-operation of all; but even here I think it best, as a general rule, to delegate the actual work of management to some economic body or board which will manage it simply and separately as a pure matter of business, and thus prevent it from being entangled in my own legal machinery. On the other hand, if I am not an agent of production, I am by my nature the supervisor of the whole process of production; and though it is not my business to manage the work of production, it certainly is my business to lay down the general rules to which such management must conform. That is the line of action which I have long been following. It is now a century and a half since I began to lay down the rules of factory legislation, in order to protect the right of every factory worker to the enjoyment of personal security. My rules have grown and grown. They are based on my two great principles of liberty and equality: they are intended to protect and secure the rights which are involved in the application of those principles; and as the social interpretation of those principles grows, my rules must continue to grow in order to keep in step with that interpretation. Today the interpretation of these principles is beginning to demand from me an

[1] *Supra*, Book IV, § 4.

adjustment of the right of the owner of capital to the double right of the worker: his right to enjoy a status of personal freedom, by virtue of being treated not as an instrument but as a collaborator; and his further right to enjoy the permanent possession of some personal property, by virtue of being made a partner or 'share-holder' in the ownership of capital. The beginnings of that adjustment have already been made in the course of the last fifty years; I started, for example, as long ago as 1909, a system of Trade Boards which gave to workers in unorganized industries an active right of helping to fix the rate of their wages, and thus enabled them to enjoy a status of greater personal freedom. Much has been done since 1909; but there is more to be done in order to improve the status of the worker, and far more to be done in order to increase the diffusion of ownership. It is all a matter for tentative experiment and progressive movement from stage to stage. It is a matter of keeping a constant watch on the whole of the process of production: a matter of noting emergent claims for new rights, and how they affect and impinge on the existing scheme of rights; a matter of observing the tentative efforts made by the parties concerned to secure some form of voluntary adjustment between new claims and old rights, until finally, at the end of the watch and the noting and the observing, the time comes for my making of a uniform rule of compulsory adjustment, in the light of all the data collected and all the experience gained. If this is the way in which I act, I shall be acting strictly within my sphere as a legal association: I shall be simply adjusting one right to another—the right of the owner of capital resources to the worker's rights both of status and property—as it always is my duty to adjust rights and to serve thereby as the organ of justice.'

There is a gloss or corollary which follows naturally on this view of the economic function of the State. Whatever the State may do in the way of securing an involuntary adjustment of rights by the method of legal compulsion and in the form of statutory rules, there also exists, and there will always exist, the way of voluntary adjustment by the method of spontaneous agreement between the parties concerned. This way of voluntary adjustment has had a long if chequered history. It has meant the formation of associations of workers, trade by trade: it has meant the long struggle of these associations, or trade unions, for recognition and for the right of bargaining and making agreements with the similar associations formed by employers. At first thwarted by the State, and repressed by Combination Acts, but afterwards recognized and even encouraged, these associations have gradually established themselves as permanent social organs, seeking to achieve by social methods a social accommodation between conflicting claims. In themselves, and by the mere fact of their existence and action, they have already given the worker a new and added enjoyment of freedom of personal status which he derives from their collective strength. They have their defects as well as their qualities. The collective strength which can give to the worker a new enjoyment of personal freedom can also be used to insist that each worker shall merge himself and his personality in the collective mass; and the adhesion of these associations of workers, in the mass and in their collective capacity, to a particular political party wedded to policies of nationalization, has had the disadvantage, whatever its gains may have been, of distracting them from that policy of the voluntary social adjustment of rights which belongs to their essential nature, and of turning their attention to the method of compulsory legal regulation through the agency of the State. Yet these may not be the permanent trends; and it is possible to hope, as has already been suggested,[1] that the future may have in store not only negotiation and voluntary adjustment between the associated workers and the associated employers in each industry, but also negotiation and voluntary adjustment, in some form of voluntary 'social parliament', between representatives of the whole body of associated workers and the whole body of associated employers over the whole of the field of production.

This is not to say that the State will tend to become less active in its own work of legal adjustment by general rules. On the contrary it may well become even more active. A country which follows simultaneously the two ways of adjustment between conflicting claims of right—the way of voluntary adjustment by social agreement, and the way of legal adjustment by means of general rules—may become increasingly busy in pursuing *both* of these ways. True, the State will normally wait for the exploration of the way of self-help and voluntary social agreement before

[1] *Supra*, Book II, § 7.

it begins to follow the way of public help and legal adjustment. True, again, the State, when it follows that way, will often, and perhaps even mainly, find itself concerned with generalizing, and making compulsory for all, what has already been tried and has already approved itself experimentally in the field of self-help and voluntary social agreement. But that only goes to prove that an increase of activity and experimentation in the social field, far from discouraging, will tend to encourage and foster an increase of activity in the legal field and the area of State-adjustment. The busier the effort of voluntary adjustment the greater will be the amount of material and the volume of suggestion on which the State can act.

The general method of advance which emerges from these considerations is a method which may be called by the name of 'experimentalism'. It is a method which begins with the ventilation of new claims to rights in the field of social thought and the forum of social discussion; with the pitting of these new claims against the old rights which they challenge; and with the demand for an adjustment between the old and the new. It is a method which then proceeds to the stage of social and voluntary adjustment, along a variety of lines and by a variety of experiments which tentatively compete with one another, and are tentatively pitted against one another, in the course of a process of social selection. It is a method which finally arrives at the stage of a legal and general adjustment, ultimately achieved by the State (through the action of its various organs of political discussion), as it works on the data before it and selects for endorsement and registration the solution which commands the adherence of general or common conviction. The whole method is a dialectical method, though it is far from being the method of 'dialectical materialism': it also is a method which has in its favour biological analogy, though it is far from being a method of natural selection of the fittest, and may rather be called a method of spiritual selection of the best—so far as the spirit of man is able to discover the best. If we call it by the name of experimentalism, which is only a shorthand name with the necessary defects of shorthand, we may plead that we mean by that name the process of gradually feeling a way, through time, by means of discussion, with the aid of the method of trial and error.

This experimentalism, if it may be so called, is something different from 'gradualism'. Gradualism means that you start from, and stick to, a preconceived plan, though you move slowly and with a Fabian cunctation towards its achievement. Experimentalism means that you start from the postulate of the sanctity of human rights—but also from the postulate of the constant growth of new rights (or the constant reinterpretation and extension of old rights) and the consequent need of adjustment between the new and the old—and that you are always seeking to discover, by fresh thought and experiment as you come to each new problem in each new generation, how you can meet the demands of your double postulate. But just as experimentalism is not gradualism, so neither is it opportunism; and just as it is not a plan or 'blue-print,' inherited from some past prophet, for the methodical shaping of the future, so neither is it a matter of immediate and extemporized expedients intended merely to meet an immediate contingency. Its essence is indeed the freedom of the present to shape and determine itself by its own motion, in the light of the situation immediately presented for decision. But it is also the essence of experimentalism that the situation so presented has itself been prepared by thought, experiment, and debate, and is thus, as it were, a 'planned situation', which as such suggests and invites a planned and deliberate decision. There is thus, after all, a plan in the method of experimentalism. But the plan is not a transcendent scheme, preconceived before the beginning of action: it is immanent in the process of action, and conceived by and during that process. To proceed by experiment is to proceed by constant planning, but not to proceed 'according to plan'.

§ 6. THE FUNCTIONS OF GOVERNMENT AND THEIR ORGANS

THE word 'function', in its political application, may be said to have two senses. It has the sense of purpose or aim, as when we say that the function of government is the maintenance of a scheme of law, or the service of rights, or some other such purpose or aim. It has also the sense of a particular mode of action, or a special kind of activity, by means of which a government seeks to fulfil its general purpose; and from this point of view we speak of the legislative, the judicial, and the executive function.

In the first of these senses, that of purpose, the course of the argument has led to the conclusion that the fundamental function of government is that of the service of Right. If we look at Right as 'objective', and as expressed in the external form of a body of general rules, we shall say that it is the function of government to render service to Right by translating social thought about the right order of human relations into a system of recognized and enforced law. If we look at Right as 'subjective', and as expressed in the form of rights which belong to persons or 'subjects' as their shares in objective Right, we shall say that it is the function of government to render service to rights by adjusting them to one another and removing obstacles to their enjoyment. In either case, and whether we regard the function of government as the service of Right or the service of rights, we shall say that the function of government is limited; limited by, and to, a service which it cannot transcend, a service which is the cause of its existence and the justification of all its action. On the other hand, just because it is service, and limited to being service, the function of government is also constantly growing. Since social thought about the right order of human relations is growing thought; since, in consequence of that growth, the system of Right and the rights of persons necessarily grow; since, in consequence of *that* growth, the service owed by government to securing the enjoyment of rights also necessarily grows; it follows that the function of government, even while it is limited to service, must be a growing function. All that has hitherto been said, in the previous course of the argument, about the extension of rights of persons involves a consequent and connected extension of the function of government.

Turning now to the second of the senses of the word 'function' in its political application, the sense of a mode of action or a kind of activity, we may begin by laying it down that there is always one great and general mode of action which government is bound to follow. It is the mode of proceeding by general rules of declared law backed by enforcement. Here again we may notice in passing that government is limited; limited by its general mode of action as well as by its general purpose; limited to acting by the one method of enforceable general rules, and limited therefore to acting in that sphere of acts of external conduct in which alone it is possible to enforce a general rule by means of an act of external compulsion.[1] But within this great and general mode of action, to which government is limited, and by which it is limited, we may now proceed to distinguish particular modes of action, or special kinds of activity. They are commonly held to be three: the legislative, the judicial, and the executive. At this point, however, there emerges something of a confusion of terms. Sometimes the three are described as 'functions'; sometimes they are described as 'powers' (*pouvoirs*); sometimes they are regarded and described as 'organs'. Before we attempt to consider them, or to discuss in what sense and to what extent they are or ought to be separate, and in what sense, and to what extent, they merge or should merge into one another, we shall do well to clarify our terms. What do we mean when we speak of the legislative, the judicial, and the executive, and what is the noun we imply when we use these adjectives?

We may identify, for our purposes, the term 'function' and the term 'power'. A mode of acting, which is the specific sense of 'function', is nothing very different from a faculty of acting, which is the specific sense of 'power'. But we must distinguish both of these terms from the term 'organ'. A function or power, such as vision, is one thing: an organ, such as the eye, is another. On this basis we may proceed to argue that while we may sometimes, or even generally, use one organ for one function and one function only, yet there is nothing to prevent us from using one organ for a number of functions, provided that it can perform them, and provided again that they are best performed by being held together and interconnected in that one organ. This may seem to be an abstract and even irrelevant argument. In fact it has a definite and practical bearing on the political doctrine and practice which goes by the name of 'separation of powers' (*la séparation des pouvoirs*). This was a doctrine expounded by Montesquieu: it was also an axiom incorporated in the French Declaration of Rights of 1789, which lays it down that 'a society in which the separation of powers is not fixed has no constitution'. But what is this 'separation of powers'? Does it only mean and involve a distinction of *modes* of action, and is that its essence? Or does it also mean and involve a distinction of

[1] *Supra*, Book II, § 2.

organs of action; and, if so, is each of the different organs confined
and limited to one mode of action, so that none of them can
possibly act except in a single mode, and each of them is entirely
debarred from acting in the mode or entering the province of
the others?

Separation of powers must certainly mean a distinction of
modes of action. There is a mode of action for legislation, which
is a distinctive mode with its own technique; a mode at once
deliberate and deliberative; a mode which proceeds slowly and
proceeds by debate, with 'reading' succeeding to 'reading' and
one chamber succeeding to another. There is a mode of action
for jurisdiction, which again is a distinctive mode, with its own
peculiar technique and its own particular rules of procedure;
a mode which is critical rather than deliberative; a mode which
mainly depends on a critical appreciation of the relevant rules
of law, a critical sifting of evidence, and a critical weighing of
the arguments tendered by the rival advocates. Finally there is
the executive mode, which is similarly a distinctive mode; a
mode which proceeds with rapidity (at any rate in comparison
with both the legislative and the judicial mode), and proceeds
by way of decisions and instructions intended to follow out
(*exsequi*) and give effect to the results of the legislative and
judicial modes. This distinction of modes is clear; and whether
each mode has its own separate and special organ, assigned to it
and confined to it, or whether there is less separation of the
organs and less confining of each to a single mode, the distinction
of modes remains. The legislative mode, with its separate
technique, is one thing: the judicial is another: the executive
another still. But even if there is thus plurality of modes, there is
also, we have to remember, a great and general mode of action
which is common to the whole of government, and which blends
the different modes in a unity of operation. Whatever the
government does, and in whatever particular mode it acts, it
always follows the general mode of acting by general rules of law
formally declared and regularly enforced. The fact of this unity
stands behind the difference of particular modes; and it is obvious
that this unity may affect and qualify the extent to which
difference and specialization can properly be carried in the
general conduct of government.

If 'separation of powers' thus means a distinction of modes of action, it also means, in any modern system of government, some sort of distinction of the organs of government. In early communities there may exist a single undifferentiated organ (the Anglo-Norman *Curia Regis* was of that order), acting in all the different modes, and simultaneously serving as a legislature, a judicature, and an executive. But in any developed community there will be a plurality of organs. There will be a legislative organ, which may not, indeed, be wholly and solely confined to the legislative mode of action, but will certainly be primarily and mainly concerned with that mode; there will equally be a judicial organ, primarily and mainly concerned with the judicial mode of action, but not necessarily confined to that mode; and there will similarly be an executive organ, which may, however, be concerned with other modes of action beside the executive. In a word we shall find three organs corresponding to the three different modes of action; but we may find none of the organs so absolutely specialized in its mode of action, or so entirely separate in its province, that it cannot also act in the mode and enter the province of the others.

It may be urged that the system just described, which combines a separation of modes of action (or 'functions' or 'powers') with a competence of each organ to act in more than one mode, is simply an inheritance from the past which is destined to disappear. On this view there has been an evolution from a primitive homogeneity, with little differentiation of modes and none of organs, towards heterogeneity and differentiation. That evolution has brought an increasingly clear differentiation of modes; but it has still left, as a sort of historical relic, a considerable confusion of organs, with each organ still showing signs of an old undifferentiated past. There may be some truth in this view; but it may also be urged, with even more justice, that a system in which each organ proceeds by more than one mode, and is concerned with more than one function, is inherent in the general unity of the operation of government, and is thus far more than a relic. In any case it is certain that such a system is still embedded in modern government; and it is also certain that, far from diminishing, it is constantly tending to increase. Instead of moving towards greater heterogeneity we are actually moving in the reverse direction. The more complicated government becomes, and the greater the service which it has to render, the greater becomes the trend to a unity of operation, and the more each organ of government tends to proceed by more than one mode of action.

The judicial organ perhaps shows this tendency less than the other two. Indeed it may be said that the judicial organ is a critic rather than an example of the tendency; in particular it is a critic of what some of its members regard as the encroachments and 'the new despotism' of the executive organ, now reverting, in their view, to the antiquated practice of medieval monarchy, by which the King in Council was a judicial and even a legislative as well as an executive organ. It is natural that a professional feeling should animate the legal profession, and should lead its members to vindicate the principle that a specific function is specifically reserved for the judicature and should not be exercised by other organs. 'The Law', in the sense of the Bar and the Bench, thus becomes the peculiar custodian of the doctrine of separation of powers, at any rate against executive encroachment. But we have already had reason to notice[1] that the judicature itself is an organ which is something more than judicial in the strict sense of that word. In addition to interpreting the law it also in some measure declares it: it has acted in the past, and it still acts in the present, by the legislative mode.[2]

Just as the judicature may thus be said to exercise more than one function, so too may the legislature. The legislative organ in England was originally a body of mixed legislative and judicial competence, proceeding indifferently by both modes; and either House of Parliament is still a Court, if in different ways and different degrees. Moreover, though the legislature does not act as an executive, or by the executive mode, it is everywhere brought into intimate contact with the executive, and it affects, if it does not control or determine, the action of the executive organ. This is not only true—though it is true to a greater extent—in countries which have adopted and follow the cabinet system of responsible government, under which the executive organ is generally answerable to the legislature and dependent

[1] *Supra*, Book IV, § 6.

[2] The judicature may also be said, not indeed to act as an executive, or by the executive mode, but at any rate to act as a control and check on the executive, in reviewing and judging the conduct of executive bodies and officers when it impinges upon the rights of the subject.

on its confidence; it is also true, if in a less measure, in countries in which the executive is independent of the legislature.

Finally, just as the legislature has been increasingly brought into contact with the executive by the modern evolution of government, and has come increasingly to exercise an influence on executive policy and action, so, conversely, the executive has also increased its scope, and has moved, or been drawn, into action proceeding not only by the executive, but also by the legislative and even by the judicial mode. The development of the executive into what may be called a multi-functioning organ (or, in other words, an organ proceeding by all the three modes) is one of the most notable features of modern government. If the growth of the legislative organ, in consequence of the development of the cabinet system, was the notable feature of the eighteenth century, it may be said that the growth of the executive organ, in consequence of the extension of rights and the corresponding extensions of services which mostly fall to the lot of the executive, is the notable feature of the twentieth. Today the executive is not only an executive: it is also, at the same time, a legislature, and that in a double sense. On the one hand it suggests and guides the process of law-making by the legislative organ. It does so even under the American system of division of functions between the executive President and the legislative Congress; and it does so even more under cabinet systems such as the British. On the other hand, the executive, apart from and in addition to its work of suggesting and guiding the process of law-making by the legislative organ, also acts itself as a legislature, when it issues supplementary rules of law in the form of 'regulations' and 'orders'. This power of the executive organ to issue supplementary rules of law is particularly evident in the sphere of the social services, and in matters such as housing and insurance; and it is to be noted that the power is often, and indeed mainly, exercised in virtue of a delegation of legislative power, made by the legislature itself, in a law which specifically authorizes an executive minister or ministers to supplement in detail its own more general prescriptions.[1]

The same extension of services (and particularly social

---

[1] In the British practice supplementary rules of law may also be issued by the executive in virtue of the prerogative of the Crown and the power of ministers to advise the Crown on its exercise.

services), which has largely caused the growth of this executive legislation, in order to cope with all the detail necessarily involved, has also caused the growth of executive jurisdiction. But such executive jurisdiction, while it is similar to, is also different from, executive legislation. It is similar, in so far as it owes its origin to a similar act of legislative authorization. A law about housing, for instance, which orders the clearing of slums, and therefore entails a decision, in any case of dispute, whether a given property belongs to the category of a slum and is therefore liable to clearance, may authorize an executive minister, as the person most likely to be familiar with the nature of the problem, to act judicially and give a decision. On the other hand, executive jurisdiction is different, in one respect, from executive legislation. When the legislative organ confers a measure of legislative power upon the executive, it takes something away from itself; but when it confers upon the executive a measure of judicial power, it is diminishing not itself, but an organ other than itself. That is one reason, though not the only reason, why the growth of executive jurisdiction is a more serious matter than is the growth of executive legislation.

The notable tendency of the executive organ to become more and more multi-functioning is itself sufficient to disprove the idea that the evolution of government is in the direction of a greater heterogeneity and an increasing differentiation of the various organs of government. On the contrary, the modern tendency would rather appear to be setting in the reverse direction. But though this tendency is a fact, it is also a problem, or a cause of problems. If the various organs overlap, and if some of them may enter the province and proceed by the modes of action which, primarily at any rate, belong to other organs, how is it possible for them to act amicably, without incessant disputes about boundaries and spheres? Again, if the executive takes to itself, or induces the legislative to allow it to take, both legislative and judicial powers in addition to its primary executive power, will not the rights of persons suffer from an authority so triply armed, and will not the principle of liberty be endangered by an overgrown and over-mighty executive?

It may be argued that the system works, and that the overlapping organs are able to act in unison, because one of these organs, the organ which is primarily concerned with the primary function of law-making, is the dominant and therefore the co-ordinating organ. In other words the legislature, as being the immediate sovereign under the constitution and therefore possessing the sovereign power of making final adjustments, is able to determine boundaries and spheres between the executive and the judicature, and between them both and itself. It may thus be said to secure a unity of operation in a system of different overlapping organs.[1] But there is another factor which must also be present, in addition to the co-ordinating and adjusting activity of the legislature, if a system of multi-functioning organs is to work without friction and without detriment to liberty. Each of the organs, when performing a function or proceeding by a mode additional to its own specific function or mode, should act in the way and according to the technique appropriate to the function or mode thus added. If the executive, for example, is vested with judicial power, and accordingly performs the judicial function and proceeds by the judicial mode, it must really and actually proceed by that mode; and discarding the technique of executive action it must adopt and follow, as far as possible, the proper and peculiar technique of judicial action. It must accept the procedure of a public hearing, with a proper confrontation of witnesses according to the regular rules of evidence: it must publish its decision and the reasons for its decision: it must also admit, if it possibly can, the possibility of appeal. The result will be that the distinction of modes will still be observed, even if there is not a separation of organs; and the executive organ, when acting judicially, will cease to follow the executive mode and adopt instead the judicial.

Granted these two conditions—the co-ordinating and adjusting activity of the sovereign legislature, and the observance of the distinction of separate modes even when the distinction of separate organs ceases to be observed—we may accept the contemporary tendency towards the confusion or overlap of multi-

[1] This is, at any rate, the British method: the American method is different. In the United States there is, to begin with, a greater separation and distinction of organs, especially between the executive and the legislature, and therefore less overlapping between multi-functioning organs. Such co-ordination as is needed, or at any rate as is possible, between the separate (and equal) organs cannot be achieved by the legislature, which is not dominant, and it is therefore remitted to the ultimate sovereign itself—that is to say the constitution, as interpreted by the judges of the supreme court. The regular and permanent activity of the ultimate sovereign is thus the peculiar feature of the American method.

functioning organs. But this is not to deny the justice and the propriety, for its time and under its conditions, of the eighteenth-century doctrine of the separation of powers. That doctrine was developed by Montesquieu in reference to French conditions. It was relative to the contemporary French facts of an over-grown royal executive organ; of the suspension of any legislative organ, and the substitution of executive decrees for legislative enactments; of the subordination of the judicial organ (the *parlement* of Paris) to the sovereign appearance of the King in person when he sat in a *lit de justice*. Under these conditions Montesquieu could argue, fairly enough, that with the executive claiming to do all things, confusing all the modes, and making its will the canon of Right and controller of rights, it was only possible to clarify confusion and to vindicate rights by asserting the titles of two other organs, the legislative and the judicial, to a separate existence and a separate power of acting inde-pendently by their own proper modes. In favour of such an assertion he could also plead, fairly enough (even if he was necessarily unaware of the nascent English system of responsible or cabinet government, and of the close connexion thereby established between the executive and the legislature), that the government of England was an example of the principle of separation of powers. The case is altered today; but if the facts are different, the principle, in its essence, remains. There is bound to be confusion, and there is bound to be a menace to rights, if it is not, in some way, observed. But that way, under our conditions, is now a different way.

Today we have in all countries, at any rate formally if not always in fact, the three separate organs which Montesquieu desired. But we have also something more than, and something different from, what he desired. There is in Britain (and there is also in other countries, in various ways and different degrees) an overlapping and an interlacing of the separate organs of govern-ment. The legislature does something more than legislation; the judicature does something more than adjudication; and the executive, in particular, does something more than executive action. But we get a co-ordination of what might seem to be confusion by the action of a dominant and sovereign legislature; we preserve a distinction of modes even if we do not maintain a clear separation of organs, and by that distinction of modes we preserve liberty and the rights of persons; and, finally, lest it succumb to the corruption of absolute power, we set bounds which it cannot overpass even to the sovereign legislature.

These bounds of the sovereign legislature are many and various. Some of them have already been traced in the previous course of the argument, and need only be summarized here. In the first place, the legislature, by its nature, is simply an organ of the legal association, or in other words the State; but besides the State and its legislature there is also Society and its social organs, with all the general play of voluntary social activity which proceeds, in the main, independently of the State.[1] Secondly, the legislature, like the whole of government, is limited both by the purpose it fulfils and by the mode of action it follows: the purpose of serving Right and the rights which issue from Right, and the mode of action which consists in proceeding by general rules of law relative to and enforceable in the sphere of external conduct.[2] Thirdly, the legislature is an organ of government acting in and under a general system of democracy, which proceeds by the method of discussion and thus reflects and repeats, at the political level, a process of debate which is already at work in the social area. Being an organ in such a system it may be said to be doubly limited, first by the play of social debate and the growth of common conviction which are precedent to its own action,[3] and secondly by the existence of other forces and foci of discussion (party and the electorate on the one hand, and the cabinet on the other) which are concurrent with its action, and to which its action must be adjusted in some sort of balance and with some measure of mutual respect.[4]

But there is a still further limit on the legislature which demands our consideration. This is the limit imposed by the development and the activity of political parties. The legislature has not only to respect the system of political parties as a force and focus of discussion parallel to and concurrent with itself. It has also to respect the system as something *within* itself; something by which its motion is *internally* affected and qualified. In

---

[1] *Supra,* Book V, § 6.

[2] *Supra,* § 6 of this Book, and also Book II, § 2. If we regard this limiting purpose and limiting mode of action as expressed in the constitution, we may proceed to add that the legislature is thus limited by the constitution, which is the ultimate sovereign behind and above its immediate sovereignty (*supra,* Book II, § 5).

[3] *Supra,* Book V, § 4.   [4] *Supra,* § 3 of this Book.

an earlier passage of the argument it has already been suggested that the democratic method of government, being as it is in its essence a method of government by discussion, necessarily requires a plurality of parties as a condition and *sine qua non* of discussion.[1] We may now go on to suggest that the legislature, as a representative body reflecting in its own composition the plurality of parties in the national community, is inherently limited by the fact of that plurality, and is bound by the necessity, which arises from it, of attaining such measure of common agreement as is required for any united action proceeding from the whole body. It may be objected that no common agreement is required; that the majority party, or combination of parties, can simply overbear the minority and force it to acquiesce; and that a majority-vote is thus sufficient to ensure the united action of the legislative body. The objection does not hold; and the operation of a representative legislative based on a plurality of parties is more than a matter of counting votes and then doing a sum in subtraction.

Whether the parties are only two, or more than two, they generally arrange themselves in two sides (there may be many *parties*, but there can be only two *sides*)—the side of the party or combination of parties which supports the executive government or cabinet, and the side of the party or combination of parties which opposes that government. The government side, under normal conditions, does not simply outvote and overbear the opposition side; nor is the opposition side always waging a war in which it is always defeated. The two sides are indeed engaged in the conflict of debate; but they are also engaged in the co-operation of managing the nation's business together. The conflict is public: the co-operation, which is unacknowledged and may even be unconscious, is hidden in the background. But it is always there. The two sides must, at the least, attain some agreement about the conduct of the current business of legislation. They must, in a grave emergency, whether of peace or of war, attain some agreement about the conduct of the general business of the nation. But even without an emergency, and even in normal conditions, they must always attain some agreement which goes beyond the conduct of current business and the routine of daily procedure. They must, in regard to all major

[1] *Supra*, Book V, § 4, *ad finem*.

measures of proposed legislation, endeavour to achieve some sort of compromise which is likely to command the general consent and to be endorsed by the common conviction of the whole community, and which is therefore likely to last even after a change of government, and even when the government side has been succeeded in office by the side now in opposition. This is the price of continuity, and continuity, in its turn, is the price of peaceful progress.

We may accordingly say that the legislature is two as well as one, and that it is inherently limited by the fact that the two have to act as one. In other words a joint effort—an effort of construction on the one side and of constructive criticism on the other; an effort which combines contradiction with co-opera- tion—is involved in the double nature of the legislative body. The necessity of this joint effort is an internal limit; and the separation of the two sides of the legislature, thus at once opposed and conjoined, is the return in a new and different form of the old eighteenth-century system of *séparation des pouvoirs*. We do not indeed now separate, or seek to oppose and balance, the executive and legislative organ: on the contrary we unite them together in a system of responsible government which brings the executive into the legislature and enables either to affect the other in a constant interaction. But within this union and inter- action we retain separation and maintain a balance. We retain a separation of two sides and the leaders of the two sides (the head of the Government and the leader of the Opposition): we maintain a balance in the sense that we require both sides and their leaders to adjust their claims and accom- modate their policies in a compromise which eventually may command our general consent. Thus the end of the argument on the functions of government is at once in favour of union and in favour of separation. You may unite the executive with the legislature; but when you have done so you must provide some element of separation and balance within that union. Again, and from another point of view, you may set your executive organ to act not only by the executive mode of action, but also by the judicial (in the exercise of executive jurisdiction) and in addition by the legislative (in the shape of executive legislation); but again when you have done so, and when you have thus united three modes in a single organ, you must ensure that there is also separation, and that the one organ uniting the modes nevertheless acts separately, and acts by a separate procedure, in each of the different modes. Union, but also separation—such is the rule which, in this way or that, is always imperative in the discharge of the functions of government.

§ 7. COLLECTIVISM AND INDIVIDUALISM

WE may now return, in conclusion, to the theme of the relation between the functions of government and the rights of individuals. However government may discharge its functions, and however those functions may be distributed among its different organs, they are always, in their nature, functions of service rendered to rights and therefore rendered to persons, *individual* persons, who own these rights as the necessary conditions of the development in action of their individual personality. From this point of view the current antithesis between collectivism and individualism is verbal rather than real. If by individualism we mean a belief in the rights of individual persons, and by collectivism we mean a belief in the collective service owed and rendered to such rights by government, we shall see no opposition, but rather a necessary connexion. It is possible, indeed, to draw a distinction, as some thinkers have done, between a period of individualism, dominated by the influence of Bentham and his followers and marked by the idea of liberation, which lasted into the third quarter of the nineteenth century, and a period of collectivism, marked by the extension of the idea of protection, which succeeded the period of individualism from 1870 onwards. But the distinction is a distinction of the study; and it may even be said to show a class or professional bias. Some classes or professions might mourn a loss of individual rights after 1870: others, and those were numerous, began to enjoy an increase. Generally the whole of the nineteenth century, far from being divided into two different parts, was a century of a single and homogeneous process; a process of the extension of personal rights, which may be called individualism, but a process entailing, at the same time, an extension of the service of government on behalf of those rights, an extension which may be called by the name of collectivism, but is really and in fact the consequence and the other side of the extension of personal rights which is called by the name of individualism.

Individualism is a word which is easily used in different and even conflicting senses. It can be used, and is often used, to denote a doctrine that the State leaves the individual alone, 'letting him do and letting him go' (*laissez faire et laissez passer*) as he himself thinks best. The phrase is a phrase of the French Free Trade economists of the eighteenth century: it originally belonged only to economics, and only to one part of that—the part concerned with commerce. It was a good enough phrase in its day, and it has its value still, in its own restricted field. But it cannot be properly applied to economics generally, or made to include the field of industry as well as the field of commerce: still less can it be applied to the whole broad field of politics. Individualism of the *laissez-faire* order in *that* field, individualism which meant that the State should leave each individual alone in the general business and whole conduct of life, would not only mean dereliction of its duty by the State; it would also mean the destruction of the individual's power to do anything freely or to go anywhere freely. A true individualism, in the field of politics, involves a recognition of the State's liberating power, coupled with a recognition of its duty to use that power according to its nature, and therefore for liberation and the removal of obstacles.

Individualism so conceived starts, indeed, from individual personality, and from the inherent title of each individual person to enjoy the conditions necessary to the development of his capacities. But just because it starts from that basis, it cannot end in any conclusion of *laissez faire*, or issue in any doctrine that it is the duty of the State to leave individuals alone. The conditions necessary for the development of each individual person are not to be had for the whistling, and they do not come of themselves in obedience to each person's call. They have to be assembled by a collective effort which is only possible to an organized State. They are assembled for the sake of the individual; but he cannot assemble them himself, or be left alone to shift for himself by his own unaided devices. On the contrary, he must be surrounded with service; a collective service which, in union with others, he himself helps to provide for others as well as himself: a service which becomes all the greater, the more fully the conditions necessary for his development are recognized and the more his rights are thereby extended. The State which is based on regard and respect for the worth of individual persons is not a 'let-alone' State: it is a State which follows and attends, 'with unperturbèd pace',[1] and with a constant office of service. To argue for individuality is not to argue for the unserved and unattended individual. It is rather the opposite: it is to argue for the general legal framework, and the whole system of collective service, which individuality needs for its development: it is to argue for the rights it requires, for the system of Right which is the other side of these rights, and for the service of the State in declaring and enforcing the common conviction about that system.

The argument seems to result in a paradox: 'the greater the liberty of the individual, the greater the interposition of government: the more rights, the more law, and therefore the more the activity of the State in declaring and enforcing law.' The statement of the paradox suggests a reflection. There is always a price to be paid for rights. That price, as has already been noted,[2] is partly financial, or a matter of payment in money; partly spiritual, or a matter of payment in the acceptance of control. We need not pause to discuss the nature and the implications of the financial price. That is a matter of economics: of national finance and the balancing of national income and national expenditure. It is the spiritual price which matters most; and the crucial balance to be struck is the balance between the spiritual profit gained in the increased enjoyment of rights and the spiritual loss incurred or involved in the increased acceptance of control. When we seek to strike this balance, we have two calculations to make. The first is a calculation of the gain and loss in the private account of each individual: it is a matter, as it were, of the private bank-book of each; it is a business of reckoning individual gain of liberty against individual loss. The second is a calculation of the gain and loss in what may be called the common account of the whole community: it is a matter of reckoning between classes or sections of the community; it is a business of computing the gain of one class or section, in liberty and personal rights, against the loss of another.

[1] The words are taken from Francis Thompson's poem *The Hound of Heaven*. The writer remembers Mr. Lionel Curtis saying to him, nearly forty years ago, that when he thought of the constant service of the democratic commonwealth to the cause of human liberty, he was always reminded of that poem.

[2] *Supra*, § 5 of this Book, *ad initium*.

The necessity of reckoning spiritual gain and spiritual loss in the private account of each individual is a necessity which may easily be forgotten; but it still remains a necessity. Men readily accept new rights and the enlargement which they immediately bring: they are less ready to remember the price and the restrictions which may be entailed. The rights comprised in a system of social security are precious; but they are necessarily accompanied by administrative control and regulation, and they necessarily involve the performance of prescribed and compulsory acts in the channels of regular routine. There is at once an increase of liberty and an increase of automatism; and the question is whether the increase of liberty is more than enough to offset the increase of automatism. To enjoy the rights of social security is to be liberated from fears and dangers; to be more of a freeman, and to have more freedom for the development of personal capacity. If the freedom is grasped and used, and if the development is actually achieved, the game is well worth the candle, and the commodity is worth far more than the price. On the other hand there *is* a price. To be liberated from a set of risks is also to be liberated from the responsibility of facing those risks: indeed it is even more, under a system of collective insurance; it is also to be subjected to the control involved in the system. Only if the liberty gained is actively grasped and used; only if it is something more than a passive acceptance of benefits; only then will there be a net gain on the whole of the transaction. The man who is formally made more free by a system of social security must actively use his freedom to make something more of himself if he is to be really and actually more free.

The necessity of reckoning gain and loss between different classes or sections is a still more obvious necessity, daily forced upon our attention by the process of class-debate. The extension of rights for one class may mean the limitation of rights for another; and it is possible that the one class may lose even more than the other gains. But that, in itself, does not necessarily mean that the bargain is bad. The previous distribution of rights between classes may have been unfair and inequitable: one class may have been entrenched in the possession of a superfluity, and the other depressed below the level of bare necessity. If the greatest number are to enjoy the greatest possible development of the capacities of personality, correction is inevitable, and it may be as just (in terms of the sovereign justice which assigns rights equally to each and all) as it is inevitable. The distribution of rights among classes is not a thing fixed for ever. It is a matter for constant adjustment and readjustment, as social thought about justice grows and as the interpretation of the principles of liberty and equality broadens with its growth. But there is still a limit to the process of adjustment and readjustment. It may be fair to ask one class, particularly when in numbers it is a small and limited class, to surrender old rights and responsibilities for the sake of another and larger class, and in order that the members of that class may enjoy new rights and responsibilities. But it will only be really fair if two conditions are satisfied.

The first of these conditions is that the rights and responsibilities surrendered should be used by those who receive them for their own higher development, and not merely accepted as prizes or trophies. Otherwise there may be no gain, and there may even be loss, in terms of that development of personality which is the final criterion. The other condition is that the class surrendering rights (such as the right to ownership of capital resources and the management of those resources on the basis of personal responsibility) should not be made to surrender so much that it becomes impotent to contribute any energy of initiative or originality of experiment to the development of the national economy and the general national culture or type of civilization. Under any system of organization a national community will always need an initiatory and experimental class which can generate and distribute the electricity of ideas. The recruiting of that class should be broad and generous; and every talent should have an open way into its ranks. But however recruited, and however broad, this class will always require the conditions necessary for the discharge of its electric work; and there will always remain a modicum of rights and responsibility which it must necessarily retain if it is to be itself and to contribute its own gifts to the cause of general development. The days of hereditary aristocracy are gone; but there is no numbering of the days of what may be called the professional aristocracy, in the widest sense of the word 'professional'. The more a national community moves towards the greatest possible development of the capacities of personality in the greatest possible number of persons, the more it needs the stimulus which professional skill and managing capacity can give to the whole development of the whole community.

It has been argued that there is no antithesis between individualism, in the sense of a belief in the development of individual personality, and collectivism in the sense of a belief in the collective service necessary for individual development. On the other hand, it has also been argued that though there is no antithesis there is or may be tension—a tension between the 'pull' of individual development and the 'pull' of a collective service which must always be in some measure also a collective control. The two may be complements to one another; but they are complements which need a nice and delicate adjustment. There is a principle of polarity in the political nature of man, as there is in human nature generally: a 'quality of exhibiting opposite or contrasted properties', a 'tendency to develop in two opposite directions'.[1] In his general nature man has the contrasted properties of privacy and sociability; and though he is one being, and though he needs them both, he is also divided between them, and he also feels the tension between their different pulls. Similarly in his political nature he has the contrasted and yet complementary properties of the individualist who would fain be himself and the collectivist who would merge himself in a fellowship of service; and though he is one being and needs both these properties, he is also divided between them and feels in himself the tension of a 'tendency to develop in two opposite directions'. Individualism and collectivism are not the banners of two separate armies, composed of two separate bodies of men. All of us fly them both, and we all serve under both. There is a polarity in each of us, as well as in the whole community to which we all belong. We need not dread the resultant tension. That would simply be to dread life; for life is tension, as tension is life. We have to accept it as it exists, both within ourselves and within the community; and we have constantly to find, in each new conjuncture, the new adjustment which the new conjuncture demands, surrendering neither individual development nor collective service, but endeavouring to find an adjustment which preserves them both and may even make them both mutually serviceable to one another.

[1] The *New English Dictionary*, under the word 'polarity'.

There is another polarity, and another tension, besides the tension within the State between the call of individual development and the call of collective service. This is the polarity or tension between the State and Society; between the community permanently organized in a single legal association, for the one legal purpose of declaring and enforcing universal and uniform rules, and the community organized, or rather constantly organizing itself, in a number of voluntary associations for a variety of purposes (religious, cultural, recreational, charitable, economic, and whatever else may be comprehended under the general designation of 'social'), which adorn and supplement, and may even stimulate or anticipate, the activity proper to the purpose of the legal organization. The question which thus emerges, and the tension thus presented, bring us back at the end to the theme from which the argument originally started. What is the province of the State, and what is the province of Society? Is there any definite boundary, or how shall we conceive their relations?

In attempting to answer this question we may begin by asking ourselves whether the goal which is set before us—the securing of the greatest amount of rights for the greatest number of persons; the providing of the conditions for the highest possible development of the capacities of personality over the widest possible range—is a goal which can be simultaneously attained by two parallel lines of action, or a goal to be attained by one and only one. Can the extension and spread of rights 'in widest commonalty' be partly secured by voluntary action in the social area, or must it be altogether secured by uniform and compulsory action in the legal area, with a large consequential growth of State-action and a large increase of the functions of government in the necessary service of rights? There is a good case to be made in favour of the first of these alternatives. Voluntary action in the social area is needed as well as, and no less than, the uniform and compulsory action of the organized State in its own legal area. Both are necessary, but the first comes first; and the prior thing, in the order of time (though not necessarily in order of importance) is the voluntary action of Society. We do our best if we do what we can for ourselves, by voluntary social co-operation, before we invoke the action of the State—which indeed is also ourselves, wherever it is democratically organized, but is ourselves engaged in the making and enforcing of compulsory rules.[1] There is a time for voluntary and varied experiment as well as for the uniform obligatory rule. Indeed the distinction between social action and the legal action of the State is perhaps rather a distinction of time than a distinction of space or area. It is not always the case that one sort of action is concerned with one area or set of subjects, and the other with another area or set: on the contrary, both sorts of action may well be concerned with the same areas or sets of subjects. Rather it is often the case that the one sort of action belongs to one time or conjuncture, the time of the laboratory and the experiment, and the other to another time or conjuncture—let us say, in a metaphor, that of mass-production, when a result of the laboratory is being put on the market as a standardized uniform commodity.

If we follow this line of thought, we shall be led to believe that a reorganization of the economic process, such as will introduce the principles of liberty and equality into this process, and will therefore secure to all who are concerned in it the rights involved by these principles, may well begin, and may even sometimes remain, as the level of voluntary agreement between voluntary associations (those of the workers and those of the employers), an agreement based on voluntary consultation and issuing in voluntary co-operation.[2] But often the matter will not end there, and there will come a time and conjuncture for acting in a different way and by a different mode. Voluntary social effort, feeling its way, making its experiments, proceeding by trial and error, may discover a best which is so obviously best that it deserves to be made the general rule. In that case the State, which is not the enemy of Society, but rather stands to it in something of the relation in which a solicitor may stand to

---

[1] It may be noted in passing, though it is a matter which deserves something more than a passing notice, that the democratically organized State is the more tempted to act at all times and in all places (in other words to become what is nowadays called 'totalitarian'), because it can plead to itself '*L'État, c'est le moi commun*—the State is just you and me, acting all together and all as one'. It is all the more important to notice that there is something more to the matter than that. The State is indeed 'just you and me'; but it is you and me acting all together and all as one *in a particular way*, which is by no means necessarily the way for doing everything 'at all times and in all places'. There may be times and places in which you and I ought to act *in another way*.

[2] *Supra*, § 5 of this Book.

a family, will register and endorse this best as a rule for general application and enforcement. But just as it is wise to avoid going to a solicitor unless or until you have a case to submit, so it may also be wise to avoid recourse to the State (to which we are perhaps too prone to carry our problems instantly) until social thought and experiment have done their preparatory work. The issue between Society and the State, if we can speak at all of an issue, is not an issue between opposites. How indeed can it be so, when the State is just Society writ legally—Society organized in the form and for the purposes of a legal association? It is either an issue between two alternatives, either of which may serve, but one of which, at a given moment, may serve better than the other, or an issue between two complements, both of which are needed, but one of which is needed as the forerunner of the other.

The conclusion to which we are thus led is not a conclusion in favour of the individualism which means leaving individuals alone, to shift for themselves by their own devices: nor again, on the other hand, is it a conclusion in favour of the form of collectivism under which the State serves individuals so much that they have little or nothing to do for themselves, and thus lose much of their liberty in the very act of their own liberation. It is rather a conclusion in favour of the maximum of voluntary self-help by groups of individuals, voluntarily acting for themselves in the social area; thinking out for themselves, in their own sphere of interest, the requirements and conditions of their own development; and, when they have thought them out *for* themselves, going on to achieve them *by* themselves, and by their own efforts, so far as in their own sphere they can. In one sense this may be called individualism; for it involves a belief in the value of the spontaneous activity of individuals, freely associated for the purpose of shifting for themselves, by their own devices, in a scheme of voluntary self-help. In another sense, however, it may also be called collectivism; for it involves a belief in the value of the concerted activity of collective groups, each knit together by a common interest of all the members in a common object, and each seeking to achieve its object by means of common effort. But on a broad view the method of voluntary self-help by the concerted effort of a voluntary association is neither individualism nor collectivism, in the ordinary sense of those terms; it is a happy bridge between them. The essence of the method is a spirit of 'voluntary community', which marries *voluntas* to *communitas;* and the essence in turn of that spirit is the power not of force but of persuasion.

The power of persuasion, issuing in the spirit of voluntary community, has studded the world in which we live with a profusion of social institutions. Professor Whitehead, in one of the most suggestive of his essays,[1] has spoken of the transformation wrought in the problem of liberty by 'a profusion of corporations originated by explicit thought'. In his view the development of these autonomous institutions, limited to special purposes, places the problem of liberty at a new angle: and he holds accordingly that the novelty of our days, and the modern method of solving the problem of liberty, 'consists in the deliberate formation of institutions, embodying purposes of special groups, and unconcerned with the general purposes of any political state'.[2] His authority and his persuasive power reinforce the argument here advanced. The future will largely lie with the development and the activity of a variety of social institutions. What such institutions can do, and what they may ultimately achieve, in the economic field, is a matter already touched upon in the previous course of the argument. But there are other fields besides the economic in which the development of social institutions may contribute greatly to the solution of the ancient problem of liberty. There is, for example, the field of education, which is not, and never can be, a monopoly of the State. Educational associations—of parents, of teachers, of workers, and of members of religious confessions—are all concerned in the development of educational experiments, and in offering that liberty of choice among types of school and forms of instruction which is essential to the growth of personal and individual capacity. Indeed on a general view, and looking beyond particular fields to the general field of the way of life and the type of civilization common to the whole community, we cannot but notice that social institutions are active in all its range and over

---

[1] The essay entitled 'Aspects of Freedom', in his *Adventures of Ideas*.

[2] Professor Whitehead ascribes the origin of the novelty to the saying of Christ: 'Render unto Caesar the things which are Caesar's: and unto God the things that are God's.' (See above, Book I, § 4, *ad initium.*) 'However limited', he writes, 'may be the original intention of the saying, very quickly God was conceived as a principle of organization in complete disjunction from Caesar' (op. cit., p. 69).

all its extent. 'Our lives are passed from the first not in a monistic, homogeneous circle, but in a number of circles. . . . we live in various social complexes which are in the last resort concentric and each of which has its own intellectual content.'[1] These circles and social complexes, each with its intellectual content, and all with their moral aim of mutual aid and common service, are essentially personal unions, enlisting personal interest and eliciting fully the initiative of their leading personalities. The greater the part which they play, on that basis and in that form, the greater their contribution to the development of the capacities of individual personality in the community at large, and thereby to the growth of a better way of life and a higher type of civilization. But they must be true to their personal basis, and retain their personal form, if they are to contribute effectively. Social institutions can easily become ossified, no less than political: they can become official organizations, in lieu of personal associations: they can dictate to their members, instead of responding to the lift and surge of their minds. They must constantly be renewed and reviewed: sometimes, when they have served and outlived their purpose, they may even have to be destroyed, in order that something new and better may be able to take their place. It might be a motto for a community: 'Never rest content with your institutions, whether social or political—but least of all with the social: there is a virtue in continuity, but there is no less virtue in change.'

All in all, the question before us is not a question of 'the man *versus* the State', or of individualism *versus* collectivism. There is no point in the question: there is no such antithesis; there is, at the most, a tension, which is as healthy as it is necessary. Nor is the question before us a question of 'Society *versus* the State', or of the voluntary principle *versus* the principle of legal control and regulation. There may be more point in that question; but again there is no antithesis, for both of the things thus opposed are needed, and both may be needed equally. Here, however, the tension is greater; and here, as we have already seen, there is a reasonable ground for debating, not so much *what* the State should do and *what* Society should do (both handle equally a number of matters, and few matters can be said to belong exclusively either to the one or to the other), as *when* and in what

[1] Ernst Troeltsch, in *Christian Thought, its History and Application*, pp. 118, 126.

conjuncture Society should be the agent, and *when* and in what conjuncture the agent should be the State.

Each mind has a drawing bias, which makes it naturally run in some particular direction. The bias of the writer has always inclined his thought—the more, the older he grows—towards a belief in the value of the social mode of action. With all its imperfections and its possible inefficiencies, it is none the less a mode of action which permits and even demands the free energy of the mind. The movement of the State is the regular revolution of steady and unfailing machinery. The movement of social institutions is a varied and irregular movement, like the movement of trees and plants as they spring from the seed in the ground: here one group, and there another, thrusts up its fresh particular idea into the varied field of social life and experiment. The humming automatism of the State is about us and all our doings, engaged in constant service and constantly intending our good. The varied field is untidy, irregular, un-regulated: it has many gaps: it has even more redundancies. But may the time never come when all our life spins round on the revolving wheels of legal regulation.

INDEX

Note: The index is an index rather of persons and things mentioned in the text than of the themes discussed. For the latter the reader is referred to the table of contents at the beginning and to the page-headings.

PRINTED IN GREAT BRITAIN
AT THE UNIVERSITY PRESS, OXFORD
BY VIVIAN RIDLER, PRINTER TO THE UNIVERSITY